To

KATHARINE BRADY LYNCH

who loves poets—and us

POET TO POET

A Treasury of Golden Criticism

Edited by HOUSTON PETERSON
and WILLIAM S. LYNCH

Granger Poetry Library

GRANGER BOOK CO., INC.
Great Neck, NY

First Published 1945
Reprinted 1979

INTERNATIONAL STANDARD BOOK NUMBER
0-89609-121-X

LIBRARY OF CONGRESS CATALOG NUMBER
78-73495

PRINTED IN THE UNITED STATES OF AMERICA

PREFACE

In the third book of his great autobiographical poem, "The Prelude," Wordsworth gives a vivid account of his college days in Cambridge—of the physical surroundings, the life of the students, the historic atmosphere.

> Beside the pleasant Mill of Trompington
> I laughed with Chaucer in the hawthorn shade;
> Heard him, while birds were warbling, tell his tales
> Of amorous passion. And that gentle Bard,
> Chosen by the muses for their Page of State—
> Sweet Spenser, moving through his clouded heaven,
> With the moon's beauty and the moon's soft pace,
> I called him Brother, Englishman, and Friend!
> Yea, our blind Poet, who, in his later day,
> Stood almost single; uttering odious truth—
> Darkness before, and danger's voice behind,
> Soul awful—if the earth has ever lodged
> An awful soul—I seemed to see him here . . .

Elsewhere in Wordsworth there are poems or passages on John Dyer, William Collins, Thomas Chatterton, Robert Burns, James Hogg and Samuel Taylor Coleridge—all warm and accurate evocations more revealing than many pages of interpretive prose. A minute anthology of golden criticism!

Would not a volume of such poetry, drawn from the whole range of literature in the English language, be novel, useful, refreshing? Our prejudiced answer is emphatically "Yes," after a long, happy adventure in collecting, sifting and arranging. We had no difficulty in finding a vast amount of sincere, earnest verse from one bard to another, but much of it is dull and platitudinous. We have put aside scores of poems that are fairly good in their way, for the laurels they proffer would fit almost any brow, the cypress they describe would adorn almost any grave.

We have asked ourselves if each selection is really illuminating. Does it shed light on some special facet of the poetry contemplated? Does it, with some poignant phrase or quick image, take us to the heart of another poet? Here is a stanza on Horace, a sequence on Dante, an "Ode to Walt Whitman." Here is a salute to a friend across the town, or to a friend across the centuries. There have been many essays on John Donne but perhaps none so penetrating as Thomas Carew's "Elegy upon the Death of Doctor Donne"; there have been many essays on Wordsworth but few equal to Matthew Arnold's "Memorial Verses."

Nearly all of these poems are contagious in that they send the reader back, not only to familiar names but to the neglected or forgotten. After a sonnet by Edwin Arlington Robinson, one simply has to browse for a while in the honest pages of George Crabbe. Even a few minor tributes to Theocritus send us back to the precious pastorals in translation, if not in the original Greek.

At the same time light is shed on the authors of these poems by their very choice of subject, and their mode of treatment. It is no accident that T. S. Eliot should write unforgettable lines on Donne and Webster, or that Elinor Wylie should lay down "a red carpet for Shelley." When we read Thomas Hardy on "A Singer Asleep," we have a deeper understanding of Swinburne —and of Hardy. When we read Ben Jonson's lines "To the Memory of My Beloved the Author, Mr. William Shakespeare: and What He Hath Left Us," we love them both the more.

In a larger sense, these selections form a kind of history of taste as they record the poetic judgment of contemporary on contemporary, or of one generation on another. Compare, for example, Keats, Arnold and Auden on Byron. Not only are the Elizabethan and the Romantic and the Victorian periods richly represented but also that long and vigorous era between "Paradise Lost" and the *Lyrical Ballads*. Dryden's ode on the pious memory of Mrs. Anne Killigrew may not resurrect that lady's verse but it communicates the sensibilities of an age; as does John Gay's hearty welcome to Mr. Pope on his return from Greece. The shifting taste of our own day is reflected in Horace Gregory's "Praise to John Skelton," laureate of Henry VIII. Indeed, one will realize again and again that the "new poetry" of the twentieth century is far from entirely new—that the most daring innovators, as Henry W. Wells has shown at length, have been inspired by some tradition, be it Middle English, Jacobean or Augustan.

Incidentally we think that it is pleasant to know the original settings of some memorable lines that come trippingly but not always accurately from the tongue of the literati.

> "He saw life steadily and saw it whole."
> or
> "the well of English undefyled"
> or
> "the large dimensions of the English tongue"
> or
> "the sun-treader"
> or
> "Teach the free man how to praise."

II

Now a little more detail as to the selections, along with some of the usual defensive gestures of every anthologist. As the language is English, most of the subjects are English, Irish or American and most of the larger clusters of poems deal with the greater figures—Chaucer and Shakespeare, Milton and Wordsworth, Shelley and Keats.

Why then four comparatively long poems, three on little-known figures, by John Dryden, who is monotonous and metallic to those reared exclusively on a romantic diet? It is at least significant that Thomas Gray and Sir Walter Scott placed Dryden only after Shakespeare and Milton in the procession of English poets. Mark Van Doren has written a brilliant volume on Dryden's poetry and says specifically: "He was partial to literary history and literary parallels as subjects for poems, and no one in English has done better criticism in verse." Bad poets are not the concern of this book but it seems fitting to include "Mac Flecknoe," the masterpiece on the poetry of dullness. And "if one is not pleased by the lines 'To the Memory of Mr. Oldham'," remarks Professor Van Doren, "one will not be pleased by anything in Dryden; they are his touchstone."

Why so many pieces by Algernon Charles Swinburne whose

flamboyant rhetoric is now out of fashion? He was dangerously fluent and prodigally generous, but he was profoundly immersed in Greek, French and English poetry. Therefore, we have included his poems to Sappho and that modern Greek, Walter Savage Landor, those to Villon, Victor Hugo and Baudelaire, and four of the twenty-one sonnets to the English dramatists. We have omitted Swinburne's tributes to Robert Burns, Walt Whitman and Robert Browning.

In the case of Matthew Arnold, there were certain obvious choices but we did not include "Thyrsis," the long elegy on his friend A. C. Clough, because it has so little to do with Clough as a poet. Fortunately, Arnold has some fine stanzas on Goethe, for there seems to be no adequate lyric tribute to the Zeus of Weimar.

It is to be regretted that there are so few poems about the Middle Ages or the entire East, and none at all on such Russians as Pushkin and Lermontov. As we have ranged widely in time and space, we have had to pass over some lively contributions, bitter and benign, of the past twenty years. But it is hardly necessary to apologize for ending with citations for D. H. Lawrence, Robert Frost, Stephen Vincent Benét and William Butler Yeats.

III

Finally, a few words as to the general pattern of this book. It is arranged chronologically by *poet as subject* of the poems, not as author, from David and Homer down to the present time. But there has been no slavery to chronology. Many poets have lived such brief lives that the date of death is more significant than the date of birth. And certainly the accident of birth should not separate, in our arrangement, Marlowe and Shakespeare, Beaumont and Fletcher, Verlaine and Rimbaud. As often as possible interchanges between two poets are placed side by side, in spite of the calendar, and frequently a poem by an author is followed immediately by a group of poems about him. A long, discursive piece may be more than balanced by a few lines of lyric concentration, but "Adonais," of course, is both long and intense, the supreme acknowledgment of a poet and of poetry.

Scattered throughout the book, as summaries or resting-places, are a number of miscellanies, dealing with many writers, such as Drayton's letter to Henry Reynolds, Pope's imitation of Horace and Mrs. Browning's vision of poets. Although not poetry on the loftiest level, they thicken the atmosphere and add historical perspective.

As the dates of the subjects and authors are given in connection with each poem, and in some instances the date of composition or first publication, few footnotes have been added and no reference marks disfigure the text. But there are four indexes which may be of use to the technical and the timid.

Like any anthology, this one may be read item by item, jewel by jewel, but it grows more exciting with the clusters centered around an individual poet or a group of poets, all falling into eight large sections. And, of course, there is always the two-way passage, the reciprocal light of poet on poet. But the proof of a book is in the reading. We can only say again that we have had great pleasure in making this collection and we hope that it will open fresh fields to Pegasus—however much he may snort at anthologies.

HOUSTON PETERSON
WILLIAM S. LYNCH

NEW YORK, NEW YORK
MARCH 6, 1945

ACKNOWLEDGMENTS

We shudder to think what this book would have been without the enthusiasm and constant assistance of the following: Henry W. Wells and Katharine B. Lynch, heroic travelers in all the realms of poetry; Harold C. Whitford, research librarian, and Leroy H. Buckingham, colleague in the humanities, at The Cooper Union; M. Elma Krumwiede, librarian of the Bronxville Public Library; and Dorothy Donnelly and Lorraine C. Carmien, flawless secretaries.

We refuse to think what this book might have been without publishing permissions from the following:

The selection from Conrad Aiken is reprinted from his *Preludes for Memnon*, published by Charles Scribner's Sons; copyright, 1930, 1931, by Conrad Aiken.

The selections from W. H. Auden are reprinted from his *Another Time* (1940) and from *Letters from Iceland* (1937), by W. H. Auden and Louis MacNeice, by permission of Random House, Inc., publishers.

The selection from Gertrude Lowthian Bell is reprinted from her *Poems from the Divan of Hafiz* (1897), by permission of William Heinemann, Limited, London, publishers.

The selection from Stephen Vincent Benét is reprinted from *Selected Works of Stephen Vincent Benét* (2 vols.), published by Farrar & Rinehart; copyright, 1935, by Stephen Vincent Benét.

The selection from William Rose Benét is reprinted from *Day of Deliverance*, copyright 1944 by William Rose Benét, by permission of Mr. Benét and Alfred A. Knopf, Inc., publishers.

The selections from Edmund Blunden are reprinted from *The Poems of Edmund Blunden* (1930), by permission of Mr. Blunden.

ACKNOWLEDGMENTS

The selection from Wilfrid Scawen Blunt is reprinted from *The Poetical Works of Wilfrid Scawen Blunt* (2 vols., 1914), by permission of The Macmillan Company, New York, publishers.

The selection from John Henry Boner is reprinted from *The Century Magazine* (November, 1889), by permission of D. Appleton-Century Company, Inc., publishers.

The selection from Robert Bridges is reprinted from his *The Testament of Beauty* (1930), by permission of Oxford University Press, New York, publishers.

The selection from William Cullen Bryant is reprinted from *The Poetical Works of William Cullen Bryant* (2 vols., 1883), by permission of D. Appleton-Century Company, Inc., publishers.

The selection from James D. Corrothers is reprinted from *The Century Magazine* (November, 1912), by permission of D. Appleton-Century Company, Inc., publishers.

The selections from Hart Crane are reprinted from *Collected Poems of Hart Crane* (1933), edited with an introduction by Waldo Frank, by permission of Liveright Publishing Corporation, publishers.

The selection from Emily Dickinson is reprinted from *The Poems of Emily Dickinson* (1930), edited by Martha Dickinson Bianchi and Alfred Leete Hampson, by permission of Little, Brown and Company, publishers.

The selections from Austin Dobson are reprinted from his *Collected Poems* (1899), by permission of Mr. A. T. A. Dobson and of Oxford University Press, London, publishers.

The selection from Lord Alfred Douglas is reprinted from *The Collected Poems of Lord Alfred Douglas* (1915), by permission of The Richards Press, Limited, London, publishers.

The selection from T. S. Eliot is reprinted from his *Collected Poems, 1909–1935*, by permission of Harcourt, Brace and Company, Inc., publishers.

The selection from Paul Engle is reprinted from his *West of Midnight*, copyright 1939, 1940, 1941, by Paul Engle, by permission of Mr. Engle, *Poetry*, and Random House, Inc., publishers.

ACKNOWLEDGMENTS

The selection from Wilfrid Wilson Gibson is reprinted from his *Collected Poems, 1905-1925*, by permission of The Macmillan Company, publishers.

The selections from Sir Edmund Gosse are reprinted from *The Collected Poems of Edmund Gosse* (1911), by permission of William Heinemann, Limited, London, publishers.

The selection from Horace Gregory is reprinted from his *Poems, 1930-1940*, by permission of Harcourt, Brace and Company, Inc., publishers.

The selections from Thomas Hardy are reprinted from *Collected Poems of Thomas Hardy* (1920), by permission of The Macmillan Company, publishers.

The selection from Frederick Robert Higgins is reprinted from his *The Gap of Brightness* (1940), by permission of The Macmillan Company, publishers.

The selections from Robert Hillyer are reprinted from *The Collected Verse of Robert Hillyer*, copyright 1933, and from his *A Letter to Robert Frost and Others*, copyright 1936, 1937, by Robert Hillyer; by permission of Alfred A. Knopf, Inc., publishers.

The selection from Alexander Hay Japp is reprinted from his *The Circle of the Year* (1893).

The selection from Lionel Pigot Johnson is reprinted from *Poetical Works of Lionel Pigot Johnson* (1915, 1917), by permission of George Allen & Unwin, Limited, London, publishers.

The selections from Thomas S. Jones, Jr., are reprinted from his *Shadow of the Perfect Rose; Collected Poems of Thomas S. Jones, Jr.*, with a Memoir by John L. Foley (1937), by permission of Mr. Foley.

The selections from Alfred Joyce Kilmer are reprinted from his *Main Street and Other Poems*, copyright 1917 by, and with permission of, Doubleday, Doran and Company, Inc., publishers.

The selections from Amy Lowell are reprinted from *Selected Poems of Amy Lowell* (1928) and from her *A Critical Fable* (1922), by permission of Houghton Mifflin Company, publishers.

The selection from Herman Melville is reprinted from his *Poems* (1924).

ACKNOWLEDGMENTS

The selection from Christopher Morley is reprinted from *Parson's Pleasure;* copyright, 1923, by Christopher Morley; published by J. B. Lippincott Company.

The selection from Thomas Sturge Moore is reprinted from *The Poems of T. Sturge Moore* (4 vols., 1931–1933), by permission of The Macmillan Company, publishers.

The selection from Edwin Muir is reprinted from his *Journeys and Places* (1937), by permission of J. M. Dent and Sons, Limited, London, publishers.

The selection from Norreys Jephson O'Conor is reprinted from his *Songs of the Celtic Past* (1918), by his permission.

The selections from Edwin Arlington Robinson are reprinted from his *Collected Poems* (1921), by permission of The Macmillan Company, publishers.

The selection from Siegfried Sassoon is reprinted from his *The Heart's Journey* (1928), by permission of Mr. Sassoon.

The selections from Karl Jay Shapiro are reprinted from *Person, Place and Thing,* copyright 1942, and from his *V-Letter and Other Poems,* copyright 1944, by permission of Reynal and Hitchcock, Inc., publishers.

The selection from Allen Tate is reprinted from his *Selected Poems* (1937), by permission of Charles Scribner's Sons, publishers.

The selection from Francis Thompson is reprinted from *The Works of Francis Thompson* (3 vols., 1914), by permission of Mr. Wilfrid Meynell.

The selection from Sir William Watson is reprinted from *The Poems of Sir William Watson, 1878–1935,* by permission of George G. Harrap & Company, Limited, publishers.

The selection from Walter Theodore Watts-Dunton is reprinted from his *The Coming of Love—and Other Poems* (1913), by permission of John Lane, the Bodley Head, Limited, London, publishers.

The selection from William Carlos Williams is reprinted from *Poetry: A Magazine of Verse* (March, 1935), by permission of Dr. Williams and *Poetry.*

The selections from Humbert Wolfe are reprinted from his *This Blind Rose,* copyright 1929 by, and with permission of,

ACKNOWLEDGMENTS

Doubleday Doran and Company, Inc., publishers; from his *Early Poems*, copyright 1930, 1931 by permission of Alfred A. Knopf, Inc., publishers; and from his *Out of Great Tribulation* (1940), by permission of Victor Gollancz, Limited, London, publishers.

The selection from Elinor Wylie is reprinted from *Collected Poems of Elinor Wylie*, copyright 1932 by and with permission of Alfred A. Knopf, Inc., publishers.

The selection from William Butler Yeats is reprinted from *The Collected Poems of W. B. Yeats* (1933), by permission of The Macmillan Company, publishers.

CONTENTS

	PAGE
PREFACE	v

I

DAVID (10th century B.C.)
    From "A SONG TO DAVID," *Christopher Smart* 1

HOMER (9th century B.C.)
    From "DRAKE," *Charles Fitz-Geffrey* 4
    TO HOMER, *John Keats* 4
    ACHILLES, *Ernest Myers* 5
    THE ODYSSEY, *Andrew Lang* 5

SAPPHO (7th century B.C.)
    SAPPHICS, *Algernon Charles Swinburne* 6

ANACREON (572?–?488 B.C.)
    ELEGIE UPON ANACREON, *Abraham Cowley* 8

PINDAR (*c.* 522?–443 B.C.)
    THE PRAISE OF PINDAR, *Abraham Cowley* 11

MISCELLANY
    From "ON LYRIC POETRY," *Mark Akenside* 13

ÆSCHYLUS (525–456 B.C.)
    ÆSCHYLOS AND SOPHOCLES, *Walter Savage Landor* . . . 15

SOPHOCLES (496–406 B.C.)
    TO A FRIEND, *Matthew Arnold* 16
    AFTER READING "AJAX," *William Cory* 16

EURIPIDES (480–406 B.C.)
    From "WINE OF CYPRUS," *Elizabeth Barrett Browning* . 17
    From "BALAUSTION'S ADVENTURE," *Robert Browning* . . 17

THEOCRITUS (3rd century B.C.)
    THEOCRITUS, *Charles Hartley Langhorne*. 19
    FOR A COPY OF THEOCRITUS, *Austin Dobson* 20
    THEOCRITUS, *Edmund Gosse* 21

CONTENTS

	PAGE
LUCRETIUS (96?–55 B.C.)	
LUCRETIUS, *Alfred, Lord Tennyson*	22
LUCRETIUS, *Lionel Johnson*	30
CATULLUS (84?–54 B.C.)	
ON CATULLUS, *Walter Savage Landor*	31
"FRATER AVE ATQUE VALE," *Alfred, Lord Tennyson*	31
VIRGIL (70–19 B.C.)	
TO VIRGIL, *Alfred, Lord Tennyson*	31
THE AENEID, *J. W. Mackail*	33
HORACE (65–8 B.C.)	
From "AN ESSAY ON CRITICISM," *Alexander Pope*	34
From "CHILDE HAROLD'S PILGRIMAGE," *Lord Byron*	34
TO Q. H. F., *Austin Dobson*	34
MARTIAL (1st century A.D.)	
MARTIAL IN TOWN, *Andrew Lang*	36
MISCELLANY	
From "THE HOUS OF FAME," *Geoffrey Chaucer*	37

II

OMAR KHAYYÁM (12th century)	
FOR OMAR, *Humbert Wolfe*	39
JACOPONE DA TODI (1230?–1306)	
AUSTERITY OF POETRY, *Matthew Arnold*	40
DANTE ALIGHIERI (1265–1321)	
DANTE, *William Cullen Bryant*	40
A DREAM, AFTER READING DANTE'S EPISODE OF PAOLO AND FRANCESCA, *John Keats*	41
DIVINA COMMEDIA, *Henry Wadsworth Longfellow*	41
From "THE TESTAMENT OF BEAUTY," *Robert Bridges*	44
FRANCESCO PETRARCA (1304–1374)	
From "ITALY," *Samuel Rogers*	46
From "CHILDE HAROLD'S PILGRIMAGE," *Lord Byron*	47
HAFIZ (14th century)	
TO HAFIZ OF SHIRAZ, *Gertrude Lowthian Bell*	48

CONTENTS

	PAGE
GEOFFREY CHAUCER (1340?–1400)	
Lament for Chaucer, *Thomas Hoccleve*	49
From "The Fall of Princes," *John Lydgate*	50
From "Garlande of Laurell," *John Skelton*	50
From "The Faerie Queene," *Edmund Spenser*	50
Written on the Blank Space at the End of Chaucer's Tale of "The Floure and the Lefe," *John Keats*	51
Chaucer, *Henry Wadsworth Longfellow*	51
From "A Dream of Fair Women," *Alfred, Lord Tennyson*	52
For Maister Geoffrey Chaucer, *Robert Hillyer*	52
FRANÇOIS VILLON (1431–1489)	
A Ballad of François Villon, *Algernon Charles Swinburne*	53

III

JOHN SKELTON (1460?–1529)	
Praise to John Skelton, *Horace Gregory*	55
SIR THOMAS WYATT (1503?–1542)	
On the Death of Sir T(homas) W(yatt), *Henry Howard, Earl of Surrey*	56
SAINT TERESA (1515–1582)	
From "Upon the Book and Picture of the Seraphical Saint Teresa," *Richard Crashaw*	58
PIERRE DE RONSARD (1524–1585)	
Ronsard, *Andrew Lang*	58
Ronsard and Hélène, *Humbert Wolfe*	59
LUIZ VAZ DE CAMOENS (1524–1580)	
Camoens, *Herman Melville*	59
TORQUATO TASSO (1544–1595)	
From "Childe Harold's Pilgrimage," *Lord Byron*	60
EDMUND SPENSER (1552?–1599)	
To the Learned Shepheard, *Gabriel Harvey*	62
A Vision upon the Conceit of "The Faery Queen," *Sir Walter Raleigh*	64
The Poets, *Leigh Hunt*	64

CONTENTS

SIR WALTER RALEIGH (1552–1618)
 To the Right Noble and Valorous Knight, Sir
  Walter Raleigh, *Edmund Spenser* 65

SIR PHILIP SIDNEY (1554–1586)
 Epitaph on Sir Philip Sidney,
  Fulke Greville, Lord Brooke 65
 On the Death of Sir Philip Sidney, *Henry Constable* 67

CHRISTOPHER MARLOWE (1564–1593)
 Christopher Marlowe, *Algernon Charles Swinburne* . 67
 After Reading "Tamburlaine the Great,"
  William Watson 68

WILLIAM SHAKESPEARE (1564–1616)
 To Our English Terence, Mr. Will. Shakespeare,
  John Davies of Hereford 68
 To the Memory of My Beloved the Author, Mr.
  William Shakespeare: and What He Hath Left Us,
  Ben Jonson 68
 Elegy on Mr. William Shakespeare, *William Basse* . . 70
 On Shakespeare, *John Milton* 71
 From "Prologue Spoken by Mr. Garrick,"
  Samuel Johnson 72
 Shakespeare and Milton, *Walter Savage Landor* . . . 73
 On Sitting Down to Read "King Lear" Once Again,
  John Keats 74
 To Shakespeare, *Hartley Coleridge* 74
 Shakespeare, *John Sterling* 75
 The Names, *Robert Browning* 76
 Shakspeare, *Matthew Arnold* 76
 The Spirit of Shakespeare, *George Meredith* 77
 To Shakespeare, *Thomas Hardy* 78
 To Shakespeare, *Hart Crane* 79

GEORGE CHAPMAN (1559?–1634)
 Sonnet 86, *William Shakespeare* 80
 To My Worthy Friend Mr. George Chapman, and His
  Translated Hesiod, *Michael Drayton* 80
 To My Worthy and Honoured Friend, Mr. George
  Chapman, On His Translation of Hesiod's Works
  and Days, *Ben Jonson* 81
 On First Looking into Chapman's Homer, *John Keats* 82

CONTENTS

THOMAS CAMPION (1567–1620)
Madrigal, *Edmund Gosse* 82

THOMAS DEKKER (1572?–1632)
Thomas Decker, *Algernon Charles Swinburne* . . . 83

BEN JONSON (1573?–1637)
Master Francis Beaumont's Letter to Ben Jonson, *Francis Beaumont* 83
An Ode for Ben Jonson, *Robert Herrick* 86
His Prayer to Ben Jonson, *Robert Herrick* 86
Upon Ben Jonson, *Robert Herrick* 87
Upon M. Ben Jonson, Epigram, *Robert Herrick* . . . 87
Ben Jonson, *Algernon Charles Swinburne* 88

FRANCIS BEAUMONT (1584–1616)
To Francis Beaumont, *Ben Jonson* 88
Bards of Passion and of Mirth, *John Keats* 89

JOHN FLETCHER (1579–1625)
Upon Master Fletchers Incomparable Playes, *Robert Herrick* 90
Upon Mr. John Fletcher's Playes, *Edmund Waller* . . 90
To Fletcher Reviv'd, *Richard Lovelace* 91
Upon Mr. Fletchers Playes, *Henry Vaughan* 93

JOHN DONNE (1573–1631)
To John Donne, *Ben Jonson* 95
An Elegy upon the Death of Doctor Donne, Dean of Paul's, *Thomas Carew* 95
On Donne's Poetry, *Samuel Taylor Coleridge* 98

JOHN WEBSTER (1580?–?1625)
John Webster, *Algernon Charles Swinburne* 98
Whispers of Immortality, *T. S. Eliot* 99

PHILIP MASSINGER (1583–1640)
Philip Massinger, *Algernon Charles Swinburne* . . . 100

JOHN FORD (1586?–?1638)
To My Friend, Master John Ford, *James Shirley* . . 101

MISCELLANY
To My Most Dearly-Loved Friend, Henry Reynolds, Esquire, of Poets and Poesy, *Michael Drayton* . . . 101

IV

PAGE

ROBERT HERRICK (1591–1674)
    For a Copy of Herrick, *Austin Dobson* 107
    With a Copy of Herrick, *Edmund Gosse* 107

MISCELLANY
    A Session of the Poets, *Sir John Suckling* 108

GEORGE HERBERT (1593–1633)
    On Mr. G. Herbert's Book, entitled The Temple of Sacred Poems, sent to a gentlewoman,
                                     Richard Crashaw 112
    George Herbert, *Thomas S. Jones, Jr.* 112

RICHARD CRASHAW (1613?–1649)
    On the Death of Mr. Crashaw, *Abraham Cowley* . . 113
    Richard Crashaw, *Thomas S. Jones, Jr.* 115

JOHN MILTON (1608–1674)
    On Mr Milton's "Paradise Lost," *Andrew Marvell* . . 115
    Epigram on Milton, *John Dryden* 117
    England, 1802, *William Wordsworth* 117
    Milton, *Henry Wadsworth Longfellow* 118
    Milton, *Alfred, Lord Tennyson* 118

ABRAHAM COWLEY (1618–1667)
    On Mr. Abraham Cowley, His Death and Burial amongst the Ancient Poets, *Sir John Denham* . . . 119

HENRY VAUGHAN (1622–1695)
    At the Grave of Henry Vaughan, *Siegfried Sassoon* . 122
    Henry Vaughan, *Thomas S. Jones, Jr.* 122
    The Age of Herbert & Vaughan, *Edmund Blunden* . . 123

V

THOMAS SHADWELL (1642?–1692)
    Mac Flecknoe, *John Dryden* 124

JOHN OLDHAM (1653–1683)
    To the Memory of Mr. Oldham, *John Dryden* . . . 130

ANNE KILLIGREW (1660–1685)
    To the Pious Memory of the accomplisht young lady, Mrs. Anne Killigrew, *John Dryden* 130

CONTENTS xxiii

PAGE

WILLIAM CONGREVE (1670–1729)
To My Dear Friend, Mr. Congreve, on His Comedy Call'd "The Double-Dealer," *John Dryden* . . . 134

JOHN DRYDEN (1631–1700)
From "An Account of the Greatest English Poets," *Joseph Addison* 136
From "The Progress of Poesy," *Thomas Gray* . . . 140

JOSEPH ADDISON (1672–1719)
To the Earl of Warwick on the Death of Mr. Addison, *Thomas Tickell* 141

JONATHAN SWIFT (1667–1745)
Swift's Epitaph, *William Butler Yeats* 144

THOMAS PARNELL (1679–1718)
Epitaph on Dr. Parnell, *Oliver Goldsmith* 145

JOHN GAY (1685–1732)
On Mr. Gay, *Alexander Pope* 145
From "Epistle to Dr. Arbuthnot," *Alexander Pope* . . 146

MISCELLANY
The First Epistle of the Second Book of Horace, *Alexander Pope* 146

ALEXANDER POPE (1688–1744)
To Mr. Pope, *Thomas Parnell* 157
From "Mr. Pope's Welcome from Greece," *John Gay* 160
From "Table Talk," *William Cowper* 163
Pope at Twickenham, *Charles Kent* 164
Mr. Pope, *Allen Tate* 166

JOHN DYER (1700?–1758)
To the Poet, John Dyer, *William Wordsworth* . . . 167

JAMES THOMSON (1700–1748)
Ode on the Death of Mr. Thomson, *William Collins* . 168

WILLIAM COLLINS (1721–1759)
Remembrance of Collins, *William Wordsworth* . . . 169

SAMUEL JOHNSON (1709–1784)
Epitaph on Dr. Johnson, *William Cowper* 170

THOMAS GRAY (1716–1771)
To Mr. Gray, *Thomas Warton, Jr.* 171

CONTENTS

JOSEPH WARTON (1722–1800)
THOMAS WARTON, JR. (1728–1790)
    THE WARTONS, *Edmund Blunden* 171
CHRISTOPHER SMART (1722–1771)
    From "PARLEYINGS WITH CERTAIN PEOPLE OF IMPORTANCE," *Robert Browning* 172
SIR WILLIAM JONES (1746–1794)
    ON THE INGENIOUS MR. JONES, *John Scott* 180
WILLIAM COWPER (1731–1800)
    COWPER, *John Clare* 180
    COWPER'S GRAVE, *Elizabeth Barrett Browning* 181

VI

THOMAS CHATTERTON (1752–1770)
    MONODY ON THE DEATH OF CHATTERTON,
                    Samuel Taylor Coleridge 184
    From "RESOLUTION AND INDEPENDENCE,"
                    William Wordsworth 187
    TO CHATTERTON, *John Keats* 187
    THOMAS CHATTERTON, *Dante Gabriel Rossetti* 187
GEORGE CRABBE (1754–1832)
    From "ENGLISH BARDS AND SCOTCH REVIEWERS,"
                          Lord Byron 188
    GEORGE CRABBE, *Edwin Arlington Robinson* 188
FRIEDRICH VON SCHILLER (1759–1805)
    TO THE AUTHOR OF "THE ROBBERS,"
                    Samuel Taylor Coleridge 189
WILLIAM BLAKE (1757–1827)
    WILLIAM BLAKE, *Dante Gabriel Rossetti* 189
    WILLIAM BLAKE, *James Thomson* 190
ROBERT BURNS (1759–1796)
    AT THE GRAVE OF BURNS, *William Wordsworth* . . . 191
    ROBERT BURNS, *Henry Wadsworth Longfellow* 193
    BURNS, *John Greenleaf Whittier* 195
FRIEDRICH HÖLDERLIN (1770–1843)
    HÖLDERLIN'S JOURNEY, *Edwin Muir* 199

CONTENTS

WILLIAM WORDSWORTH (1770–1850)
To William Wordsworth, *Samuel Taylor Coleridge* . 201
To Wordsworth, *Percy Bysshe Shelley* 204
The Lost Leader, *Robert Browning* 205
On a Portrait of Wordsworth by B. R. Haydon,
  Elizabeth Barrett Browning 206
William Wordsworth, *Francis Turner Palgrave* . . . 206
From "Stanzas in Memory of the Author of 'Obermann,'" *Matthew Arnold* 208
Memorial Verses, *Matthew Arnold* 209

SAMUEL TAYLOR COLERIDGE (1772–1834)
From "The Prelude," *William Wordsworth* 211
Samuel Taylor Coleridge, *Dante Gabriel Rossetti* . . 213
Coleridge, *Walter Theodore Watts-Dunton* 214

ROBERT SOUTHEY (1774–1843)
From "Don Juan," *Lord Byron* 214
To Southey, 1833, *Walter Savage Landor* 216

WALTER SAVAGE LANDOR (1775–1864)
Landor, *Alexander Hay Japp* 218
In Memory of Walter Savage Landor,
  Algernon Charles Swinburne 218

THOMAS MOORE (1779–1852)
To Thomas Moore [1816], *Lord Byron* 220
To Thomas Moore [1817], *Lord Byron* 221

GEORGE GORDON, LORD BYRON (1788–1824)
To [Byron], *Percy Bysshe Shelley* 221
Sonnet to Byron, *Percy Bysshe Shelley* 222
To Byron, *John Keats* 222
From "Stanzas from the Grande Chartreuse,"
  Matthew Arnold 223
From "Letter to Lord Byron," *W. H. Auden* . . . 223

PERCY BYSSHE SHELLEY (1792–1822)
From "Pauline," *Robert Browning* 225
Memorabilia, *Robert Browning* 227
Percy Bysshe Shelley, *Dante Gabriel Rossetti* . . . 228
Shelley's Skylark, *Thomas Hardy* 228
A Red Carpet for Shelley, *Elinor Wylie* 229

JOHN KEATS (1795–1821)

To John Keats, *Leigh Hunt* 231
Adonais, *Percy Bysshe Shelley* 232
Popularity, *Robert Browning* 247
After a Lecture on Keats, *Oliver Wendell Holmes* . . 249
John Keats, *Dante Gabriel Rossetti* 251
To John Keats, *Amy Lowell* 251
On Reading Keats in War Time, *Karl Jay Shapiro* . . 252

JAMES HOGG (1770–1835)

Extempore Effusion upon the Death of James Hogg, *William Wordsworth* 252

VII

GIACOMO LEOPARDI (1798–1837)

To Giacomo Leopardi, *T. S. Moore* 254

HEINRICH HEINE (1797–1856)

Heine's Grave, *Matthew Arnold* 255

THOMAS HOOD (1799–1845)

To the Memory of Hood, *James Russell Lowell* . . . 261
Thomas Hood, *Edwin Arlington Robinson* 262

MISCELLANY

From "A Vision of Poets," *Elizabeth Barrett Browning* 263

ELIZABETH BARRETT BROWNING (1806–1861)

[Her "Last Poems"–], *Emily Dickinson* 267
E. B. B., *James Thomson* 268

MISCELLANY

From "A Fable for Critics," *James Russell Lowell* . . 269

EDGAR ALLAN POE (1809–1849)

Poe's Cottage at Fordham, *John Henry Boner* . . . 274
Israfel, *Karl Jay Shapiro* 276

HENRY WADSWORTH LONGFELLOW (1807–1882)

To H. W. L., *James Russell Lowell* 277

MISCELLANY

The Crystal, *Sidney Lanier* 278

ALFRED, LORD TENNYSON (1809–1892)

Wapentake, *Henry Wadsworth Longfellow* 281
Alfred Tennyson, *Wilfrid Scawen Blunt* 282

CONTENTS

ROBERT BROWNING (1812–1889)
    To ROBERT BROWNING, *Walter Savage Landor* 282
    From "SONNETS FROM THE PORTUGUESE,"
        Elizabeth Barrett Browning 283

EDWARD FITZGERALD (1809–1883)
    To E. FITZGERALD, *Alfred, Lord Tennyson* 284

EDWARD LEAR (1812–1888)
    EDWARD LEAR, *W. H. Auden* 285

VICTOR HUGO (1802–1885)
    To VICTOR HUGO, *Alfred, Lord Tennyson* 286
    To VICTOR HUGO, *Algernon Charles Swinburne* . . . 286

CHARLES BAUDELAIRE (1821–1867)
    AVE ATQUE VALE, *Algernon Charles Swinburne* . . . 292
    BAUDELAIRE, *Humbert Wolfe* 297

WALT WHITMAN (1819–1892)
    ODE TO WALT WHITMAN, *Stephen Vincent Benét* . . . 298

EMILY DICKINSON (1830–1886)
    To EMILY DICKINSON, *Hart Crane* 309
    EMILY DICKINSON, *Paul Engle* 309

PAUL VERLAINE (1844–1896)
    VERLAINE, *Edwin Arlington Robinson* 310

JEAN ARTHUR RIMBAUD (1854–1891)
    RIMBAUD, *W. H. Auden* 310
    PRELUDES FOR MEMNON, LVI, *Conrad Aiken* 311

OSCAR WILDE (1856–1900)
    THE DEAD POET, *Lord Alfred Douglas* 312

LIONEL JOHNSON (1867–1902)
    LIONEL JOHNSON, *Joyce Kilmer* 312

MISCELLANY
    From "ODE FOR THE DIAMOND JUBILEE OF QUEEN
        VICTORIA, 1897," *Francis Thompson* 313

VIII

PAUL LAURENCE DUNBAR (1872–1906)
    PAUL LAURENCE DUNBAR, *James D. Corrothers* 315

CONTENTS

PAGE

ALGERNON CHARLES SWINBURNE (1837–1909)
A Singer Asleep, *Thomas Hardy* 316

RUPERT BROOKE (1887–1915)
Rupert Brooke, *Wilfrid Wilson Gibson* 317

FRANCIS LEDWIDGE (1891–1917)
For Francis Ledwidge, *Norreys Jephson O'Conor* . . 319

GERARD MANLEY HOPKINS (1844–1889)
Father Gerard Hopkins, S. J., *Joyce Kilmer* 320

AUSTIN DOBSON (1840–1921)
Austin Dobson, *Christopher Morley* 320

ALICE MEYNELL (1847–1922)
On Looking at a Copy of Alice Meynell's Poems Given Me Years Ago by a Friend, *Amy Lowell* . . 321

THOMAS STEARNS ELIOT (1888–)
EZRA POUND (1885–)
From "A Critical Fable," *Amy Lowell* 323

PADRAIC O'CONAIRE (1881–1928)
Padraic O'Conaire—Gaelic Storyteller, *Frederick Robert Higgins* 328

ROBERT BRIDGES (1844–1930)
Robert Bridges, *Humbert Wolfe* 329

DAVID HERBERT LAWRENCE (1885–1930)
An Elegy for D. H. Lawrence, *William Carlos Williams* 330

ROBERT FROST (1875–)
A Letter to Robert Frost, *Robert Hillyer* 333

STEPHEN VINCENT BENÉT (1898–1943)
S. V. B., *William Rose Benét* 339

WILLIAM BUTLER YEATS (1865–1939)
In Memory of W. B. Yeats, *W. H. Auden* 341

INDEX OF SUBJECTS 345

INDEX OF AUTHORS 349

INDEX OF TITLES 357

INDEX OF FIRST LINES 363

I

DAVID (10th century B.C.)

From "A Song to David"

O thou, that sit'st upon a throne,
With harp of high majestic tone,
   To praise the King of kings;
And voice of heav'n-ascending swell,
Which, while its deeper notes excel,
   Clear, as a clarion, rings:

To bless each valley, grove and coast,
And charm the cherubs to the post
   Of gratitude in throngs;
To keep the days on Zion's mount,
And send the year to his account,
   With dances and with songs:

O servant of God's holiest charge,
The minister of praise at large,
   Which thou mayst now receive;
From thy blest mansion hail and hear,
From topmost eminence appear
   To this the wreath I weave.

Great, valiant, pious, good, and clean,
Sublime, contemplative, serene,
   Strong, constant, pleasant, wise!
Bright effluence of exceeding grace;
Best man!—the swiftness and the race,
   The peril, and the prize!

* * * * *

DAVID (10th century B.C.)

His Muse, bright angel of his verse,
Gives balm for all the thorns that pierce,
   For all the pangs that rage;
Blest light, still gaining on the gloom
The more than Michal of his bloom,
   Th' Abishag of his age.

He sung of God—the mighty source
Of all things—the stupendous force
   On which all strength depends;
From whose right arm, beneath whose eyes,
All period, pow'r, and enterprise
   Commences, reigns, and ends.

Angels—their ministry and meed,
Which to and fro with blessing speed,
   Or with their citterns wait;
Where Michael with his millions bows,
Where dwells the seraph and his spouse,
   The cherub and her mate.

Of Man—the semblance and effect
Of God and Love—the Saint elect
   For infinite applause—
To rule the land, and briny broad,
To be laborious in his laud,
   And heroes in his cause.

The world—the clust'ring spheres he made,
The glorious light, the soothing shade,
   Dale, champaign, grove, and hill;
The multitudinous abyss,
Where secrecy remains in bliss,
   And wisdom hides her skill.

Trees, plants, and flow'rs—of virtuous root;
Gem yielding blossom, yielding fruit,
   Choice gums and precious balm;
Bless ye the nosegay in the vale,
And with the sweetness of the gale
   Enrich the thankful psalm.

DAVID (10th century B.C.)

Of fowl—e'en ev'ry beak and wing
Which cheer the winter, hail the spring,
   That live in peace or prey;
They that make music, or that mock,
The quail, the brave domestic cock,
   The raven, swan, and jay.

Of fishes—ev'ry size and shape,
Which Nature frames of light escape,
   Devouring man to shun:
The shells are in the wealthy deep,
The shoals upon the surface leap,
   And love the glancing sun.

Of beasts—the beaver plods his task;
While the sleek tigers roll and bask,
   Nor yet the shades arouse;
Her cave the mining coney scoops;
Where o'er the mead the mountain stoops,
   The kids exult and browse.

Of gems—their virtue and their price,
Which hid in earth from man's device,
   Their darts of lustre sheathe;
The jasper of the master's stamp,
The topaz blazing like a lamp
   Among the mines beneath.

Blest was the tenderness he felt
When to his graceful harp he knelt,
   And did for audience call;
When Satan with his hand he quell'd,
And in serene suspense he held
   The frantic throes of Saul.

His furious foes no more malign'd
As he such melody divin'd,
   And sense and soul detain'd;
Now striking strong, now soothing soft,
He sent the godly sounds aloft,
   Or in delight refrain'd.

* * * * *

DAVID (10th century B.C.)

O David, scholar of the Lord!
Such is thy science, whence reward
  And infinite degree;
O strength, O sweetness, lasting ripe!
God's harp thy symbol, and thy type
  The lion and the bee!

CHRISTOPHER SMART
(1722–1771)

HOMER (9th century B.C.)

From "Drake"

Heart-stealing Homer, marrow of the Muses,
Chief grace of Greece, best pearl of poetry,
Drowner of souls in art's o'erwhelming sluices,
Embellished with Phoebus lunary,
Decked with the Graces' rich embroidery,
  Sweet honey-suckle, whence all poets' sprights
  Suck the sweet honey of divine delights.

CHARLES FITZ-GEFFREY
(1575?–1638)

To Homer

Standing aloof in giant ignorance,
  Of thee I hear and of the Cyclades,
As one who sits ashore and longs perchance
  To visit dolphin-coral in deep seas.
So thou wast blind!—but then the veil was rent,
  For Jove uncurtain'd Heaven to let thee live,
And Neptune made for thee a spumy tent,
  And Pan made sing for thee his forest-hive;
Ay on the shores of darkness there is light,
  And precipices show untrodden green;
There is a budding morrow in midnight;
  There is a triple sight in blindness keen:
Such seeing hadst thou, as it once befell
To Dian, Queen of Earth, and Heaven, and Hell.

JOHN KEATS
(1795–1821)

HOMER (9th century B.C.)

Achilles

Athwart the sunrise of our western day
  The form of great Achilles, high and clear,
  Stands forth in arms, wielding the Pelian spear.
The sanguine tides of that immortal fray,
Swept on by gods, around him surge and sway,
  Wherethrough the helms of many a warrior peer,
  Strong men and swift, their tossing plumes uprear.
But stronger, swifter, goodlier he than they,
More awful, more divine. Yet mark anigh;
  Some fiery pang hath rent his soul within,
  Some hovering shade his brows encompasseth.
What gifts hath Fate for all his chivalry?
  Even such as hearts heroic oftenest win;
  Honour, a friend, anguish, untimely death.

                        ERNEST MYERS
                        (1844–1921)

The Odyssey

As one that for a weary space has lain
Lulled by the song of Circe and her wine
In gardens near the pale of Proserpine,
Where that Ægean isle forgets the main,
And only the low lutes of love complain,
And only shadows of wan lovers pine,
As such an one were glad to know the brine
Salt on his lips, and the large air again,—
So gladly, from the songs of modern speech
Men turn, and see the stars, and feel the free
Shrill wind beyond the close of heavy flowers,
And through the music of the languid hours,
They hear like ocean on a western beach
The surge and thunder of the Odyssey.

                        ANDREW LANG
                        (1844–1912)

SAPPHO (7th century B.C.)

Sapphics

All the night sleep came not upon my eyelids,
Shed not dew, nor shook nor unclosed a feather,
Yet with lips shut close and with eyes of iron
    Stood and beheld me.

Then to me so lying awake a vision
Came without sleep over the seas and touched me,
Softly touched mine eyelids and lips; and I too,
    Full of the vision,

Saw the white implacable Aphrodite,
Saw the hair unbound and the feet unsandalled
Shine as fire of sunset on western waters;
    Saw the reluctant

Feet, the straining plumes of the doves that drew her,
Looking always, looking with necks reverted,
Back to Lesbos, back to the hills whereunder
    Shone Mitylene;

Heard the flying feet of the Loves behind her
Make a sudden thunder upon the waters,
As the thunder flung from the strong unclosing
    Wings of a great wind.

So the goddess fled from her place, with awful
Sound of feet and thunder of wings around her;
While behind a clamour of singing women
    Severed the twilight.

Ah the singing, ah the delight, the passion!
All the Loves wept, listening; sick with anguish,
Stood the crowned nine Muses about Apollo;
    Fear was upon them,

While the tenth sang wonderful things they knew not.
Ah the tenth, the Lesbian! the nine were silent,
None endured the sound of her song for weeping;
    Laurel by laurel,

SAPPHO (7th century B.C.)

Faded all their crowns; but about her forehead,
Round her woven tresses and ashen temples
White as dead snow, paler than grass in summer,
   Ravaged with kisses,

Shone a light of fire as a crown for ever.
Yea, almost the implacable Aphrodite
Paused, and almost wept; such a song was that song.
   Yea, by her name too

Called her, saying, "Turn to me, O my Sappho;"
Yet she turned her face from the Loves, she saw not
Tears for laughter darken immortal eyelids,
   Heard not about her

Fearful fitful wings of the doves departing,
Saw not how the bosom of Aphrodite
Shook with weeping, saw not her shaken raiment,
   Saw not her hands wrung;

Saw the Lesbians kissing across their smitten
Lutes with lips more sweet than the sound of lute-strings,
Mouth to mouth and hand upon hand, her chosen,
   Fairer than all men;

Only saw the beautiful lips and fingers,
Full of songs and kisses and little whispers,
Full of music; only beheld among them
   Soar, as a bird soars

Newly fledged, her visible song, a marvel,
Made of perfect sound and exceeding passion,
Sweetly shapen, terrible, full of thunders,
   Clothed with the wind's wings.

Then rejoiced she, laughing with love, and scattered
Roses, awful roses of holy blossom;
Then the Loves thronged sadly with hidden faces
   Round Aphrodite,

Then the Muses, stricken at heart, were silent;
Yea, the gods waxed pale; such a song was that song.

SAPPHO (7th century B.C.)

All reluctant, all with a fresh repulsion,
   Fled from before her.

All withdrew long since, and the land was barren,
   Full of fruitless women and music only.
Now perchance, when winds are assuaged at sunset,
   Lulled at the dewfall,

By the grey sea-side, unassuaged, unheard of,
Unbeloved, unseen in the ebb of twilight,
Ghosts of outcast women return lamenting,
   Purged not in Lethe,

Clothed about with flame and with tears, and singing
Songs that move the heart of the shaken heaven,
Songs that break the heart of the earth with pity,
   Hearing, to hear them.

                 ALGERNON CHARLES SWINBURNE
                           (1837–1909)

Professor J. W. Mackail speaks of the "splendid but hardly exaggerated language" of Swinburne's "Sapphics," "that early poem where, alone among the moderns, he has mastered and all but reproduced one of her favorite metres, the Sapphic stanza which she invented and to which she gave her name." The reader may now experience a double delight in turning to "A Singer Asleep" by Thomas Hardy. See p. 316.

ANACREON (572?–?488 B.C.)

Elegie upon Anacreon
Who was choaked by a GRAPE-STONE

Spoken by the God of LOVE

How shall I lament thine end,
My best *Servant*, and my *Friend*?
Nay and, if from a *Deity*
So much *Deif'ed* as I,
It sound not too profane and odd,
Oh my *Master*, and my *God*!
For 'tis true, most mighty *Poet*,
(Though I like not Men should know it)
I am in naked *Nature* less,
Less by much then in thy *Dress*.

ANACREON (572?–?488 B.C.)

All thy Verse is softer far
Then the downy Feathers are,
Of my Wings, or of my *Arrows*,
Of my Mothers *Doves*, or *Sparrows*.
Sweet as Lovers freshest *kisses*,
Or their riper following blisses,
Graceful, cleanly, smooth and round,
All with *Venus Girdle* bound,
And thy *Life* was all the while
Kind and gentle as thy *Stile*.
The smooth-pac'd *Hours* of ev'ry day
Glided numerously away.
Like thy *Verse* each *Hour* did pass,
Sweet and short, like that it was.
 Some do but their *Youth* allow me,
Just what they by *Nature* owe me,
The Time that's *mine*, and not their *own*,
The certain *Tribute* of my *Crown*,
When they grow old, they grow to be
Too *Busie*, or too *wise* for me.
Thou wert *wiser*, and did'st know
None too *wise* for Love can grow,
Love was with thy *Life* entwin'd
Close as *Heat* with *Fire* is joyn'd,
A powerful *Brand* prescrib'd the date
Of thine, like *Meleagers* Fate.
Th' *Antiperistasis* of *Age*
More enflam'd thy amorous rage,
Thy *silver Hairs* yielded me more
Then even *golden curls* before.
 Had I the power of *Creation*,
As I have of *Generation*,
Where I the matter must obey,
And cannot work *Plate* out of *Clay*,
My *Creatures* should be all like *Thee*,
'Tis *Thou* shouldst their *Idæa* be.
They, like Thee, should throughly hate
Bus'iness, Honor, Title, State.
Other wealth they should not know
But what my *Living Mines* bestow;

[9]

ANACREON (572?–?488 B.C.)

The pomp of *Kings* they should confess
At their *Crownings* to be less
Then a Lovers humblest guise,
When at his *Mistress* feet he lies.
Rumour they no more should mind
Then Men safe-landed do the *Wind*,
Wisdom it self they should not hear
When it presumes to be *Severe*.
Beauty alone they should admire;
Nor look at *Fortunes* vain attire,
Nor ask what *Parents* it can shew;
With *Dead* or *Old* t'has nought to do.
They should not love yet *All*, or *Any*,
But very *Much*, and very *Many*.
All their Life should gilded be
With Mirth, and Wit, and Gayety,
Well remembring, and *Applying*
The *Necessity* of *Dying*.
Their chearful Heads should always wear
All that crowns the flowry year.
They should always laugh, and sing,
And dance, and strike th'harmonious string.
Verse should from their Tongue so flow,
As if it in the *Mouth* did *grow*,
As swiftly answering their command,
As tunes obey the artful *Hand*.
And whilst I do thus discover
Th'ingredients of a happy *Lover*,
'Tis, my *Anacreon*, for thy sake
I of the *Grape* no mention make.

    Till my' *Anacreon* by thee fell,
Cursed Plant, I lov'd thee well.
And 'twas oft my wanton use
To dip my *Arrows* in thy juice.
Cursed Plant, 'tis true I see,
Th'old report that goes of Thee,
That with *Gyants* blood the Earth
Stain'd and poys'ned gave thee birth,
And now thou wreak'st thy ancient spight

ANACREON (572?–?488 B.C.)

On *Men* in whom *the Gods* delight.
Thy *Patron Bacchus*, 'tis no wonder,
Was brought forth in *Flames* and *Thunder*,
In rage, in quarrels, and in fights,
Worse then his *Tygers* he delights;
In all our heaven I think there be
No such *ill-natur'd God* as He.
Thou pretendest, *Trayt'erous Wine*,
To be the *Muses* friend and *Mine*.
With *Love* and *Wit* thou dost begin,
False Fires, alas, to draw us in.
Which, if our course we by them keep,
Misguide to *Madness*, or to *Sleep*.
Sleep were well; thou'hast learnt a way
To *Death* it self now to betray.
  It grieves me when I see what Fate
Does on the best of *Mankind* wait.
Poets or *Lovers* let them be,
'Tis neither *Love* nor *Poesie*
Can arm against *Deaths* smallest dart
The *Poets Head*, or *Lovers Heart*.
But when their *Life* in its decline,
Touches th'*Inevitable Line*,
All the *Worlds Mortal* to 'em then,
And *Wine* is *Aconite* to men.
Nay in *Deaths Hand* the *Grape-stone* proves
As strong as *Thunder* is in *Joves*.
              FINIS   ABRAHAM COWLEY
                                            (1618–1667)

PINDAR (c. 522?–443 B.C.)

The Praise of Pindar
In Imitation of Horace his second *Ode*, B. 4.

1.

Pindar is imitable by none;
  The *Phœnix Pindar* is a vast *Species* alone.
Who e're but *Dædalus* with waxen wings could fly
And neither *sink* too low, nor *soar* too high?

PINDAR (c. 522?–443 B.C.)

What could he who *follow'd* claim,
But of vain *boldness* the unhappy fame,
And by his fall a *Sea* to name?
Pindars unnavigable Song
Like a swoln *Flood* from some steep *Mountain* pours along,
The *Ocean* meets with such a *Voice*
From his enlarged *Mouth*, as drowns the *Oceans* noise.

2.

So *Pindar* does new *Words* and *Figures* roul
Down his impetuous *Dithyrambique Tide*,
Which in no *Channel* deigns t'abide,
Which neither *Banks* nor *Dikes* controul.
Whether th' *Immortal Gods* he sings
In a no less *Immortal strain*,
Or the great Acts of *God-descended Kings*,
Who in his Numbers still survive and *Reign*.
Each rich embroidered *Line*,
Which their triumphant *Brows* around,
By his sacred Hand is bound,
Does all their *starry Diadems* outshine.

3.

Whether at *Pisa's* race he please
To *carve* in polisht *Verse* the *Conque'rors Images*,
Whether the *Swift*, the *Skilful*, or the *Strong*,
Be crowned in his *Nimble*, *Artful*, *Vigorous* Song:
Whether some brave young man's untimely fate
In words worth *Dying for* he celebrate,
Such *mournful*, and such *pleasing* words,
As *joy* to'his *Mothers* and his *Mistress grief* affords:
He bids him *Live* and *Grow* in fame,
Among the *Stars* he sticks his *Name*:
The *Grave* can but the *Dross* of him devour,
So *small* is *Deaths*, so *great* the *Poets* power.

4.

Lo, how th'obsequious *Wind*, and swelling *Ayr*
The *Theban Swan* does upwards bear
Into the *walks* of *Clouds*, where he does play,
And with extended *Wings* opens his liquid way.

PINDAR (c. 522?–443 B.C.)

Whilst, alas, my *tim'erous Muse*
Unambitious tracks pursues;
Does with weak unballast wings,
About the *mossy Brooks* and *Springs*;
About the *Trees* new-blossom'ed *Heads*,
About the *Gardens* painted *Beds*,
About the *Fields* and flowry *Meads*,
And all *inferior beauteous things*
  Like the laborious *Bee*,
  For little drops of *Honey* flee,
And there with *Humble Sweets* contents her *Industrie*.

ABRAHAM COWLEY
(1618–1667)

[MISCELLANY]

From "On Lyric Poetry"

I. 1

Once more I join the Thespian choir,
And taste th'inspiring fount again;
O parent of the Grecian lyre,
Admit me to thy pow'rful strain.
And lo! with ease my step invades
The pathless vale and op'ning shades,
Till now I spy her verdant seat;
And now at large I drink the sound,
While these her offspring, list'ning round,
By turns her melody repeat.

I. 2

I see Anacreon smile and sing,
His silver tresses breathe perfume;
His cheek displays a second spring
Of roses, taught by wine to bloom.
Away, deceitful Cares! away,
And let me listen to his lay;
Let me the wanton pomp enjoy,
While in smooth dance the light-wing'd Hours
Lead round his lyre its patron pow'rs,
Kind Laughter and convivial Joy.

[ON LYRIC POETRY]

I. 3

Broke from the fetters of his native land,
Devoting shame and vengeance to her lords,
With louder impulse, and a threat'ning hand,
The Lesbian patriot smites the sounding chords.
Ye wretches! Ye perfidious train!
Ye curs'd of gods and free-born men!
Ye murderers of the laws!
Though now ye glory in your lust,
Though now ye tread the feeble neck in dust,
Yet Time and righteous Jove will judge your dreadful cause.

II. 1

But lo! to Sappho's melting airs
Descends the radiant Queen of Love:
She smiles, and asks what fonder cares
Her suppliant's plaintive measures move?
Why is my faithful maid distrest?
Who, Sappho, wounds thy tender breast?
Say, flies he?—Soon he shall pursue:
Shuns he thy gifts?—He soon shall give:
Slights he thy sorrows?—He shall grieve,
And soon to all thy wishes bow.

II. 2

But, O Melpomene! for whom
Awakes thy golden shell again?
What mortal breath shall e'er presume
To echo that unbounded strain?
Majestic in the frown of years,
Behold the man of Thebes appears
For some there are whose mighty frame
The hand of Jove at birth endow'd
With hopes that mock the gazing crowd,
As eagles drink the noontide flame.

1745
the Lesbian patriot] Alcaeus
the man of Thebes] Pindar

MARK AKENSIDE
(1721–1770)

ÆSCHYLUS (525–456 B.C.)

Aeschylos and Sophocles

Sophocles. Thou goest then, and leavest none behind
Worthy to rival thee!

Æschylos.   Nay, say not so.
Whose is the hand that now is pressing mine?
A hand I may not ever press again!
What glorious forms hath it brought boldly forth
From Pluto's realm! The blind old Œdipos
Was led on one side by Antigone,
Sophocles propped the other.

Sophocles.   Sophocles
Soothed not Prometheus chained upon his rock,
Keeping the vultures and the Gods away;
Sophocles is not greater than the chief
Who conquered Ilion, nor could he revenge
His murder, or stamp everlasting brand
Upon the brow of that adulterous wife.

Æschylos. Live, and do more. Thine is the Lemnian isle,
And thou has placed the arrows in the hand
Of Philoctetes, has assuaged his wounds
And given his aid without which Greece had failed.

Sophocles. I did indeed drive off the pest of flies;
We also have our pest of them which buzz
About our honey, darken it, and sting;
We laugh at them, for under hands like ours,
Without the wing that Philoctetes shook,
One single feather crushes the whole swarm.
I must be grave. Hath Sicily such charms
Above our Athens? Many charms hath she,
But she hath kings. Accursed be the race!

Æschylos. But where kings honor men better than they
Let kings be honored too. The laurel crown
Surmounts the golden; wear it; and farewell.
                              WALTER SAVAGE LANDOR
                                  (1775–1864)

SOPHOCLES (496?–406 B.C.)

To A Friend

Who prop, thou ask'st, in these bad days, my mind?—
He much, the old man, who, clearest-soul'd of men,
Saw The Wide Prospect, and the Asian Fen,
And Tmolus hill, and Smyrna bay, though blind.
Much he, whose friendship I not long since won,
That halting slave, who in Nicopolis
Taught Arrian, when Vespasian's brutal son
Clear'd Rome of what most shamed him. But be his
My special thanks, whose even-balanced soul,
From first youth tested up to extreme old age,
Business could not make dull, nor passion wild;
Who saw life steadily, and saw it whole;
The mellow glory of the Attic stage,
Singer of sweet Colonus, and its child.

1849
MATTHEW ARNOLD
(1822–1888)

After Reading "Ajax"

The world may like, for all I care,
  The gentler voice, the cooler head,
That bows a rival to despair,
  And cheaply compliments the dead;

That smiles at all that's coarse and rash,
  Yet wins the trophies of the fight,
Unscathed, in honour's wreck and crash,
  Heartless, but always in the right,

Thanked for good counsel by the judge
  Who tramples on the bleeding brave,
Thanked too by him who will not budge
  From claims thrice hallowed by the grave.

Thanked, and self-pleased: aye, let him wear
  What to that noble breast was due;
And I, dear passionate Teucer, dare
  Go through the homeless world with you.

WILLIAM CORY
(1823–1892)

EURIPIDES (480–406 B.C.)

From "Wine of Cyprus"

Our Euripides, the Human,
  With his droppings of warm tears,
And his touches of things common
  Till they rose to touch the spheres.

ELIZABETH BARRETT BROWNING
(1806–1861)

From "Balaustion's Adventure"

So were we at destruction's very edge,
When those o' the galley, as they had discussed
A point, a question raised by somebody,
A matter mooted in a moment,—"Wait!"
Cried they (and wait we did, you may be sure).
"That song was veritable Aischulos,
Familiar to the mouth of man and boy,
Old glory: how about Euripides?
The newer and not yet so famous bard,
He that was born upon the battle-day
While that song and the salpinx sounded him
Into the world, first sound, at Salamis—
Might you know any of his verses too?"

Now, some one of the Gods inspired this speech:
Since ourselves knew what happened but last year—
How, when Gulippos gained his victory
Over poor Nikias, poor Demosthenes,
And Syracuse condemned the conquered force
To dig and starve i' the quarry, branded them—
Freeborn Athenians, brute-like in the front
With horse-head brands,—ah, "Region of the Steed"!—
Of all these men immersed in misery,
It was found none had been advantaged so
By aught in the past life he used to prize
And pride himself concerning,—no rich man
By riches, no wise man by wisdom, no
Wiser man still (as who loved more the Muse)
By storing, at brain's edge and tip of tongue,
Old glory, great plays that had long ago

EURIPIDES (480–406 B.C.)

Made themselves wings to fly about the world,—
Not one such man was helped so at his need
As certain few that (wisest they of all)
Had, at first summons, oped heart, flung door wide
At the new knocking of Euripides,
Nor drawn the bolt with who cried "Decadence!
And, after Sophokles, be nature dumb!"
Such,—and I see in it God Bacchos' boon
To souls that recognized his latest child,
He who himself, born latest of the Gods,
Was stoutly held impostor by mankind,—
Such were in safety: any who could speak
A chorus to the end, or prologize,
Roll out a rhesis, wield some golden length
Stiffened by wisdom out into a line,
Or thrust and parry in bright monostich,
Teaching Euripides to Syracuse—
Any such happy man had prompt reward:
If he lay bleeding on the battlefield
They stanched his wounds and gave him drink and food;
If he were slave i' the house, for reverence
They rose up, bowed to who proved master now,
And bade him go free, thank Euripides!
Ay, and such did so: many such, he said,
Returning home to Athens, sought him out,
The old bard in the solitary house,
And thanked him ere they went to sacrifice.
I say, we knew that story of last year!

ROBERT BROWNING
(1812–1889)

THEOCRITUS (3rd century B.C.)

Theocritus

Theocritus! Theocritus! ah, thou hadst pleasant dreams
Of the crystal spring Burinna, and the Haleus' murmuring streams;
Of Physcus, and Neaethus, and fair Arethusa's fount,
Of Lacinion's beetling crag, and Latymnus' woody mount;
Of the fretted rocks and antres hoar that overhang the sea,
And the sapphire sky and thymy plains of thy own sweet Sicily;
And of the nymphs of Sicily, that dwelt in oak and pine—
Theocritus! Theocritus! what pleasant dreams were thine!

And of the merry rustics who tend the goats and sheep,
And the maids who trip to milk the cows at morning's dewy peep,
Of Clearista with her locks of brightest sunny hair,
And the saucy girl Eunica, and sweet Chloe kind and fair;
And of those highly favor'd ones, Endymion and Adonis,
Loved by Selena the divine, and the beauteous Dionis;
Of the silky-hair'd caprella, and the gentle lowing kine—
Theocritus! Theocritus! what pleasant dreams were thine!

Of the spring time, and the summer, and the zephyr's balmy breeze;
Of the dainty flowers, and waving elms, and the yellow humming bees;
Of the rustling poplar and the oak, the tamarisk and the beech,
The dog-rose and anemone,—thou hadst a dream of each!
Of the galingale and hyacinth, and the lily's snowy hue,
The couch-grass, and green maiden-hair, and celandine pale blue,
The gold-bedropt cassidony, the fern, and sweet woodbine—
Theocritus! Theocritus! what pleasant dreams were thine!

Of the merry harvest-home, all beneath the good green tree,
The poppies and the spikes of corn, the shouting and the glee
Of the lads so blithe and healthy, and the girls so gay and neat,
And the dance they lead around the tree with ever twinkling feet;
And the bushy piles of lentisk to rest the aching brow,
And reach and pluck the damson down from the overladen bough,
And munch the roasted bean at ease, and quaff the Ptelean wine—
Theocritus! Theocritus! what pleasant dreams were thine!

THEOCRITUS (3rd century B.C.)

And higher dreams were thine to dream—of Heracles the brave,
And Polydeukes good at need, and Castor strong to save;
Of Dionysius and the woe he wrought the Theban king;
And of Zeus the mighty centre of Olympus' glittering ring;
Of Tiresias, the blind old man, the fam'd Aonian seer;
Of Hecatè, and Cthonian Dis, whom all mankind revere;
And of Daphnis lying down to die beneath the leafy vine—
Theocritus! Theocritus! what pleasant dreams were thine!

But mostly sweet and soft thy dreams—of Cypris' loving kiss,
Of the dark-haired maids of Corinth, and the feasts of Sybaris;
Of alabaster vases of Assyrian perfume,
Of ebony, and gold, and pomp, and softly-curtain'd room;
Of Faunus piping in the woods to the Satyrs' noisy rout,
And the saucy Panisks mocking him with many a jeer and flout;
And of the tender-footed Hours, and Pieria's tuneful Nine—
Theocritus! Theocritus! what pleasant dreams were thine!

CHARLES HARTLEY LANGHORNE
(1818–1845)

For a Copy of Theocritus

O Singer of the field and fold,
Theocritus! Pan's pipe was thine,—
Thine was the happier Age of Gold.

For thee the scent of new-turned mould,
The bee-hives, and the murmuring pine,
O Singer of the field and fold!

Thou sang'st the simple feasts of old,—
The beechen bowl made glad with wine . . .
Thine was the happier Age of Gold.

Thou bad'st the rustic loves be told,—
Thou bad'st the tuneful reeds combine,
O Singer of the field and fold!

THEOCRITUS (3rd century B.C.)

And round thee, ever-laughing, rolled
The blithe and blue Sicilian brine . . .
Thine was the happier Age of Gold.

Alas for us! Our songs are cold;
Our Northern suns too sadly shine:—
O Singer of the field and fold,
Thine was the happier Age of Gold!

AUSTIN DOBSON
(1840–1921)

Theocritus

The poplars and the ancient elms
  Make murmurous noises high in air;
The noon-day sunlight overwhelms
  The brown cicalas basking there;
But here the shade is deep, and sweet
  With new-mown grass and lentisk-shoots,
And far away the shepherds meet
    With noisy fifes and flutes.

Their clamor dies upon the ear;
  So now bring forth the rolls of song,
Mouth the rich cadences, nor fear
  Your voice may do the poet wrong;
Lift up the chalice to our lips,—
  Yet see, before we venture thus,
A stream of red libation drips
    To great Theocritus.

We are in Sicily to-day;
  And, as the honeyed metre flows,
Battos and Corydon, at play,
  Will lose the syrinx, gain the rose;
Soft Amaryllis, too, will bind
  Dark violets round her shining hair,
And in the fountain laugh to find
    Her sun-browned face so fair.

THEOCRITUS (3rd century B.C.)

> We are in Sicily to-day;
>   Ah! foolish world, too sadly wise,
> Why didst thou e'er let fade away
>   Those ancient, innocent ecstasies?
> Along the glens, in checkered flight,
>   Hither to-day the nymphs shall flee,
> And Pan forsake for our delight
>   The tomb of Helice.

EDMUND GOSSE
(1849–1928)

LUCRETIUS (96?–55 B.C.)

Lucretius

Lucilia, wedded to Lucretius, found
Her master cold; for when the morning flush
Of passion and the first embrace had died
Between them, tho' he lov'd her none the less,
Yet often when the woman heard his foot
Return from pacings in the field, and ran
To greet him with a kiss, the master took
Small notice, or austerely, for—his mind
Half buried in some weightier argument,
Or fancy-borne perhaps upon the rise
And long roll of the hexameter—he past
To turn and ponder those three hundred scrolls
Left by the Teacher, whom he held divine.
She brook'd it not, but wrathful, petulant,
Dreaming some rival, sought and found a witch
Who brew'd the philtre which had power, they said,
To lead an errant passion home again.
And this, at times, she mingled with his drink,
And this destroy'd him; for the wicked broth
Confused the chemic labor of the blood,
And tickling the brute brain within the man's
Made havoc among those tender cells, and check'd
His power to shape. He loathed himself, and once
After a tempest woke upon a morn
That mock'd him with returning calm, and cried:

[22]

LUCRETIUS (96?–55 B.C.)

'Storm in the night! for thrice I heard the rain
Rushing; and once the flash of a thunderbolt—
Methought I never saw so fierce a fork—
Struck out the streaming mountain-side, and show'd
A riotous confluence of watercourses
Blanching and billowing in a hollow of it,
Where all but yester-eve was dusty-dry.

'Storm, and what dreams, ye holy Gods, what dreams!
For thrice I waken'd after dreams. Perchance
We do but recollect the dreams that come
Just ere the waking. Terrible: for it seem'd
A void was made in Nature; all her bonds
Crack'd; and I saw the flaring atom-streams
And torrents of her myriad universe,
Ruining along the illimitable inane,
Fly on to clash together again, and make
Another and another frame of things
For ever. That was mine, my dream, I knew it—
Of and belonging to me, as the dog
With inward yelp and restless forefoot plies
His function of the woodland; but the next!
I thought that all the blood by Sylla shed
Came driving rainlike down again on earth,
And where it dash'd the reddening meadow, sprang
No dragon warriors from Cadmean teeth,
For these I thought my dream would show to me,
But girls, Hetairai, curious in their art,
Hired animalisms, vile as those that made
The mulberry-faced Dictator's orgies worse
Than aught they fable of the quiet Gods.
And hands they mixt, and yell'd and round me drove
In narrowing circles till I yell'd again
Half-suffocated, and sprang up, and saw—
Was it the first beam of my latest day?

'Then, then, from utter gloom stood out the breasts,
The breasts of Helen, and hoveringly a sword
Now over and now under, now direct,
Pointed itself to pierce, but sank down shamed

LUCRETIUS (96?–55 B.C.)

At all that beauty; and as I stared, a fire,
The fire that left a roofless Ilion,
Shot out of them, and scorch'd me that I woke.

'Is this thy vengeance, holy Venus, thine,
Because I would not one of thine own doves,
Not even a rose, were offer'd to thee? thine
Forgetful how my rich prœmion makes
Thy glory fly along the Italian field,
In lays that will outlast thy deity?

'Deity? nay, thy worshippers. My tongue
Trips, or I speak profanely. Which of these
Angers thee most, or angers thee at all?
Not if thou be'st of those who, far aloof
From envy, hate and pity, and spite and scorn,
Live the great life which all our greatest fain
Would follow, centre'd in eternal calm.

'Nay, if thou canst, O Goddess, like ourselves
Touch, and be touch'd, then would I cry to thee
To kiss thy Mavors, roll thy tender arms
Round him, and keep him from the lust of blood
That makes a steaming slaughter-house of Rome.

'Ay, but I meant not thee; I meant not her
Whom all the pines of Ida shook to see
Slide from that quiet heaven of hers, and tempt
The Trojan, while his neatherds were abroad;
Nor her that o'er her wounded hunter wept
Her deity false in human-amorous tears;
Nor whom her beardless apple-arbiter
Decided fairest. Rather, O ye Gods,
Poet-like, as the great Sicilian called
Calliope to grace his golden verse—
Ay, and this Kypris also—did I take
That popular name of thine to shadow forth
The all-generating powers and genial heat
Of Nature, when she strikes thro' the thick blood
Of cattle, and light is large, and lambs are glad

LUCRETIUS (96?–55 B.C.)

Nosing the mother's udder, and the bird
Makes his heart voice amid the blaze of flowers;
Which things appear the work of mighty Gods.

'The Gods! and if I go *my* work is left
Unfinish'd—*if* I go. The Gods, who haunt
The lucid interspace of world and world,
Where never creeps a cloud, or moves a wind,
Nor ever falls the least white star of snow,
Nor ever lowest roll of thunder moans,
Nor sound of human sorrow mounts to mar
Their sacred everlasting calm! and such,
Not all so fine, nor so divine a calm,
Not such, nor all unlike it, man may gain
Letting his own life go. The Gods, the Gods!
If all be atoms, how then should the Gods
Being atomic not be dissoluble,
Not follow the great law? My master held
That Gods there are, for all men so believe.
I prest my footsteps into his, and meant
Surely to lead my Memmius in a train
Of flowery clauses onward to the proof
That Gods there are, and deathless.
    Meant? I meant?
I have forgotten what I meant; my mind
Stumbles, and all my faculties are lamed.

'Look where another of our Gods, the Sun,
Apollo, Delius, or of older use
All-seeing Hyperion—what you will—
Has mounted yonder; since he never sware,
Except his wrath were wreak'd on wretched man,
That he would only shine among the dead
Hereafter—tales! for never yet on earth
Could dead flesh creep, or bits of roasting ox
Moan round the spit—nor knows he what he sees;
King of the East altho' he seem, and girt
With song and flame and fragrance, slowly lifts
His golden feet on those empurpled stairs
That climb into the windy halls of heaven

LUCRETIUS (96?-55 B.C.)

And here he glances on an eye new-born,
And gets for greeting but a wail of pain;
And here he stays upon a freezing orb
That fain would gaze upon him to the last;
And here upon a yellow eyelid fallen
And closed by those who mourn a friend in vain,
Not thankful that his troubles are no more.
And me, altho' his fire is on my face
Blinding, he sees not, nor at all can tell
Whether I mean this day to end myself.
Or lend an ear to Plato where he says,
That men like soldiers may not quit the post
Allotted by the Gods. But he that holds
The Gods are careless, wherefore need he care
Greatly for them, nor rather plunge at once,
Being troubled, wholly out of sight, and sink
Past earthquake—ay, and gout and stone, that break
Body toward death, and palsy, death-in-life,
And wretched age—and worst disease of all,
These prodigies of myriad nakednesses,
And twisted shapes of lust, unspeakable,
Abominable, strangers at my hearth
Not welcome, harpies miring every dish,
The phantom husks of something foully done,
And fleeting thro' the boundless universe,
And blasting the long quiet of my breast
With animal heat and dire insanity?

'How should the mind, except it loved them, clasp
These idols to herself? or do they fly
Now thinner, and now thicker, like the flakes
In a fall of snow, and so press in, perforce
Of multitude, as crowds that in an hour
Of civic tumult jam the doors, and bear
The keepers down, and throng, their rags and they
The basest, far into that council-hall
Where sit the best and stateliest of the land?

'Can I not fling this horror off me again,
Seeing with how great ease Nature can smile,

LUCRETIUS (96?-55 B.C.)

Balmier and nobler from her bath of storm,
At random ravage? and how easily
The mountain there has cast his cloudy slough,
Now towering o'er him in serenest air,
A mountain o'er a mountain,—ay, and within
All hollow as the hopes and fears of men?

'But who was he that in the garden snared
Picus and Faunus, rustic Gods? a tale
To laugh at—more to laugh at in myself—
For look! what is it? there? yon arbutus
Totters; a noiseless riot underneath
Strikes through the wood, sets all the tops quivering—
The mountain quickens into Nymph and Faun,
And here an Oread—how the sun delights
To glance and shift about her slippery sides,
And rosy knees and supple roundedness,
And budded bosom-peaks—who this way runs
Before the rest!—A satyr, a satyr, see,
Follows; but him I proved impossible;
Twy-natured is no nature. Yet he draws
Nearer and nearer, and I scan him now
Beastlier than any phantom of his kind
That ever butted his rough brother-brute
For lust or lusty blood or provender.
I hate, abhor, spit, sicken at him; and she
Loathes him as well; such a precipitate heel,
Fledged as it were with Mercury's ankle-wing,
Whirls her to me—but will she fling herself
Shameless upon me? Catch her, goat-foot! nay,
Hide, hide them, million-myrtled wilderness,
And cavern-shadowing laurels, hide! do I wish—
What?—that the bush were leafless? or to whelm
All of them in one massacre? O ye Gods,
I know you careless, yet, behold, to you
From childly wont and ancient use I call—
I thought I lived securely as yourselves—
No lewdness, narrowing envy, monkey-spite,
No madness of ambition, avarice, none;

LUCRETIUS (96?-55 B.C.)

No larger feast than under plane or pine
With neighbors laid along the grass, to take
Only such cups as left us friendly-warm,
Affirming each his own philosophy—
Nothing to mar the sober majesties
Of settled, sweet, Epicurean life.
But now it seems some unseen monster lays
His vast and filthy hands upon my will,
Wrenching it backward into his, and spoils
My bliss in being; and it was not great,
For save when shutting reasons up in rhythm,
Or Heliconian honey in living words,
To make a truth less harsh, I often grew
Tired of so much within our little life,
Or of so little in our little life—
Poor little life that toddles half an hour
Crown'd with a flower or two, and there an end—
And since the nobler pleasure seems to fade,
Why should I, beastlike as I find myself,
Not manlike end myself?—our privilege—
What beast has heart to do it? And what man,
What Roman would be dragg'd in triumph thus?
Not I; not he, who bears one name with her
Whose death-blow struck the dateless doom of kings,
When, brooking not the Tarquin in her veins,
She made her blood in sight of Collatine
And all his peers, flushing the guiltless air,
Spout from the maiden fountain in her heart.
And from it sprang the Commonwealth, which breaks
As I am breaking now!

             'And therefore now
Let her, that is the womb and tomb of all,
Great Nature, take, and forcing far apart
Those blind beginnings that have made me man,
Dash them anew together at her will
Thro' all her cycles—into man once more,
Or beast or bird or fish, or opulent flower.
But till this cosmic order everywhere

LUCRETIUS (96?–55 B.C.)

Shatter'd into one earthquake in one day
Cracks all to pieces,—and that hour perhaps
Is not so far when momentary man
Shall seem no more a something to himself,
But he, his hopes and hates, his homes and fanes,
And even his bones long laid within the grave,
The very sides of the grave itself shall pass,
Vanishing, atom and void, atom and void,
Into the unseen for ever,—till that hour,
My golden work in which I told a truth
That stays the rolling Ixionian wheel,
And numbs the Fury's ringlet-snake, and plucks
The mortal soul from out immortal hell,
Shall stand. Ay, surely; then it fails at last
And perishes as I must; for O Thou,
Passionless bride, divine Tranquility,
Yearn'd after by the wisest of the wise,
Who fail to find thee, being as thou art
Without one pleasure and without one pain,
Howbeit I know thou surely must be mine
Or soon or late, yet out of season, thus
I woo thee roughly, for thou carest not
How roughly men may woo thee so they win—
Thus—thus—the soul flies out and dies in the air.'

With that he drove the knife into his side.
She heard him raging, heard him fall, ran in,
Beat breast, tore hair, cried out upon herself
As having fail'd in duty to him, shriek'd
That she but meant to win him back, fell on him,
Clasp'd, kiss'd him, wail'd. He answer'd,
    'Care not thou!
Thy duty? What is duty? Fare thee well!'

                      ALFRED, LORD TENNYSON
                            (1809–1892)

LUCRETIUS (96?–55 B.C.)

Lucretius

Lucretius! King of men, that are
    No more, they think, than men:
Who, past the flaming walls afar,
    Find nought within their ken:

The cruel draught, that wildered thee,
    And drove thee upon sleep,
Was kinder than Philosophy,
    Who would not let thee weep.

Thou knowest now, that life and death
    Are wondrous intervals:
The fortunes of a fitful breath,
    Within the flaming walls.

Without them, an eternal plan,
    Which life and death obey:
Divinity, that fashions man,
    Its high, immortal way.

Or was he right, thy past compare,
    Thy one true voice of Greece?
Then, whirled about the unconscious air,
    Thou hast a vehement peace.

No calms of light, no purple lands,
    No sanctuaries sublime:
Like storms of snow, like quaking sands,
    Thine atoms drift through time.

                  LIONEL JOHNSON
                    (1867–1902)

CATULLUS (84?-54 B.C.)

On Catullus

Tell me not what too well I know
About the bard of Sirmio.
 Yes, in Thalia's son
Such stains there are—as when a Grace
Sprinkles another's laughing face
 With nectar, and runs on.
WALTER SAVAGE LANDOR
(1775-1864)

"Frater Ave atque Vale"

Row us out from Desenzano, to your Sirmione row!
So they row'd, and there we landed—'O venusta Sirmio!'
There to me thro' all the groves of olive in the summer glow,
There beneath the Roman ruin where the purple flowers grow,
Came that 'Ave atque Vale' of the Poet's hopeless woe,
Tenderest of Roman poets nineteen hundred years ago,
'Frater Ave atque Vale'—as we wander'd to and fro
Gazing at the Lydian laughter of the Garda Lake below
Sweet Catullus's all-but-island, olive-silvery Sirmio!
ALFRED, LORD TENNYSON
(1809-1892)

VIRGIL (70-19 B.C.)

To Virgil

*Written at the Request of the Mantuans
for the Nineteenth Centenary
of Virgil's Death*

I

Roman Virgil, thou that singest
 Ilion's lofty temples robed in fire,
Ilion falling, Rome arising,
 wars, and filial faith, and Dido's pyre;

[31]

VIRGIL (70–19 B.C.)

II

Landscape-lover, lord of language
   more than he that sang the 'Works and Days,'
All the chosen coin of fancy
   flashing out from many a golden phrase;

III

Thou that singest wheat and woodland,
   tilth and vineyard, hive and horse and herd;
All the charm of all the Muses
   often flowering in a lonely word;

IV

Poet of the happy Tityrus
   piping underneath his beechen bowers;
Poet of the poet-satyr
   whom the laughing shepherd bound with flowers;

V

Chanter of the Pollio, glorying
   in the blissful years again to be,
Summers of the snakeless meadow,
   unlaborious earth and oarless sea;

VI

Thou that seest Universal
   Nature moved by Universal Mind;
Thou majestic in thy sadness
   at the doubtful doom of human kind;

VII

Light among the vanish'd ages;
   star that gildest yet this phantom shore;
Golden branch amid the shadows,
   kings and realms that pass to rise no more;

VIII

Now thy Forum roars no longer,
   fallen every purple Caesar's dome—

VIRGIL—(70–19 B.C.)

    Tho' thine ocean-roll of rhythm
      sound forever of Imperial Rome—

IX

Now the Rome of slaves hath perish'd,
    and the Rome of freemen holds her place,
I, from out the Northern Island
    sunder'd once from all the human race,

X

I salute thee, Mantovano,
    I that loved thee since my day began,
Wielder of the stateliest measure
    ever moulded by the lips of man.

ALFRED, LORD TENNYSON
(1809–1892)

The Aeneid

From pastoral meads, from tasks of field and fold,
To war, to love, to death by land and sea
He turned, and sang in soft Parthenope
Heroic deeds, and peoples great of old,
Who dwelt where Nar and Amasenus rolled
By Sabine slope or Volscian low-country,
Mingling the dimly-shadowed days to be
With days long dead in his high verse of gold.
Yet even sickening at loves ill allied,
Thwart fates, vext wanderings, waste of princely blood,
Harsh trumpet-notes and tossing fields of foam,
In twilight visions of the mystic wood
He sought, with longing eyes unsatisfied,
The immortality he gave to Rome.

J. W. MACKAIL
(1859–   )

HORACE (65–8 B.C.)

From "An Essay on Criticism"

Horace still charms with graceful negligence,
And without method talks us into sense;
Will, like a friend, familiarly convey
The truest notions in the easiest way.
He who, supreme in judgment as in wit,
Might boldly censure as he boldly writ,
Yet judg'd with coolness, though he sung with fire;
His precepts teach but what his works inspire.
Our critics take a contrary extreme,
They judge with fury, but they write with phlegm;
Nor suffers Horace more in wrong translations
By Wits, than Critics in as wrong quotations.

ALEXANDER POPE
(1688–1744)

From "Childe Harold's Pilgrimage"

Canto IV
LXXVII

Then farewell, Horace; whom I hated so,
Not for thy faults, but mine; it is a curse
To understand, not feel thy lyric flow,
To comprehend, but never love thy verse,
Although no deeper Moralist rehearse
Our little life, nor Bard prescribe his art,
Nor livelier Satirist the conscience pierce,
Awakening without wounding the touch'd heart;—
Yet fare thee well—upon Soracte's ridge we part.

LORD BYRON
(1788–1824)

To Q. H. F.

"Horatius Flaccus, B.C. 8,"
There's not a doubt about the date,—
  You're dead and buried:
As you observed, the seasons roll;

HORACE (65–8 B.C.)

And 'cross the Styx full many a soul
  Has Charon ferried,
Since, mourned of men and Muses nine,
They laid you on the Esquiline.

And that was centuries ago!
You'd think we'd learned enough, I know,
  To help refine us,
Since last you trod the Sacred Street,
And tacked from mortal fear to meet
  The bore Crispinus;
Or, by your cold Digentia, set
The web of winter birding-net.

Ours is so far-advanced an age!
Sensation tales, a classic stage,
  Commodious villas!
We boast high art, an Albert Hall,
Australian meats, and men who call
  Their sires gorillas!
We have a thousand things, you see,
Not dreamt in your philosophy.

And yet, how strange! Our "world," today,
Tried in the scale, would scarce outweigh
  Your Roman cronies;
Walk in the Park—you'll seldom fail
To find a Sybaris on the rail
  By Lydia's ponies,
Or hap on Barrus, wigged and stayed,
Ogling some unsuspecting maid.

The great Gargilius, then, behold!
His "long-bow" hunting tales of old
  Are now but duller;
Fair Neobule too! Is not
One Hebrus here,—from Aldershot?
  Aha, you colour!
Be wise. There old Canidia sits;
No doubt she's tearing you to bits.

[35]

HORACE (65–8 B.C.)

    And look, dyspeptic, brave, and kind,
    Comes dear Maecenas, half behind
        Terentia's skirting;
    Here's Pyrrha, "golden-haired" at will;
    Prig Damasippus, preaching still;
        Asterie flirting,—
    Radiant, of course. We'll make her black,—
    Ask her when Gyges' ship comes back.

    So with the rest. Who will may trace
    Behind the new each elder face
        Defined as clearly;
    Science proceeds, and man stands still;
    Our "world" today's as good or ill,—
        As cultured (nearly),
    As yours was, Horace! You alone,
    Unmatched, unmet, we have not known.

                      AUSTIN DOBSON
                        (1840–1921)

MARTIAL (1st century A.D.)

Martial in Town

    Last night, within the stifling train,
        Lit by the foggy lamp o'erhead,
    Sick of the sad Last News, I read
        Verse of that joyous child of Spain,

    Who dwelt when Rome was waxing cold,
        Within the Roman din and smoke.
    And like my heart to me they spoke,
        These accents of his heart of old:—

    Brother, had we but time to live,
        And fleet the careless hours together,
    With all that leisure has to give
        Of perfect life and peaceful weather,

    The Rich Man's halls, the anxious faces,
    The weary Forum, courts, and cases

MARTIAL (1st century A.D.)

Should know us not; but quiet nooks,
But summer shade by field and well,
But country rides, and talk of books,
At home, with these, we fain would dwell!

Now neither lives, but day by day
Sees the sun's wasting in the west,
And feels their flight, and doth delay
To lead the life he loveth best.

So from thy city prison broke,
    Martial, thy wail for life misspent,
And so, through London's noise and smoke
    My heart replies to the lament.

For dear as Tagus with his gold,
    And swifter Salo, were to thee,
So dear to me the woods that fold
    The streams that circle Fernielea!

ANDREW LANG
(1844–1912)

[MISCELLANY]

From "The Hous of Fame"

There saugh I stonden, out of drede,
Upon an yren piler strong
That peynted was, al endelong,
With tigres blod in every place,
The Tholosan that highte Stace,
That bar of Thebes up the fame
Upon his shuldres, and the name
Also of cruel Achilles.
And by him stood, withouten les,
Ful wonder hy on a piler
Of yren, he, the gret Omer;
And with him Dares and Tytus
Before, and eke he Lollius,
And Guydo eke de Columpnis,
And Englyssh Gaufride eke, ywis;

[FROM "THE HOUS OF FAME"]

And ech of these, as have I joye,
Was besy for to bere up Troye.
So hevy therof was the fame
That for to bere hyt was no game.
But yet I gan ful wel espie,
Betwex hem was a litil envye.
Oon seyde that Omer made lyes,
Feynynge in hys poetries,
And was to Grekes favorable;
Therfor held he hyt but fable.
   Tho saugh I stonde on a piler,
That was of tynned yren cler,
The Latyn poete, Virgile,
That bore hath up a longe while
The fame of Pius Eneas.
   And next hym on a piler was,
Of coper, Venus clerk, Ovide,
That hath ysowen wonder wide
The grete god of Loves name.
And ther he bar up wel hys fame
Upon his piler, also hye
As I myghte see hyt with myn ye;
For-why this halle, of which I rede,
Was woxen on highte, length, and brede,
Wel more, be a thousand del,
Than hyt was erst, that saugh I wel.
   Thoo saugh I on a piler by,
Of yren wroght ful sternely,
The grete poete, daun Lucan,
And on hys shulders bar up than,
As high as that y myghte see,
The fame of Julius and Pompe.
And by him stoden alle these clerkes
That writen of Romes myghty werkes,
That yf y wolde her names telle,
Al to longe most I dwelle.

Geoffrey Chaucer
(1340?–1400)

II

OMAR KHAYÝAM (12th century)

For Omar

When dawn no longer, with the hunters use,
    for you flung a bright noose,
and darkness in its everlasting net
    trapped dome and minaret,
was there a voice upon the further side
    in some dim tavern cried:
"All you, whose landlord is the Lord of Hosts,
    fill up your glasses, ghosts,
and, as you drain the shadow-bumper, feel
    how through veins stricken steal
the summer-heats that are the gift of verse
    and its great vintagers."
It is all over—life and love and song,
    you thought, and you were wrong!
For as the door flings open, the grey mist
    breaks for the lutanist!
Yes! from high-piping Pehlevi the rose
    about his footing grows,
and through his garden to the moon ascending,
    world without ending,
in Hell and over silence shall prevail
    the Persian nightingale.
Ghosts to your feet! No heel-taps, drink and cry
    "Mud in the devil's eye!"
When song and wine and Omar to their Hell come,
the place is heaven and the password, "Welcome!"

                    HUMBERT WOLFE
                    (1885–1940)

JACOPONE DA TODI (1230?–1306)

Austerity of Poetry

That son of Italy who tried to blow,
Ere Dante came, the trump of sacred song,
In his light youth amid a festal throng
Sate with his bride to see a public show.
Fair was the bride, and on her front did glow
Youth like a star; and what to youth belong—
Gay raiment, sparkling gauds, elation strong.
A prop gave way! crash fell a platform! lo,
'Mid struggling sufferers, hurt to death, she lay!
Shuddering, they drew her garments off—and found
A robe of sackcloth next the smooth, white skin.
Such, poets, is your bride, the Muse! young, gay,
Radiant, adorn'd outside; a hidden ground
Of thought and of austerity within.

MATTHEW ARNOLD
(1822–1888)

DANTE ALIGHIERI (1265–1321)

Dante

Who, mid the grasses of the field,
    That spring beneath our careless feet,
First found the shining stems that yield
    The grains of life-sustaining wheat:

Who first, upon the furrowed land,
    Strewed the bright grains to sprout, and grow,
And ripen for the reaper's hand—
    We know not, and we cannot know.

But well we know the hand that brought
    And scattered, far as sight can reach,
The seeds of free and living thought
    On the broad field of modern speech.

DANTE ALIGHIERI (1265–1321)

Mid the white hills that round us lie,
  We cherish that Great Sower's fame,
And, as we pile the sheaves on high,
  With awe we utter Dante's name.

Six centuries, since the poet's birth,
  Have come and flitted o'er our sphere:
The richest harvest reaped on earth
  Crowns the last century's closing year.

WILLIAM CULLEN BRYANT
(1794–1878)

A Dream, after Reading Dante's Episode of Paolo and Francesca

As Hermes once took to his feathers light,
  When lulled Argus, baffled, swoon'd and slept,
So on a Delphic reed, my idle spright
  So play'd, so charm'd, so conquer'd, so bereft
The dragon-world of all its hundred eyes;
  And, seeing it asleep, so fled away—
Not to pure Ida with its snow-cold skies,
  Nor unto Tempe where Jove grieved a day;
But to that second circle of sad hell,
  Where 'mid the gust, the whirlwind, and the flaw
Of rain and hail-stones, lovers need not tell
  Their sorrows. Pale were the sweet lips I saw,
Pale were the lips I kiss'd, and fair the form
I floated with, about that melancholy storm.

JOHN KEATS
(1795–1821)

Divina Commedia

I

Oft have I seen at some cathedral door
  A laborer, pausing in the dust and heat,
  Lay down his burden, and with reverent feet
Enter, and cross himself, and on the floor

DANTE ALIGHIERI (1265-1321)

    Kneel to repeat his paternoster o'er;
        Far off the noises of the world retreat;
        The loud vociferations of the street
        Become an undistinguishable roar.
    So, as I enter here from day to day,
        And leave my burden at this minster gate,
        Kneeling in prayer, and not ashamed to pray,
    The tumult of the time disconsolate
        To inarticulate murmurs dies away,
        While the eternal ages watch and wait.

II

    How strange the sculptures that adorn these towers!
        This crowd of statues, in whose folded sleeves
        Birds build their nests; while canopied with leaves
        Parvis and portal bloom like trellised bowers,
    And the vast minster seems a cross of flowers!
        But fiends and dragons on the gargoyled eaves
        Watch the dead Christ between the living thieves,
        And, underneath, the traitor Judas lowers!
    Ah! from what agonies of heart and brain,
        What exultations trampling on despair,
        What tenderness, what tears, what hate of wrong,
    What passionate outcry of a soul in pain,
        Uprose this poem of the earth and air,
        This mediaeval miracle of song!

III

    I enter, and I see thee in the gloom
        Of the long aisles, O poet saturnine!
        And strive to make my steps keep pace with thine.
        The air is filled with some unknown perfume;
    The congregation of the dead make room
        For thee to pass; the votive tapers shine;
        Like rooks that haunt Ravenna's groves of pine
        The hovering echoes fly from tomb to tomb.
    From the confessionals I hear arise
        Rehearsals of forgotten tragedies,
        And lamentations from the crypts below;
    And then a voice celestial that begins

DANTE ALIGHIERI (1265-1321)

With the pathetic words, "Although your sins
As scarlet be," and ends with "as the snow."

IV

With snow-white veil and garments as of flame,
  She stands before thee, who so long ago
  Filled thy young heart with passion and the woe
From which thy song and all its splendors came;
And while with stern rebuke she speaks thy name,
  The ice about thy heart melts as the snow
  On mountain heights, and in swift overflow
Comes gushing from thy lips in sobs of shame.
Thou makest full confession; and a gleam,
  As of the dawn on some dark forest cast,
  Seems on thy lifted forehead to increase;
Lethe and Eunoë—the remembered dream
  And the forgotten sorrow—bring at last
  That perfect pardon which is perfect peace.

V

I lift mine eyes, and all the windows blaze
  With forms of Saints and holy men who died,
  Here martyred and hereafter glorified;
And the great Rose upon its leaves displays
Christ's Triumph, and the angelic roundelays,
  With splendor upon splendor multiplied;
  And Beatrice again at Dante's side
No more rebukes, but smiles her words of praise.
And then the organ sounds, and unseen choirs
  Sing the old Latin hymns of peace and love
  And benedictions of the Holy Ghost;
And the melodious bells among the spires
  O'er all the house-tops and through heaven above
  Proclaim the elevation of the Host!

VI

O star of morning and of liberty!
  O bringer of the light, whose splendor shines
  Above the darkness of the Apennines,
Forerunner of the day that is to be!

DANTE ALIGHIERI (1265-1321)

    The voices of the city and the sea,
      The voices of the mountains and the pines,
      Repeat thy song, till the familiar lines
      Are footpaths for the thought of Italy!
    Thy flame is blown abroad from all the heights,
      Through all the nations, and a sound is heard,
      As of a mighty wind, and men devout,
    Strangers of Rome, and the new proselytes,
      In their own language hear thy wondrous word,
      And many are amazed and many doubt.
                       HENRY WADSWORTH LONGFELLOW
                                   (1807-1882)

From "The Testament of Beauty"

    In higher natures, poetic or mystical,
sense is transfigur'd quite; as once with Dante it was
who saw the grace of a fair Florentine damsel
as WISDOM UNCREATE: for it happen'd to him
in thatt awakening miracle of Love at first sight,
which is to many a man his only miracle,
his one divine Vision, his one remember'd dream—
it happ'd to Dante, I say, as with no other man
in the height of his vision and for his faith therein:
the starry plentitude of his radiant soul,
searching for tenement in the bounties of life,
encounter'd an aspect of spiritual beauty
at the still hour of dawn which is holier than day:
as when a rose-bud first untrammeleth the shells
of her swathing petals and looseneth their embrace,
so the sunlight may enter to flush the casket
of her virgin promise, fairer than her full bloom
shall ever be, ere its glories lie squander'd in death:—
'Twas of thatt silent meeting his high vision came
rapturous as any vision ever to poet given;
since in thatt Sacrament he rebaptized his soul
and lived thereafter in Love, by the merit of Faith
toiling to endow the world: and on those feather'd wings
his mighty poem mounted panting, and lieth now

[44]

DANTE ALIGHIERI (1265-1321)

with all its earthly tangle by the throne of God.
So to Lucretius also seeking Order in Chance
some frenzy of Beauty came, neath which constraint he left
his atoms in the lurch and fell to worshipping
Aphroditè, the naked Goddess of man's breed·
and waving the oriflamme of her divinity
above the march of his slow-trooping argument
he attributeth to her the creation and being
of all Beauty soe'er: NEC SINE TE QUICQUAM
DIAS IN LUMINIS ORAS EXORITUR,
NEQUE FIT LATEUM NEQUE: AMABILE QUICQUAM.
So well did he in his rapture: such is Beauty's power
physical or spiritual; and if it be the cause
of spiritual emotion (as hath been said), 'tis plain
that Beauty wil be engaged in man's love, in so far
as 'tis a proper and actual attribute of man:
first, as in animals, of his physical form,
to which, when beauty of soul is added, the addition
but marketh more specially its human character.
    Thus Shakespeare, *in the sessions of sweet silent thought*
gathering from memory the idealization of love,
when he launch'd from their dream-sheds those golden sonnets
that swim like gondolas i' the wake of his drama.
fashion'd for their ensignry a pregnant axiom,
and wrote: *From fairest creatures we desire increase
That thereby Beauty's Rose might never die;* wherein
he asserteth beauty to be of love the one motiv,
and thatt in double meaning of object and cause.
    And tho' blind instinct wer full puissant of itself
for propagation of man, yet the attraction of beauty
bettereth the species, nor without it coud ther hav been
effect in spirit; and that the poet guarded this
showeth in his lyric, where of Sylvia 'tis enquired
why all the swains commend her, and he replyeth thereto
Holy fair and wise is she, thus giving to Soul
first place, thereafter to Body and last of the trine
Intelligence; and thatt is their right order in Love.

                                                    Robert Bridges
                                                     (1844-1930)

FRANCESCO PETRARCA (1304-1374)

From "Italy"

Arqua

There is, within three leagues and less of Padua
(The Paduan student knows it, honours it),
A lonely tomb-stone in a mountain churchyard,
And I arrived there as the sun declined
Low in the west. The gentle airs, that breathe
Fragrance at eve, were rising, and the birds
Singing their farewell song—the very song
They sung the night that tomb received a tenant;
When, as alive, clothed in his Canon's habit,
And, slowly winding down the narrow path
He came to rest there. Nobles of the land,
Princes and prelates mingled in his train,
Anxious by any act, while yet they could,
To catch a ray of glory by reflection;
And from that hour have kindred spirits flocked
From distant countries, from the north, the south,
To see where he is laid.
                              Twelve years ago,
When I descended the impetuous Rhone,
Its vineyards of such great and old renown,
Its castles, each with some romantic tale,
Vanishing fast—the pilot at the stern,
He who had steer'd so long, standing aloft,
His eyes on the white breakers, and his hands
On what at once served him for oar and rudder,
A huge misshapen plank—the bark itself
Frail and uncouth, launch'd to return no more,
Such as a shipwreck'd man might hope to build,
Urged by the love of home—when I descended
Two long, long days' silence, suspense on board,
It was to offer at thy fount, Valclusa,
Entering the arched Cave, to wander where
Petrarch had wander'd, in a trance to sit
Where in his peasant-dress he loved to sit,
Musing, reciting—on some rock moss-grown,
Or the fantastic root of some old fig tree,

FRANCESCO PETRARCA (1304-1374)

That drinks the living waters as they stream
Over their emerald-bed; and could I now
Neglect to visit Arqua, where, at last,
When he had done and settled with the world,
When all the illusions of his Youth were fled,
Indulged perhaps too long, cherish'd too fondly,
He came for the conclusion? Halfway up
He built his house, whence as by stealth he caught
Among the hills, a glimpse of busy life,
That soothed, not stirr'd.—But knock, and enter in.
This was his chamber. 'Tis as when he left it;
As if he now were busy in his garden.
And this his closet. Here he sate and read.
This was his chair; and in it, unobserved,
Reading, or thinking of his absent friends,
He pass'd away as in a quiet slumber.

Peace to this region! Peace to all who dwell here:
They know his value—every coming step,
That gathers round the children from their play,
Would tell them if they knew not.—But could aught,
Ungentle or ungenerous, spring up
Where he is sleeping; where, and in an age
Of savage warfare and blind bigotry,
He cultured all that could refine, exalt;
Leading to better things?

SAMUEL ROGERS
(1763-1855)

From "Childe Harold's Pilgrimage"
Canto IV
XXX

There is a tomb in Arqua;—rear'd in air,
Pillar'd in their sarcophagus, repose
The bones of Laura's lover: here repair
Many familiar with his well-sung woes,
The pilgrims of his genius. He arose
To raise a language, and his land reclaim

[47]

FRANCESCO PETRARCA (1304-1374)

> From the dull yoke of her barbaric foes;
> Watering the tree which bears his lady's name
> With his melodious tears, he gave himself to fame.
>
> LORD BYRON
(1788-1824)

HAFIZ (14th century)

To Hafiz of Shiraz

Thus said the Poet: "When Death comes to you,
All ye whose life-sand through the hour-glass slips,
He lays two fingers on your ears, and two
Upon your eyes he lays, one on your lips,
Whispering: Silence!" Although deaf thine ear,
Thine eye, my Hafiz, suffer Time's eclipse,
The songs thou sangest still all men may hear.

Songs of dead laughter, songs of love once hot,
Songs of a cup once flushed rose-red with wine,
Songs of a rose whose beauty is forgot,
A nightingale that piped hushed lays divine:
And still a graver music runs beneath
The tender love notes of those songs of thine,
Oh, Seeker of the keys of Life and Death!

While thou wert singing, the soft summer wind
That o'er Mosalla's garden blew, the stream
Of Ruknabad flowing where roses twined,
Carried thy voice farther than thou could'st dream.
To Isfahan and Baghdad's Tartar horde,
O'er waste and sea to Yezd and distant Ind;
Yea; to the sun-setting they bore thy word.

Behold we laugh, we warm us at Love's fire,
We thirst and scarce dare tell what wine we crave,
We lift our voices in Grief's dark-robed choir,
Sing thou the wisdom joy and sorrow gave!

HAFIZ (14th century)

If my poor rhymes held aught of the heart's lore,
Fresh wreaths were theirs to lay upon thy grave—
Master and Poet, all was thine before!
GERTRUDE LOWTHIAN BELL
(1868–1926)

GEOFFREY CHAUCER (1340?–1400)

Lament for Chaucer

Allas! my worthy maister honorable,
This londes verray tresour and richesse!
Dethe by thy dethe hath harm irreparable
Unto us done: hir vengeable duresse
Despoiled hath this lond of the swetnesse
Of rethoryk; for unto Tullius
Was never man so like amonges us.

Also who was heyr in philosofye
To Aristotle in our tunge but thou?
The steppes of Virgile in poesye
Thou folwedest eke, men wote wel ynow.
That combre-worlde that my maister slow—
Wolde I slayn were!—Dethe was to hastyf
To renne on thee and reve thee thy lyf . . .

She might han tarried hir vengeance a whyle
Til that some man had egal to thee be;
Nay, let be that! she knew wel that this yle
Nay never man bring forthe like to thee,
And her office nedes do mote she:
God bade hir do so, I truste for the beste;
O maister, maister, God thy soule reste!
THOMAS HOCCLEVE
(1370?–?1450)

combre-worlde] encumberer of earth.

[49]

GEOFFREY CHAUCER (1340?-1400)

From "The Fall of Princes"

Sith of our language he was the lode-star. . . .
Sith he in Englishmaking was the best
Pray unto God to give his soul good rest.

JOHN LYDGATE
(1370?-?1451)

From "Garlande of Laurell"

POETA SKELTON *answeryth*

O noble Chaucer whos pullisshyd eloquence
  Our Englysshe rude so fresshely hath set out
That bounde are we with all deu reverence
  With all our strength that we can brynge about
  To owe to yow our servyce and more if we mowte
But what sholde I say? ye wote what I entende
Which glad am to please and loth to offende.

JOHN SKELTON
(1460?-1529)

From "The Faerie Queene"

Book IV, Canto II
XXXII

Whylome, as antique stories tellen us,
Those two were foes the fellonest on ground,
And battell made the dreddest daungerous
That ever shrilling trumpet did resound;
Though now their acts be no where to be found,
  As that renowmed poet them compyled
With warlike numbers and heroicke sound,
Dan Chaucer, well of English undefyled,
On Fames eternall beadroll worthie to be fyled.

EDMUND SPENSER
(1552-1599)

GEOFFREY CHAUCER (1340?–1400)

Written on the Blank Space at the End of Chaucer's Tale of "The Floure and the Lefe"

> This pleasant tale is like a little copse:
>   The honied lines so freshly interlace,
>   To keep the reader in so sweet a place,
> So that he here and there full-hearted stops;
> And oftentimes he feels the dewy drops
>   Come cool and suddenly against his face,
>   And, by the wandering melody, may trace
> Which way the tender-legged linnet hops.
> Oh! what a power has white simplicity!
>   What mighty power has this gentle story!
>   I, that do ever feel athirst for glory,
> Could at this moment be content to lie
>   Meekly upon the grass, as those whose sobbings
>   Were heard of none beside the mournful robins.

JOHN KEATS
(1795–1821)

Chaucer

> An old man in a lodge within a park;
>   The chamber walls depicted all around
>   With portraitures of huntsman, hawk, and hound,
> And the hurt deer. He listeneth to the lark,
> Whose song comes with the sunshine through the dark
>   Of painted glass in leaden lattice bound;
>   He listeneth and he laugheth at the sound,
> Then writeth in a book like any clerk.
> He is the poet of the dawn, who wrote
>   The Canterbury Tales, and his old age
>   Made beautiful with song; and as I read
> I hear the crowing cock, I hear the note
>   Of lark and linnet, and from every page
>   Rise odors of ploughed field or flowery mead.

HENRY WADSWORTH LONGFELLOW
(1807–1882)

GEOFFREY CHAUCER (1340?–1400)

From "A Dream of Fair Women"

I read, before my eyelids dropt their shade,
  'The Legend of Good Women,' long ago
Sung by the morning star of song, who made
    His music heard below;

Dan Chaucer, the first warbler, whose sweet breath
  Preluded those melodious bursts that fill
The spacious times of great Elizabeth
    With sounds that echo still.

And, for a while, the knowledge of his art
  Held me above the subject, as strong gales
Hold swollen clouds from raining, tho' my heart,
    Brimful of those wild tales,

Charged both mine eyes with tears. In every land
  I saw, wherever light illumineth,
Beauty and anguish walking hand in hand
    The downward slope to death.

Those far-renowned brides of ancient song
  Peopled the hollow dark, like burning stars,
And I heard sounds of insult, shame, and wrong,
    And trumpets blown for wars.
                    ALFRED, LORD TENNYSON
                        (1809–1892)

For Maister Geoffrey Chaucer

A bard there was, and that a worthy wight,
Who, from the time that he began to write,
Served God and beauty with an humble mind,
And most of all he knew and loved mankind.
Laughing he was, and quick at many a jest,
The Lord loves mirth,—the devil take the rest!
A simple grace ere wine be poured at dinner,
A ready hand outstretched to saint and sinner,
A prayer at times, not lengthy but devout,
This was our poet's faith without a doubt.

GEOFFREY CHAUCER (1340?-1400)

Travel he loved, and wonders had to tell
Of royal France and Italy as well,
And everywhere he went, his furtive pen
Took down the secrets of his fellow men,
Their faces and their stories, high and low,
From lordly Petrarch and Boccaccio
Unto the meanest villein who could hold
A tavern audience with the tales he told.
But with his scrivening, he never swerved
From duty to King Edward whom he served,
And though he roamed both France and Italy,
England was where he always longed to be,
And thither he returned with magic spoils
That England might have pleasure of his toils,
And hear his brave, chivalric stories sung
By English pilgrims in the English tongue.
Noble his spirit was, and gay his heart.
A judge of wine, a master of his art,
He loved all men, nor was ashamed to show it;
He was a very parfit gentil poet,
Gentil in life and parfit in his rhyme,—
God send us such another in our time!

          Robert Hillyer
           (1895-)

FRANÇOIS VILLON (1431-1489)

A Ballad of François Villon
Prince of All Ballad-Makers

Bird of the bitter bright grey golden morn
 Scarce risen upon the dusk of dolorous years,
First of us all and sweetest singer born
  Whose far shrill note the world of new men hears
  Cleave the cold shuddering shade as twilight clears;
When song new-born put off the old world's attire
And felt its tune on her changed lips expire,
 Writ foremost on the roll of them that came
Fresh grit for service of the latter lyre,
 Villon, our sad bad glad mad brother's name!

FRANÇOIS VILLON (1431–1489)

Alas the joy, the sorrow, and the scorn,
   That clothed thy life with hopes and sins and fears,
And gave thee stones for bread and tares for corn
   And plume-plucked gaol-birds for thy starveling peers
   Till death clipt close their flight with shameful shears;
Till shifts came short and loves were hard to hire,
When lilt of song nor twitch of twangling wire
   Could buy thee bread or kisses; when light fame
Spurned like a ball and haled through brake and briar,
   Villon, our sad bad glad mad brother's name!

Poor splendid wings so frayed and soiled and torn!
   Poor kind wild eyes so dashed with light quick tears!
Poor perfect voice, most blithe when most forlorn,
   That rings athwart the sea whence no man steers
   Like joy-bells crossed with death-bells in our ears!
What far delight has cooled the fierce desire
That like some ravenous bird was strong to tire
   On that frail flesh and soul consumed with flame,
But left more sweet than roses to respire,
   Villon, our sad bad glad mad brother's name?

Envoi

Prince of sweet songs made out of tears and fire,
A harlot was thy nurse, a God thy sire;
   Shame soiled thy song, and song assoiled thy shame.
But from thy feet now death has washed the mire,
Love reads out first at head of all our quire,
   Villon, our sad bad glad mad brother's name.

                          ALGERNON CHARLES SWINBURNE
                                 (1837–1909)

III

JOHN SKELTON (1460?–1529)

Praise to John Skelton

Praise to John Skelton and
his naked sinewy rhyme:
the frosty bitten seed
furrowed from his right hand—
root trunk and branches speed
to flower in our time.

John Skelton laureate,
doctor divinity,
stripped grandeur from the great
towered in simony,
uncloaked the cardinal
and Wolsey's skeleton
sloughed lace and crook and pall,
thigh bone and carrion
meat for a carousel:

Skull and charred ribs disclose
how the worm eats the rose,
how the worm jew'led and fat
dressed in Apostle's creed
sits with a mitrèd hat
eats at the king's right side . . .
Sing loud Magnificat!

John Skelton laureate
(whose sun has risen late
never to close its eye
in our eternity)

JOHN SKELTON (1460?-1529)

  thrust wide the lips that preach
  virtue in English speech
  the ragged, adder's tongue
  sharp deep and venomous
  iron and mirth,
  then tart and ruddy song
  heard when spring's morning wakes
  April whose blossom shakes
  birds over earth.

  Here is no epitaph—
  wreathed coffin, yew and hearse
  poet, to sink your verse
  in burial again,
  for these lines celebrate
  your quick immortal state:
  body hands lips and eyes
  speak metered gold
    Amen.

        HORACE GREGORY
         (1898–   )

SIR THOMAS WYATT (1503?-1542)

On the Death of Sir T(homas) W(yatt)

W(yatt) resteth here that quick could never rest;
 Whose heavenly gifts increased by disdain.
And virtue sank the deeper in his breast;
 Such profit he by envy could obtain.

A head where wisdom mysteries did frame,
 Whose hammers beat still in that lively brain,
As on a stithe where that some work of fame
 Was daily wrought, to turn to Britain's gain.

A visage stern and mild: where both did grow
 Vice to contemn, in virtue to rejoice;
Amid great storms whom grace assured so
 To live upright, and smile at fortune's choice.

SIR THOMAS WYATT (1503?-1542)

    A hand that taught what might be said in rhyme;
       That reft Chaucer the glory of his wit;
    A mark, the which (unperfected for time)
       Some may approach, but never none shall hit.

    A tongue that served in foreign realms his king;
       Whose courteous talk to virtue did inflame
    Each noble heart: a worthy guide to bring
       Our English youth by travail into fame.

    An eye who judgment none affect could blind,
       Friends to allure and foes to reconcile,
    Whose piercing look did represent a mind
       With virtue fraught reposed void of guile.

    A heart where dread was never so imprest
       To hide the thought that might the truth advance;
    In neither fortune loft, nor yet represt,
       To swell in wealth, or yield unto mischance.

    A valiant corpse, where force and beauty met,
       Happy alas, too happy but for foes,
    Lived, and ran the race that nature set;
       Of manhood's shape where she the mould did lose.

    But to the heavens that simple soul is fled,
       Which left with such as covet Christ to know
    Witness of faith that never shall be dead,
       Sent for our health, but not received so.
    Thus, for our guilt, this jewel have we lost;
    The earth his bones, the heavens possess his ghost!
                  HENRY HOWARD, EARL OF SURREY
                          (1517?-1547)

Loft] proud

SAINT TERESA (1515–1582)

From "Upon the Book and Picture of the Seraphical Saint Teresa"

O thou undaunted daughter of desires!
By all thy dower of lights and fires;
By all the eagle in thee, all the dove;
By all thy lives and deaths of love;
By thy large draughts of intellectual day,
And by thy thirsts of love more large than they;
By all thy brim-fill'd bowls of fierce desire,
By thy last morning's draught of liquid fire;
By the full kingdom of that final kiss
That seized thy parting soul, and seal'd thee His;
By all the Heav'n thou hast in Him
(Fair sister of the seraphim!);
By all of Him we have in thee;
Leave nothing of myself in me.
Let me so read thy life, that I
Unto all life of mine may die!

RICHARD CRASHAW
(1613–1649)

PIERRE DE RONSARD (1524–1585)

Ronsard

Master, I see thee with the locks of grey,
   Crowned by thy Muses with the laurel-wreath;
   I see the roses hiding underneath,
Cassandra's gift; she was less dear than they.
Thou, Master first, hast roused the lyric lay,
   The sleeping song that the dead years bequeath,
   Hast sung thine answers to the lays that breathe
Through ages, and through ages far away.
And thou hast heard the pulse of Pindar beat,
   Known Horace by the fount Bandusian!
Their deathless line thy living strains repeat,
   But ah, thy voice is sad, thy roses wan,

PIERRE DE RONSARD (1524-1585)

    But ah, thy honey is not honey-sweet,
    Thy bees have fed on yews Sardinian!
ANDREW LANG
(1844-1912)

Ronsard and Hélène

You sang, Ronsard, in your imperial lay
    Hélène, and sang as only you would dare
That she would cry, in reading, old and grey
    "Ronsard sang this of me when I was fair."
That was youth spoke, Ronsard, who will not stay
    To wonder if his own divine despair
May not with losing loveliness outweigh
    Kisses, that given, melt upon the air.
If youth but knew, Ronsard! The things that seem
    Would he not barter for the things that are,
And leave his mistress to embrace her dream
    Exchange her lips for her lost beauty's star?
Losing Hélène youth finds the lovelier truth,
If youth but knew! But then he were not youth.
HUMBERT WOLFE
(1885-1940)

LUIZ VAZ DE CAMOENS (1524-1580)

Camoens

(Before)

    And ever must I fan this fire?
    Thus ever in flame on flame aspire?
    Ever restless, restless, craving rest—
    The Imperfect toward Perfection pressed!
    Yea, for the God demands thy best.
    The world with endless beauty teems,
        And thought evokes new worlds of dreams:
    Hunt then the flying herds of themes!
    And fan, still fan, thy fervid fire,

LUIZ VAZ DE CAMOENS (1524–1580)

Until thy crucibled gold shall show
That fire can purge as well as glow.
In ordered ardour, nobly strong,
Flame to the height of epic song.

(After)
Camoens in the Hospital

What now avails the pageant verse,
Trophies and arms with music borne?
Base is the world; and some rehearse
Now noblest meet ignoble scorn,
Vain now thy ardour, vain thy fire,
Delirium mere, unsound desire;
Fate's knife hath ripped thy corded lyre.
Exhausted by the exacting lay,
Thou dost but fall a surer prey
To wile and guile ill understood;
While they who work them, fair in face,
Still keep their strength in prudent place,
And claim they worthier run life's race,
Serving high God with useful good.

HERMAN MELVILLE
(1819–1891)

TORQUATO TASSO (1544–1595)

From "Childe Harold's Pilgrimage"
Canto IV
XXXV

Ferrara! in thy wide and grass-grown streets,
Whose symmetry was not for solitude,
There seems as 'twere a curse upon the seats
Of former sovereigns, and the antique brood
Of Este, which for many an age made good
Its strength within thy walls, and was of yore
Patron or tyrant, as the changing mood
Of petty power impell'd, of those who wore
The wreath which Dante's brow alone had worn before.

TORQUATO TASSO (1544-1595)

XXXVI

And Tasso is their glory and their shame:
Hark to his strain and then survey his cell!
And see how dearly earn'd Torquato's fame,
And where Alfonso bade his poet dwell.
The miserable despot could not quell
The insulted mind he sought to quench, and blend
With the surrounding maniacs, in the hell
Where he had plunged it. Glory without end
Scatter'd the clouds away, and on that name attend

XXXVII

The tears and praise of all time; while thine
Would rot in its oblivion—in the sink
Of worthless dust which from thy boasted line
Is shaken into nothing—but the link
Thou formest in his fortunes bids us think
Of thy poor malice, naming thee with scorn.
Alfonso! how thy ducal pageants shrink
From thee! if in another station born,
Scarce fit to be the slave of him thou madest to mourn:—

XXXVIII

Thou! form'd to eat, and be despised, and die,
Even as the beasts that perish, save that thou
Hadst a more splendid trough and wider sty;
He! with a glory round his furrow'd brow,
Which emanated then, and dazzles now,
In face of all his foes, the Cruscan quire,
And Boileau, whose rash envy could allow
No strain which shamed his country's creaking lyre,
That whetstone of the teeth—monotony in wire!

XXXIX

Peace to Torquato's injured shade! 'twas his
In life and death to be the mark where Wrong
Aim'd with her poison'd arrows, but to miss.
Oh, victor unsurpass'd in modern song!
Each year brings forth its millions; but how long
The tide of generation shall roll on,

TORQUATO TASSO (1544-1595)

And not the whole combined and countless throng
Compose a mind like thine?   Though all in one
Condensed their scatter'd rays, they would not form a sun.

XL

Great as thou art, yet parallel'd by those,
Thy countrymen, before thee born to shine,
The Bards of Hell and Chivalry: first rose
The Tuscan father's comedy divine;
Then, not unequal to the Florentine
The southern Scott, the minstrel who call'd forth
A new creation with his magic line,
And like the Ariosto of the North,
Sang ladye-love and war, romance and knightly worth.

XLI

The lightning rent from Ariosto's bust
The iron crown of laurel's mimic'd leaves;
Nor was the ominous element unjust,
For the true laurel-wreath which Glory weaves
Is of the tree no bolt of thunder cleaves,
And the false semblance but disgraced his brow;
Yet still, if fondly Superstition grieves,
Know, that the lightning sanctifies below
What'er it strikes;—yon head is doubly sacred now.

LORD BYRON
(1788-1824)

EDMUND SPENSER (1552?-1599)

To the Learned Shepheard

Collyn, I see, by thy new taken taske,
Some sacred fury hath enricht thy braynes,
That leades thy Muse in haughty verse to maske,
And loathe the layes that longs to lowly swaynes;
That liftes thy notes from shepheardes unto kinges:
So like the lively larke that mounting singes.

EDMUND SPENSER (1552?–1599)

Thy lovely Rosalinde seemes now forlorne;
And all thy gentle flockes forgotten quight;
Thy chaunged hart now holdes thy pypes in scorne,
Those prety pypes that did thy mates delight;
Those trusty mates, that loved thee so well;
Whom thou gav'st mirth, as they gave thee the bell.
Yet as thou earst with thy sweete roundelayes,
Didst stirre to glee our laddes in homely bowers;
So moughtst thou now in these refyned layes
Delight the daintie eares of higher powers.
And so mought they, in their deepe skanning skill,
Alow and grace our Collyns flowing quill.

And faire befall that Faery Queene of thine!
In whose faire eyes Love linckt with Vertue sittes
Enfusing, by those bewties fyers divine,
Such high conceites into thy humble wittes,
As raised hath poore pastors oaten reedes
From rusticke tunes, to chaunt heroique deedes.

So mought thy Redcrosse knight with happy hand
Victorious be in that faire ilands right,
(Which thou dost vayle in type of Faery Land,)
Elizas blessed field, that Albion hight:
That shieldes her friendes, and warres her mightie foes,
Yet still with people, peace, and plentie, flowes.

But, iolly shepheard, though with pleasing stile
Thou feast the humour of the courtly trayne;
Let not conceipt thy settled sence beguile,
Ne daunted be through envy or disdaine.
Subiect thy doome to her empyring spright,
From whence thy Muse, and all the world, takes light.
                    GABRIEL HARVEY
                    (1545?–?1630)

EDMUND SPENSER (1552?-1599)

A Vision Upon the Conceit of "The Faery Queen"

Methought I saw the grave where Laura lay,
Within that Temple where the vestal flame
Was wont to burn; and passing by that way
To see that buried dust of living fame,
Whose tomb fair love, and fairer virtue kept,
All suddenly I saw the Faery Queen:
At whose approach the soul of Petrarch wept,
And from thenceforth those graces were not seen;
For they this Queen attended, in whose stead
Oblivion laid him down on Laura's hearse.
Hereat the hardest stones were seen to bleed,
And groans of buried ghosts the heavens did pierce:
Where Homer's spright did tremble all for grief,
And cursed the access of that celestial thief.

SIR WALTER RALEIGH
(1552?-1618)

The Poets

Were I to name, out of the times gone by,
 The poets dearest to me, I should say,
  Pulci for spirits, and a fine, free way;
Chaucer for manners, and close, silent eye;
Milton for classic taste, and harp strung high;
 Spenser for luxury, and sweet, sylvan play;
  Horace for chatting with, from day to day;
Shakespeare for all, but most, society.

But which take with me, could I take but one?
 Shakespeare,—as long as I was unoppressed
  With the world's weight, making sad
   thoughts intenser;
But did I wish, out of the common sun,
 To lay a wounded heart in leafy rest,
  And dream of things far off and healing,—Spenser.

LEIGH HUNT
(1784-1859)

SIR WALTER RALEIGH (1552–1618)

To the Right Noble and Valorous Knight, Sir Walter Raleigh

To thee that art the sommers Nightingale,
   Thy soveraine Goddesses most deare delight,
   Why doe I send this rusticke madrigale,
   That may thy tunefull ear unseason quite?
Thou onely fit this argument to write,
   In whose high thoughts Pleasure hath built her bowre,
   And dainty Love learnd sweetly to endite.
My rimes I know unsavory and sowre,
   To tast the streames, that like a golden showre
   Flow from thy fruitfull head, of thy loves praise;
   Fitter perhaps to thonder martiall stowre,
   When so thee list thy lofty Muse to raise:
Yet till that thou thy poeme wilt make knowne,
Let thy faire Cinthias praises bee thus rudely showne.

                              EDMUND SPENSER
                                 (1552?–1599)

SIR PHILIP SIDNEY (1554–1586)

Epitaph on Sir Philip Sidney

Silence augmenteth grief, writing increaseth rage,
Staled are my thoughts, which loved and lost the wonder of our age:
Yet quickened now with fire, though dead with frost ere now,
Enraged I write I know not what; dead, quick, I know not how.

Hard-hearted minds relent and rigour's tears abound,
And envy strangely rues his end, in whom no fault she found.
Knowledge her light hath lost; valour hath slain her knight,
Sidney is dead; dead is my friend; dead is the world's delight.

Place, pensive, wails his fall whose presence was her pride;
Time crieth out, "My ebb is come; his life was my spring tide."
Fame mourns in that she lost the ground of her reports;
Each living wight laments his lack, and all in sundry sorts.

SIR PHILIP SIDNEY (1554-1586)

He was (woe worth that word!) to each well-thinking mind
A spotless friend, a matchless man, whose virtue ever shined,
Declaring in his thoughts, his life, and that he writ,
Highest conceits, longest foresights, and deepest works of wit.

He, only like himself, was second unto none,
Whose death (though life) we rue, and wrong, and all in vain do moan.
Their loss, not him, wail they, that fill the world with cries,
Death slew not him, but he made death his ladder to the skies.

Now sink of sorrow I, who live, the more the wrong!
Who wishing death, whom death denies, whose thread is all too long;
Who tied to wretched life, who looks for no relief,
Must spend my ever dying days in never ending grief.

Heart's ease and only I, like parallels, run on,
Whose equal length keep equal breadth, and never meet in one;
Yet for not wronging him, my thoughts, my sorrow's cell,
Shall not run out, though leak they will, for liking him so well.

Farewell to you, my hopes, my wonted waking dreams,
Farewell, sometimes enjoyed joy; eclipsed are thy beams.
Farewell, self-pleasing thoughts, which quietness brings forth;
And farewell, friendship's sacred league, uniting minds of worth.

And farewell, merry heart, the gift of guiltless minds,
And all sports which for life's restore variety assigns;
Let all that sweet is void; in me no mirth may dwell.
Philip, the cause of all this woe, my life's content, farewell!

Now rhyme, the son of rage, which art no kin to skill,
And endless grief, which deads my life, yet knows not how to kill,
Go, seek that hapless tomb, which if ye hap to find,
Saluate the stones, that keep the limbs, that held so good a mind.

FULKE GREVILLE, LORD BROOKE
(1554-1628)

SIR PHILIP SIDNEY (1554-1586)

On the Death of Sir Philip Sidney

Give pardon, blessèd soul, to my bold cries,
  If they, importune, interrupt thy song,
Which now with joyful notes thou sing'st among
The angel-quiristers of th' heavenly skies.
Give pardon eke, sweet soul, to my slow eyes,
That since I saw thee now it is so long,
And yet the tears that unto thee belong
To thee as yet they did not sacrifice.
I did not know that thou wert dead before;
I did not feel the grief I did sustain;
The greater stroke astonisheth the more;
Astonishment takes from us sense of pain;
  I stood amazed when others' tears begun,
  And now begin to weep when they have done.
HENRY CONSTABLE
(1562-1613)

CHRISTOPHER MARLOWE (1564-1593)

Christopher Marlowe

Crowned, girdled, garbed and shod with light and fire,
  Son first-born of the morning, sovereign star!
  Soul nearest ours of all, that wert most far,
Most far off in the abysm of time, thy lyre
Hung highest above the dawn-enkindled quire
  Where all ye sang together, all that are,
  And all the starry songs behind thy car
Rang sequence, all our souls acclaim thee sire.

"If all the pens that ever poets held
  Had fed the feeling of their masters' thoughts,"
And as with rush of hurtling chariots
The flight of all their spirits were impelled
  Toward one great end, thy glory—nay, not then,
  Not yet might'st thou be praised enough of men.
ALGERNON CHARLES SWINBURNE
(1837-1909)

CHRISTOPHER MARLOWE (1564–1593)

After Reading "Tamburlaine the Great"

Yon page being closed, my Shakespeare's let me ope.
How welcome—after gong and cymbal's din—
The continuity, the long slow slope
And vast curves of the gradual violin!

WILLIAM WATSON
(1858–1935)

WILLIAM SHAKESPEARE (1564–1616)

To Our English Terence, Mr. Will. Shakespeare

Some say, good Will, (which I in sport do sing)
  Hadst thou not played some kingly parts in sport,
Thou hadst been a companion for a king,
And been a king among the meaner sort.
Some others rail; but, rail as they think fit,
Thou hast no railing, but a reigning, wit;
  And honesty thou sow'st, which they do reap,
  So to increase their stock—which they do keep.

JOHN DAVIES OF HEREFORD
(1565?–1618)

To the Memory of My Beloved the Author, Mr. William Shakespeare: and What He Hath Left Us

To draw no envy (Shakespeare) on thy name,
  Am I thus ample to thy booke, and fame;
While I confesse thy writings to be such
  As neither man, nor muse, can praise too much.
'Tis true, and all mens suffrage. But these wayes
  Were not the paths I meant unto thy praise;
For seemliest ignorance on these may light,
  Which, when it sounds at best, but eccho's right;
Or blind affection, which doth ne're advance
  The truth, but gropes, and urgeth all by chance;
Or crafty malice might pretend this praise,
  And think to ruine, where it seem'd to raise.

WILLIAM SHAKESPEARE (1564-1616)

    These are, as some infamous baud, or whore,
        Should praise a matron. What could hurt her more?
    But thou art proofe against them and indeed
        Above th'ill fortune of them, or the need.
    I, therefore, will begin. Soule of the age!
        The applause! delight! the wonder of our stage!
    My Shakespeare, rise; I will not lodge thee by
        Chaucer, or Spenser, or bid Beaumont lye
    A little further, to make thee a roome;
        Thou art a monument, without a tombe,
    And art alive still, while thy booke doth live,
        And we have wits to reade, and praise to give.
    That I not mixe thee so, my braine, excuses;
        I meane with great, but disproportion'd muses:
    For, if I thought my judgement were of yeeres,
        I should commit thee surely with thy peeres,
    And tell how farre thou didst our Lily outshine,
        Or sporting Kid, or Marlowes mighty line.
    And though thou hadst small Latine, and lesse Greeke,
        From thence to honour thee I would not seeke
    For names; but call forth thundring Æschilus,
        Euripides, and Sophocles to us,
    Paccuvius, Accius, him of Cordova dead,
        To life againe, to heare thy buskin tread
    And shake a stage: or, when thy sockes were on,
        Leave thee alone for the comparison
    Of all that insolent Greece or haughtie Rome
        Sent forth, or since did from their ashes come.
    Triumph, my Britaine, thou hast one to showe
        To whom all scenes of Europe homage owe.
    He was not of an age, but for all time!
        And all the Muses still were in their prime,
    When like Apollo he came forth to warme
        Our eares, or like a Mercury to charme!
    Nature her selfe was proud of his designes,
        And joy'd to weare the dressing of his lines,
    Which were so richly spun, and woven so fit,
        As, since, she will vouchsafe no other wit.

him of Cordova] Seneca, Roman tragic poet

WILLIAM SHAKESPEARE (1564–1616)

> The merry Greeke, tart Aristophanes,
>   Neat Terence, witty Plautus, now not please,
> But antiquated and deserted lye
>   As they were not of natures family.
> Yet must I not give nature all; thy art,
>   My gentle Shakespeare, must enjoy a part;
> For though the poet's matter nature be,
>   His art doth give the fashion. And that he
> Who casts to write a living line, must sweat,
>   (Such as thine are) and strike the second heat
> Upon the Muses anvile, turne the same,
>   (And himselfe with it) that he thinkes to frame;
> Or for the lawrell he may gaine a scorne,
>   For a good poet's made, as well as borne;
> And such wert thou. Looke how thy fathers face
>   Lives in his issue; even so the race
> Of Shakespeares minde and manners brightly shines
>   In his well tornéd, and true-filéd lines;
> In each of which he seemes to shake a lance,
>   As brandish't at the eyes of ignorance.
> Sweet swan of Avon! what a sight it were
>   To see thee in our waters yet appeare,
> And make those flights upon the bankes of Thames,
>   That so did take Eliza, and our James!
> But stay, I see thee in the hemisphere
>   Advanc'd, and make a constellation there!
> Shine forth, thou starre of poets, and with rage
>   Or influence, chide, or cheere the drooping stage;
> Which, since thy flight from hence, hath mourn'd like night,
>   And despaires day, but for thy volumes light.
>
>   BEN JONSON
>   (1573?–1637)

Elegy on Mr. William Shakespeare

> Renownèd Spenser, lie a thought more nigh
> To learned Chaucer, and rare Beaumont lie
> A little nearer Spenser, to make room
> For Shakespeare in your threefold, fourfold tomb.

WILLIAM SHAKESPEARE (1564-1616)

> To lodge all four in one bed, make a shift
> Until Doomsday, for hardly will a fifth
> Betwixt this day and that by Fate be slain,
> For whom your curtains may be drawn again.
> If your precedency in death doth bar
> A fourth place in your sacred sepulchre,
> Under this carved marble of thine own,
> Sleep, rare tragedian, Shakespeare, sleep alone;
> Thy unmolested peace, unshared cave
> Possess as lord, not tenant of thy grave,
>   That unto us and others it may be
>   Honour thereafter to be laid by thee.
> WILLIAM BASSE
(1583-1653)

On Shakespeare

> What needs my Shakespeare for his honoured bones
> The labour of an age in pilèd stones?
> Or that his hallowed reliques should be hid
> Under a star-ypointing pyramid?
> Dear son of memory, great heir of fame,
> What need'st thou such weak witness of thy name?
> Thou in our wonder and astonishment
> Hast built thyself a livelong monument.
> For whilst, to the shame of slow-endeavouring art,
> Thy easy numbers flow, and that each heart
> Hath from the leaves of thy unvalued book
> Those Delphic lines with deep impression took,
> Then thou, our fancy of itself bereaving,
> Dost make us marble with too much conceiving,
> And so sepúlchred in such pomp dost lie
> That kings for such a tomb would wish to die.
> JOHN MILTON
(1608-1674)

WILLIAM SHAKESPEARE (1564–1616)

from "Prologue"

Spoken by Mr. Garrick at the Opening of the Theatre Royal, Drury Lane, 1747

When Learning's triumph o'er her barb'rous foes
First rear'd the stage, immortal Shakespeare rose;
Each change of many-colour'd life he drew,
Exhausted worlds, and then imagin'd new:
Existence saw him spurn her bounded reign,
And panting Time toil'd after him in vain.
His pow'rful strokes presiding Truth impress'd,
And unresisted Passion storm'd the breast.
   Then Jonson came, instructed from the school,
To please in method, and invent by rule;
His studious patience and laborious art,
By regular approach essay'd the heart:
Cold Approbation gave the ling'ring bays;
For those who durst not censure, scarce could praise.
A mortal born, he met the gen'ral doom,
But left, like Egypt's kings, a lasting tomb.
   The wits of Charles found easier ways to fame,
Nor wish'd for Jonson's art, or Shakespeare's flame.
Themselves they studied; as they felt, they writ:
Intrigue was plot, obscenity was wit.
Vice always found a sympathetic friend;
They pleas'd their age, and did not aim to mend.
Yet bards like these aspir'd to lasting praise,
And proudly hop'd to pimp in future days.
Their cause was gen'ral, their supports were strong,
Their slaves were willing, and their reign was long:
Till Shame regain'd the post that Sense betray'd,
And Virtue call'd Oblivion to her aid.
   Then, crush'd by rules, and weaken'd as refin'd,
For years the pow'r of tragedy declin'd;
From bard to bard the frigid caution crept,
Till Declamation roar'd whilst Passion slept;
Yet still did Virtue deign the stage to tread,
Philosophy remain'd though Nature fled.
But forc'd, at length, her ancient reign to quit,

WILLIAM SHAKESPEARE (1564-1616)

She saw great Faustus lay the ghost of Wit;
Exulting Folly hail'd the joyful day,
And Pantomime and Song confirm'd her sway.
  But who the coming changes can presage,
And mark the future periods of the stage?
Perhaps if skill could distant times explore,
New Behns, new Durfeys, yet remain in store;
Perhaps where Lear has rav'd, and Hamlet dy'd,
On flying cars new sorcerers may ride;
Perhaps (for who can guess th' effects of chance)
Here Hunt may box, or Mahomet may dance.
  Hard is his lot that here by fortune plac'd,
Must watch the wild vicissitudes of taste;
With ev'ry meteor of caprice must play,
And chase the new-blown bubbles of the day.
Ah! let not censure term our fate our choice,
The stage but echoes back the public voice;
The drama's laws, the drama's patrons give,
For we that live to please, must please to live.
  Then prompt no more the follies you decry,
As tyrants doom their tools of guilt to die;
'Tis yours, this night, to bid the reign commence
Of rescued Nature and reviving Sense;
To chase the charms of Sound, the pomp of Show,
For useful Mirth and salutary Woe;
Bid scenic Virtue form the rising age,
And Truth diffuse her radiance from the stage.

SAMUEL JOHNSON
(1709-1784)

Shakespeare and Milton

The tongue of England, that which myriads
Have spoken and will speak, were paralyz'd
Hereafter, but two mighty men stand
    forth
Above the flight of ages, two alone;
One crying out,
        All nations spoke through me.

WILLIAM SHAKESPEARE (1564-1616)

The other:
> *True; and through this trumpet burst
> God's word; the fall of Angels, and the
>   doom
> First of immortal, then of mortal, Man,
> Glory! be glory! not to me, to God.*

WALTER SAVAGE LANDOR
(1775-1864)

On Sitting Down to Read "King Lear" Once Again

O Golden-tongued Romance, with serene lute!
Fair plumèd Syren, Queen of far away!
Leave melodizing on this wintry day,
Shut up thine olden pages, and be mute:
Adieu! for once again the fierce dispute
Betwixt damnation and impassioned clay,
Must I burn through; once more humbly essay
The bitter sweet of this Shakespearian fruit:
Chief Poet! and ye clouds of Albion,
Begetters of our deep eternal theme!
When through the old oak forest I am gone,
Let me not wander in a barren dream,
But when I am consumèd in the Fire,
Give me new Phœnix-wings to fly at my desire.

JOHN KEATS
(1795-1821)

To Shakespeare

The soul of man is larger than the sky,
Deeper than ocean or the abysmal dark
Of the unfathom'd centre. Like that Ark
Which in its sacred hold uplifted high,
O'er the drown'd hills, the human family,
And stock reserv'd of every living kind,
So, in the compass of the single mind,
The seeds and pregnant forms in essence lie,

WILLIAM SHAKESPEARE (1564–1616)

That make all worlds. Great Poet, 'twas thy art
To know thyself, and in thyself to be
Whate'er love, hate, ambition, destiny,
Or the firm, fatal purpose of the heart,
Can make the Man. Yet thou wert still the same,
Serene of thought, unhurt by thy own flame.

Hartley Coleridge
(1796–1849)

Shakespeare

How little fades from earth when sink to rest
The hours and cares that mov'd a great man's breast!
Though naught of all we saw the grave may spare,
His life pervades the world's impregnate air;
Though Shakespeare's dust beneath our footsteps lies,
His spirit breathes amid his native skies;
With meaning won from him forever glows
Each air that England feels, and star it knows;
His whisper'd words from many a mother's voice
Can make her sleeping child in dreams rejoice,
And gleams from spheres he first conjoin'd to earth
Are blent with rays of each new morning's birth.
Amid the sights and tales of common things,
Leaf, flower, and bird, and wars, and deaths of kings,
Of shore, and sea, and nature's daily round,
Of life that tills, and tombs that load the ground,
His visions mingle, swell, command, pace by,
And haunt with living presence heart and eye;
And tones from him by other bosoms caught
Awaken flush and stir of mounting thought,
And the long sigh, and deep impassion'd thrill,
Rouse custom's trance, and spur the faltering will.
Above the goodly land more his than ours
He sits supreme enthron'd in skyey towers,
And sees the heroic brood of his creation
Teach larger life to his ennobled nation.

WILLIAM SHAKESPEARE (1564-1616)

O shaping brain!   O flashing fancy's hues!
O boundless heart kept fresh by pity's dews!
O wit humane and blithe!   O sense sublime
For each dim oracle of mantled Time!
Transcendent Form of Man! in whom we read
Mankind's whole tale of Impulse, Thought, and Deed;
Amid the expanse of years beholding thee,
We know how vast our world of life may be;
Wherein, perchance, with aims as pure as thine,
Small tasks and strengths may be no less divine.

JOHN STERLING
(1806-1844)

The Names

Shakespeare!—to such name's sounding, what succeeds
   Fitly as silence?   Falter forth the spell,—
   Act follows word, the speaker knows full well,
Nor tampers with its magic more than needs.
Two names there are: That which the Hebrew reads
   With his soul only; if from lips it fell,
   Echo, back thundered by earth, heaven and hell,
Would own "Thou didst create us!"   Naught impedes
We voice the other name, man's most of might,
   Awesomely, lovingly: let awe and love
Mutely await their working, leave to sight
   All of the issue as—below—above—
   Shakespeare's creation rises: one remove,
Though dread—this finite from that infinite.

ROBERT BROWNING
(1812-1889)

Shakspeare

Others abide our question.   Thou art free.
We ask and ask—Thou smilest and art still,
Out-topping knowledge.   For the loftiest hill,
Who to the stars uncrowns his majesty,

WILLIAM SHAKESPEARE (1564–1616)

Planting his steadfast footsteps in the sea,
Making the heaven of heavens his dwelling-place,
Spares but the cloudy border of his base
To the foil'd searching of mortality;

And thou, who didst the stars and sunbeams know,
Self-school'd, self-scann'd, self-honour'd, self-secure,
Didst walk on earth unguess'd at.—Better so!

All pains the immortal spirit must endure,
All weakness which impairs, all griefs which bow,
Find their sole speech in that victorious brow.

MATTHEW ARNOLD
(1822–1888)

The Spirit of Shakespeare

I

Thy greatest knew thee, Mother Earth; unsour'd
He knew thy sons. He prob'd from hell to hell
Of human passions, but of love deflower'd
His wisdom was not, for he knew thee well.
Thence came the honey'd corner at his lips,
The conquering smile wherein his spirit sails
Calm as the God who the white sea-wave whips,
Yet full of speech and intershifting tales,
Close mirrors of us: thence had he the laugh
We feel is thine; broad as ten thousand beeves
At pasture! thence thy songs, that winnow chaff
From grain, bid sick Philosophy's last leaves
Whirl, if they have no response—they enforced
To fatten Earth when from her soul divorced.

II

How smiles he at a generation rank'd
In gloomy noddings over life! They pass.
Not he to feed upon a breast unthank'd,
Or eye a beauteous face in a crack'd glass.
But he can spy that little twist of brain
Which mov'd some weighty leader of the blind,

WILLIAM SHAKESPEARE (1564–1616)

Unwitting 't was the goad of personal pain,
To view in curs'd eclipse our Mother's mind,
And show us of some rigid harridan
The wretched bondmen till the end of time.
O liv'd the Master now to paint us Man,
That little twist of brain would ring a chime
Of whence it came and what it caus'd, to start
Thunders of laughter, clearing air and heart.

GEORGE MEREDITH
(1828–1909)

To Shakespeare
After Three Hundred Years

Bright baffling Soul, least capturable of themes,
Thou, who display'dst a life of common-place,
Leaving no intimate word or personal trace
Of high design outside the artistry
    Of thy penned dreams,
Still shalt remain at heart unread eternally.

Through human orbits thy discourse today,
Despite thy formal pilgrimage, throbs on
In harmonies that cow Oblivion,
And, like the wind, with all-uncared effect
    Maintain a sway
Not fore-desired, in tracks unchosen and unchecked.

And yet, at thy last breath, with mindless note
The borough clocks but samely tongued the hour,
The Avon just as always glassed the tower,
Thy age was published on thy passing-bell
    But in due rote,
With other dwellers' deaths accorded a like knell.

And at the strokes some townsman (met, maybe,
And thereon queried by some squire's good dame
Driving in shopward) may have given thy name,
With, "Yes, a worthy man and well-to-do;
    Though, as for me,
I knew him but by just a neighbour's nod, 'tis true.

WILLIAM SHAKESPEARE (1564–1616)

"I' faith, few knew him much here, save by word,
He having elsewhere led his busier life;
Though to be sure he left with us his wife."
—"Ah, one of the tradesmen's sons, I now recall. . . .
Witty, I've heard. . . .
We did not know him. . . . Well, good-day.
Death comes to all."

So, like a strange bright bird we sometimes find
To mingle with the barn-door brood awhile,
Then vanish from their homely domicile—
Into man's poesy, we wot not whence,
   Flew thy strange mind,
Lodged there a radiant guest, and sped for
   ever thence.

THOMAS HARDY
(1840–1928)

To Shakespeare

Through torrid entrances, past icy poles
A hand moves on the page! Who shall again
Engrave such hazards as thy might controls—
  Conflicting, purposeful yet outcry vain
Of all our days, being pilot,—tempest, too!
  Sheets that mock lust and thorns that scribble hate
Are lifted from torn flesh with human rue,
  And laughter, burnished brighter than our fate,
Thou wieldest with such tears that every faction
  Swears high in Hamlet's throat, and devils throng
Where angels beg for doom in ghast distraction
  And fall, both! Yet thine Ariel holds his song:
And that serenity that Prospero gains
Is justice that has cancelled earthly chains.

HART CRANE
(1899–1932)

GEORGE CHAPMAN (1559?–1634)

Sonnet 86

Was it the proud full sail of his great verse,
Bound for the prize of all too precious you,
That did my ripe thoughts in my brain inhearse,
Making their tomb the womb wherein they grew?
Was it his spirit, by spirits taught to write
Above a mortal pitch, that struck me dead?
No, neither he nor his compeers by night
Giving him aid, my verse astonished.
He nor that affable familiar ghost
Which nightly gulls him with intelligence,
As victors of my silence cannot boast;
I was not sick of any fear from thence:
  But when your countenance filled up his line,
  Then lack'd I matter; that enfeebled mine.

WILLIAM SHAKESPEARE
(1564–1616)

To My Worthy Friend Mr. George Chapman, and His Translated Hesiod

Chapman, we find, by thy past-prized fraught,
What wealth thou dost upon this land confer,
Th' old Grecian prophets hither that has brought,
Of their full words the true interpreter;
And by thy travell strongly hast exprest
The large dimensions of the English tongue,
Delivering them so well, the first and best
That to the world in numbers ever sung.
Thou hast unlock'd the treasury wherein
All art and knowledge have so long been hidden;
Which, till the graceful Muses did begin
Here to inhabit, was to us forbidden.
  In best Elysium, (in a place most fit)
Under that tree due to the Delphian God,
MUSÆUS and that ILIAD SINGER sit,
And near to them that noble HESIOD,

GEORGE CHAPMAN (1559?–1634)

Smoothing their rugged foreheads; and do smile,
After so many hundred years, to see
Their Poems read in this far western isle,
Translated from their ancient Greek by thee;
Each his good Genius whispering in his ear,
That with so lucky and auspicious fate
Did still attend them whilst they living were,
And gave their verses such a lasting date.
  Where, slightly passing by the Thespian spring,
Many long after did but only sup;
Nature, then fruitful, forth these men did bring,
To fetch deep roses from Jove's plenteous cup.
  In thy free labours, friend, then rest content,
Fear not Detraction, neither fawn on Praise;
When idle Censure all her force hath spent,
Knowledge can crown herself with her own bays.
Their lines that have so many lives outworn,
Clearly expounded, shall base Envy scorn.

MICHAEL DRAYTON
(1563–1631)

To My Worthy and Honoured Friend, Mr. George Chapman, On His Translation of Hesiod's Works and Days

Whose work could this be, CHAPMAN, to refine
Old HESIOD's ore, and give it us, but thine,
Who had'st before wrought in rich HOMER's mine?

What treasure hast thou brought us! and what store
Still, still, dost thou arrive with at our shore,
To make thy honour and our wealth the more!

If all the vulgar tongues that speak this day
Were ask'd of thy discoveries, they must say,
To the Greek coast thine only knew the way.

GEORGE CHAPMAN (1559?-1634)

Such passage hast thou found, such returns made,
As, now of all men, it is called thy trade;
And who make thither else rob, or invade!

BEN JONSON
(1573?-1637)

On First Looking into Chapman's Homer

Much have I travell'd in the realms of gold,
  And many goodly states and kingdoms seen;
  Round many western islands have I been
Which bards in fealty to Apollo hold.
Oft of one wide expanse had I been told
  That deep-brow'd Homer ruled as his demesne:
  Yet did I never breathe its pure serene
Till I heard Chapman speak out loud and bold:
Then felt I like some watcher of the skies
  When a new planet swims into his ken;
Or like stout Cortez when with eagle eyes
  He star'd at the Pacific—and all his men
Look'd at each other with a wild surmise—
  Silent, upon a peak in Darien.

JOHN KEATS
(1795-1821)

THOMAS CAMPION (1567-1620)

Madrigal

*Set Forth to be Sung to the Bass Viol
In Praise on Mr. Bullen   His Edition
Of the Works of Dr. Thomas Campion*

  He comes again!
    The latest, not the least desired!
    Too long in mouldering tomes retired,
  We sought in vain
  Those breathing airs
    Which, from his instrument,
    Like vocal winds of perfume, blent
  To soothe man's piercing cares.

THOMAS CAMPION (1567–1620)

> Bullen, well done!
> Where Campion lies in London-land,
> Lulled by the thunders of the Strand,
> Screened from the sun,
> Surely there must
> Now pass some pleasant gleam
> Across his music-haunted dream
> Whose brain and lute are dust.
> EDMUND GOSSE
(1849–1928)

THOMAS DEKKER (1572?–1632)

Thomas Decker

> Out of the depths of darkling life where sin
>   Laughs piteously that sorrow should not know
>   Her own ill name, nor woe be counted woe;
> Where hate and craft and lust make drearier din
> Than sounds through dreams that grief holds revel in;
>   What charm of joy-bells ringing, streams that flow,
>   Winds that blow healing in each note they blow,
> Is this that the outer darkness hears begin?
> O sweetest heart of all thy time save one,
> Star seen for love's sake nearest to the sun,
>   Hung lamplike o'er a dense and doleful city,
> Not Shakespeare's very spirit, howe'er more great,
> Than thine toward man was more compassionate,
>   Nor gave Christ praise from lips more sweet with pity.
> ALGERNON CHARLES SWINBURNE
(1837–1909)

BEN JONSON (1573?–1637)

Master Francis Beaumont's Letter to Ben Jonson

> The sun (which doth the greatest comfort bring
> To absent friends, because the selfsame thing
> They know they see, however absent) is
> Here our best haymaker! Forgive me this;

[83]

BEN JONSON (1573?–1637)

It is our country's style! In this warm shine
I lie and dream of your full Mermaid Wine!
Oh, we have water mixed with claret lees,
Drink apt to bring in drier heresies
Than beer, good only for the sonnet's strain,
With fustia in metaphors to stuff the brain;
So mixed, that, given to the thirstiest one,
'Twill not prove alms, unless he have the stone.
I think that with one draught man's invention fades,
Two cups had quite spoiled Homer's Iliads.
'Tis liquor that will find out Sutcliff's wit,
Lie where he will, and make him write worse yet.
Filled with such moisture, in most grievous qualms,
Did Robert Wisdom write his singing psalms;
And so must I do this: And yet I think
It is a potion sent us down to drink,
By special Providence, keeps us from fights,
Makes us not laugh when we make legs to knights.
'Tis this that keeps our minds fit for our states,
A medicine to obey our magistrates:
For we do live more free than you; no hate,
No envy at one another's happy state,
Moves us; we are all equal; every whit
Of land that God gives men here is their wit,
If we consider fully; for our best
And gravest man will with his main house-jest,
Scarce please you; we want subtlety to do
The city-tricks, lie, hate, and flatter too.
Here are none that can bear a painted show,
Strike when you wink, and then lament the blow;
Who, like mills set the right way for to grind,
Can make their gains alike with every wind:
Only some fellows, with the subtlest pate
Amongst us, may perchance equivocate
At selling of a horse, and that's the most.
   Methinks the little wit I had is lost
Since I saw you! For wit is like a rest
Held up at tennis, which men do the best
With the best gamesters. What things have we seen

BEN JONSON (1573?–1637)

Done at the Mermaid! heard words that have been
So nimble and so full of subtle flame,
As if that every one from whence they came
Had meant to put his whole wit in a jest
And had resolved to live a fool the rest
Of his dull life! Then, when there hath been thrown
Wit able enough to justify the town
For three days past! Wit, that might warrant be
For the whole city to talk foolishly
Till that were cancelled! And, when we were gone,
We left an air behind us, which alone
Was able to make the two next companies
Right witty! though but downright fools, more wise!
   When I remember this, and see that now
The country gentlemen begin to allow
My wit for dry bobs; then I needs must cry,
"I see my days of ballading grow nigh!"
   I can already riddle; and can sing
Catches, sell bargains; and I fear shall bring
Myself to speak the hardest words I find
Over as oft as any, with one wind,
That takes no medicines! But one thought of thee
Makes me remember all these things to be
The wit of our young men, fellows that show
No part of good, yet utter all they know!
Who, like trees of the guard, have growing souls.
   Only strong Destiny, which all controls,
I hope hath left a better fate in store
For me, thy friend, than to live ever poor,
Banished unto this home! Fate, once again,
Bring me to thee, who canst make smooth and plain
The way of knowledge for me; and then I,
Who have no good but in thy company,
Protest it will my greatest comfort be
To acknowledge all I have to flow from thee!
   Ben, when these scenes are perfect, we'll taste wine!
I'll drink thy Muse's health! thou shalt quaff mine!

FRANCIS BEAUMONT
(1584–1616)

BEN JONSON (1573?–1637)

An Ode for Ben Jonson

Ah, Ben!
Say how, or when
Shall we, thy guests,
Meet at those lyric feasts
Made at the Sun,
The Dog, the Triple Tun?
Where we such clusters had,
As made us nobly wild, not mad;
And yet each verse of thine
Out-did the meat, out-did the frolic wine.

My Ben!
Or come again,
Or send to us
Thy wit's great overplus;
But teach us yet
Wisely to husband it,
Lest we that talent spend;
And having once brought to an end
That precious stock, the store
Of such a wit the world should have no more.

ROBERT HERRICK
(1591–1674)

His Prayer to Ben Jonson

When I a verse shall make,
 Know I have prayed thee,
For old religion's sake,
 Saint Ben, to aid me.

Make the way smooth for me,
 When I, thy Herrick,
Honouring thee, on my knee
 Offer my lyric.

BEN JONSON (1573?-1637)

> Candles I'll give to thee,
>   And a new altar;
>   And thou, Saint Ben, shalt be
>   Writ in my psalter.
>
> ROBERT HERRICK
> (1591-1674)

Upon Ben Jonson

> Here lyes Jonson with the rest
> Of the poets; but the best.
> Reader, wo'dst thou more have known?
> Aske his story, not this stone.
> That will speake what this can't tell
> Of his glory. So *farewell*.
>
> ROBERT HERRICK
> (1591-1674)

Upon M. Ben Jonson, Epigram

> After the rare arch-poet Jonson died,
> The sock grew loathsome, and the buskin's pride,
> Together with the stage's glory, stood
> Each like a poor and pitied widowhood.
> The cirque prophaned was, and all postures racked,
> For men did strut and stride and stare, not act.
> Then temper flew from words, and men did squeak,
> Look red, and blow, and bluster, but not speak;
> No holy rage or frantic fires did stir,
> Or flash about the spacious theater.
> No clap of hands, or shout, or praise's proof
> Did crack the playhouse sides, or cleave her roof.
> Artless the scene was, and that monstrous sin
> Of deep and arrant ignorance came in;
> Such ignorance as theirs was who once hissed
> At thy unequalled play, the *Alchemist*.
> Oh fie upon 'em! Lastly too, all wit
> In utter darkness did, and still will sit

BEN JONSON (1573?–1637)

    Sleeping the luckless age out, till that she
    Her resurrection has again with thee.
ROBERT HERRICK
(1591–1674)

Ben Jonson

Broad-based, broad-fronted, bounteous, multiform,
    With many a valley impleached with ivy and vine,
    Wherein the springs of all the streams run wine,
And many a crag full-faced against the storm,
The mountain where thy Muse's feet made warm
    Those lawns that revelled with her dance divine
    Shines yet with fire as it was wont to shine
From tossing torches round the dance aswarm.
Nor less, high-stationed on the grey grave heights,
High-thoughted seers with heaven's heart-kindling lights
    Hold converse: and the herd of meaner things
Knows or by fiery scourge or fiery shaft
When wrath on thy broad brows has risen, and laughed,
    Darkening thy soul with shadow of thunderous wings.
ALGERNON CHARLES SWINBURNE
(1837–1909)

FRANCIS BEAUMONT (1584–1616)

To Francis Beaumont

How I doe love thee, Beaumont, and thy Muse,
    That unto me dost such religion use!
How I doe feare my selfe, that am not worth
    The least indulgent thought thy pen drops forth!
At once thou mak'st me happie, and unmak'st;
    And giving largely to me, more thou tak'st.
What fate is mine, that so it selfe bereaves?
    What art is thine, that so thy friend deceives?
When even there, where most thou praisest mee,
    For writing better, I must envie thee.
BEN JONSON
(1573?–1637)

FRANCIS BEAUMONT (1584-1616)

Bards of Passion and of Mirth

Written on the Blank Page before Beaumont and Fletcher's Tragi-Comedy "The Fair Maid of the Inn"

Bards of Passion and of Mirth,
Ye have left your souls on earth!
Have ye souls in heaven too,
Double-lived in regions new?
Yes, and those of heaven commune
With the spheres of sun and moon;
With the noise of fountains wond'rous,
And the parle of voices thund'rous;
With the whisper of heaven's trees
And one another, in soft ease
Seated on Elysian lawns
Browsed by none but Dian's fawns;
Underneath large blue-bells tented,
Where the daisies are rose-scented,
And the rose herself has got
Perfume which on earth is not;
Where the nightingale doth sing
Not a senseless, trancèd thing,
But divine melodious truth;
Philosophic numbers smooth;
Tales and golden histories
Of heaven and its mysteries.

Thus ye live on high, and then
On the earth ye live again;
And the souls ye left behind you
Teach us, here, the way to find you,
Where your other souls are joying,
Never slumber'd, never cloying.
Here, your earth-born souls still speak
To mortals, of their little week;
Of their sorrows and delights;
Of their passions and their spites;
Of their glory and their shame;
What doth strengthen and what maim.

FRANCIS BEAUMONT (1584–1616)

> Thus ye teach us, every day,
> Wisdom, though fled far away.
>
> Bards of Passion and of Mirth,
> Ye have left your souls on earth!
> Ye have souls in heaven too,
> Double-lived in regions new!

JOHN KEATS
(1795–1821)

JOHN FLETCHER (1579–1625)

Upon Master Fletchers Incomparable Playes

Apollo sings, his harpe resounds; give roome,
For now behold the golden Pompe is come,
The Pompe of Playes which thousands come to see,
With admiration both of them and thee,
O Volume worthy leafe, by leafe and cover
To be with juice of Cedar washt all over;
Here's words with lines, and lines with Scenes consent,
To raise an Act to full astonishment;
Here melting numbers, words of power to move
Young men to swoone, and Maides to dye for love.
Love lyes a bleeding here. *Evadne* there
Swells with brave rage, yet comely every where,
Here's a *mad lover*, there that high designe
Of *King* and no *King* (and the rare Plot thine)
So that when 'ere wee circumvolve our Eyes,
Such rich, such fresh, such sweet varietyes,
Ravish our spirits, that entranc't we see
None writes lov's passion in the world, like Thee.

ROBERT HERRICK
(1591–1674)

Upon Mr. John Fletcher's Playes

Fletcher, to thee, wee doe not only owe
All these good Playes, but those of others too:
Thy wit repeated, does support the Stage,
Credits the last and entertaines this age.

JOHN FLETCHER (1579-1625)

No Worthies form'd by any Muse but thine
Could purchase Robes to make themselves so fine:
What brave Commander is not proud to see
The brave *Melantius* in his Gallantry,
Our greatest Ladyes love to see their scorne
Out done by Thine, in what themselves have worne:
Th'impatient Widow ere the yeare be done
Sees thy Aspasia weeping in her Gowne:
I never yet the Tragick straine assay'd
Deterr'd by that inimitable *Maid:*
And when I venture at the Comick stile
Thy *Scornfull Lady* seemes to mock my toile:
Thus has thy Muse, at once, improv'd and marr'd
Our Sport in Playes, by rendring it too hard.
So when a sort of lusty Shepheards throw
The barre by turns, and none of the rest outgoe
So farre, but that the best are measuring casts,
Their emulation and their pastime lasts;
But if some Brawny yeoman, of the guard
Step in and tosse the Axeltree a yard
Or more beyond the farthest Marke, the rest
Despairing stand, their sport is at the best.
Edmund Waller
(1606-1687)

To Fletcher Reviv'd

How have I been Religious? what strange Good
   Ha's scap't me that I never understood?
Have I Hell guarded *Hæresie* o'rethrowne?
Heald wounded States? made Kings and Kingdomes
   one?
That *Fate* should be so mercifull to me,
To let me live t'have said I have read thee.
   Faire Star ascend; the Joy! the Life! the Light
Of this tempestuous Age, this darke worlds sight!
Oh from thy Crowne of Glory dart one flame
May strike a sacred Reverence, whilest thy Name
(Like holy *Flamens* to their God of Day)
We bowing, sing; and whilst we praise, we pray.

JOHN FLETCHER (1579–1625)

    Bright Spirit! whose Æternall motion
Of Wit, like Time, still in it selfe did runne;
Binding all others in it and did give
Commission, how far this, or that shall live:
Like *Destinie* of Poems, who, as she
Signes death to all, her selfe can never dye.
    And now thy purple-robed *Tragoedie*,
In her imbroider'd Buskins, calls mine eye,
Valentinian.   Where brave *Aëtius* we see betray'd,
T'obey his Death, whom thousand lives obey'd;
Whilst that the *Mighty Foole* his Scepter breakes,
And through his *Gen'rals* wounds his owne doome speaks,
Weaving thus richly *Valentinian*
The costliest Monarch with the cheapest man.
    Souldiers may here to their old glories adde
The Mad   *The Lover* love, and be with reason *mad*:
Lover.   Not as of old, *Alcides* furious,
Who wilder then his Bull did teare the house,
(Hurling his Language with the Canvas stone)
'Twas thought the Monster roar'd the sob'rer Tone.
Tragi-   But ah, when thou thy sorrow didst inspire
comedies.   With Passions, blacke as is her darke attire,
Arcas.   Virgins as *Sufferers* have wept to see
Bellario.   So white a Soule, so red a Crueltie;
That thou hast griev'd, and with unthought redresse,
Dri'd their wet eyes who now thy mercy blesse;
Comedies.   Yet loth to lose thy watry jewell, when
The Spanish   Joy wip't it off, Laughter straight sprung't agen.
Curate.   Now ruddy-cheeked *Mirth* with Rosie wings,
The Humo-   Fanns ev'ry brow with gladnesse, whilest she sings
rous Lieu-   Delight to all, and the whole Theatre
tenant.   A Festivall in Heaven doth appeare:
The Tamer   Nothing but Pleasure, Love, and (like the Morne)
Tam'd.   Each face a generall smiling doth adorne.
The little   Heare ye foule Speakers, that pronounce the Aire
French   Of Stewes and Shores, I will informe you where
Lawyer.   And how to cloathe aright your wanton wit,
Without her nasty Bawd attending it.

JOHN FLETCHER (1579–1625)

The custom View here a loose thought said with such a grace,
of the *Minerva* might have spoke in *Venus* face;
Countrey. So well disguis'd, that t'was conceiv'd by none
But *Cupid* had *Diana's* linnen on;
And all his naked parts so vail'd, th' expresse
The Shape with clowding the uncomlinesse;
That if this Reformation which we
Receiv'd, had not been buried with thee,
The Stage (as this work) might have liv'd and lov'd;
Her Lines; the austere Skarlet had approved,
And th' Actors wisely been from that offence
As cleare, as they are now from *Audience*.
   Thus with thy *Genius* did the *Scæne* expire,
Wanting thy Active and inliv'ning fire,
That now (to spread a darknesse over all,)
Nothing remaines but *Poesie* to fall.
And though from these thy *Embers* we receive
Some warmth, so much as may be said, we live,
That we dare praise thee, blushlesse, in the head
Of the best piece *Hermes* to *Love* e're read,
That We rejoyce and glory in thy Wit,
And feast each other with remembring it,
That we dare speak thy thought, thy Acts recite:
Yet all men henceforth be afraid to write.
RICHARD LOVELACE
(1618–1658)

Upon Mr. Fletchers Playes, published, 1647

I knew thee not, nor durst *attendance* strive
Labell to *wit*, *Verser remonstrative*,
And in some *Suburb-page* (scandal to thine)
Like *Lent* before a *Christmasse* scatter mine.
This speaks thee not, since at the utmost rate
Such *remnants* from thy *peece* Intreat their date;
Nor can I *dub* the *Coppy*, or afford
Titles to *swell* the *reare* of *Verse* with Lord,
Nor politickly big to *Inch* low fame
Stretch in the *glories* of a strangers name,

[93]

JOHN FLETCHER (1579–1625)

And Clip those *Bayes* I Court, weak *striver* I,
But a faint *Echo* unto *Poetrie*.
I have not *Clothes* t'adopt me, nor must sit
For *Plush* and *Velvets* sake *Esquire* of wit,
Yet *Modestie* these *Crosses* would improve,
And *Rags* neer thee, some *Reverence* may move.
I did believe (great *Beaumont* being dead,)
The *Widow'd Muse* slept on his *flowrie bed;*
But I am *richly* Cosen'd, and can see
Wit *transmigrates*, his *Spirit* stayd with thee,
Which *doubly* advantag'd by thy *single* pen
In *life* and *death* now treads the *Stage* agen;
And thus are wee freed from that *dearth* of wit
Which *starv'd* the Land since into *Schismes* split,
Wherein th'hast done so much, wee must needs guesse
Wits last *Edition* is now i'th' *Presse*,
For thou hast *drain'd* Invention, and he
That writes hereafter, doth but *pillage* thee.
But thou hast *plotts;* and will not the *Kirk* strain
At the *Designes* of such a *Tragick brain?*
Will they themselves think safe, when they shall see
Thy most *abominable policie?*
Will not the *Eares* assemble, and think't fit
Their *Synod fast*, and *pray*, against thy wit?
But they'le not *tyre* in such an *idle Quest*,
Thou doest but *kill*, and *Circumvent* in *Jest*,
And when thy anger'd Muse *swells* to a blow
'Tis but for *Field's*, or *Swansteed's* overthrow.
Yet shall these *Conquests* of thy *Bayes* outlive
Their *Scotish zeale*, and *Compacts* made to grieve
The *Peace of Spirits*, and when such deeds fayle
Of their foule Ends, a *faire name* is thy *Bayle*.
But (happy thou!) ne'r saw'st these *stormes*, our *aire*
Teem'd with even in thy time, though *seeming faire;*
Thy gentle *Soule* meant for the *shade*, and *ease*
Withdrew betimes into the *Land of Peace;*
So *neasted* in some Hospitable shore
The *Hermit-angler*, when the *mid-Seas* roare

JOHN FLETCHER (1579–1625)

Packs up his *lines*, and (ere the tempest *raves,*)
Retyres, and leaves his *station* to the *waves.*
Thus thou diedst almost with our *peace*, and wee
This *breathing time* thy last fair *Issue* see,
Which I think such (if *needless Ink* not soyle
So *Choice a Muse,*) others are but thy *foile;*
This, or that *age* may write, but never see
A *Wit* that dares run *Paralell* with thee.
True, B E N must live! but bate *him*, and thou hast
Undone all *future wits*, and match'd the *past.*

HENRY VAUGHAN
(1622–1695)

JOHN DONNE (1573–1631)

To John Donne

Donne, the delight of Phœbus and each muse,
  Who, to thy one, all other braines refuse;
Whose every work, of thy most early wit,
  Came forth example, and remaines so, yet:
Longer a knowing, than most wits do live;
  And which no affection praise enough can give!
To it, thy language, letters, arts, best life,
  Which might with halfe mankind maintaine a strife;
All which I meane to praise, and yet I would;
  But leave, because I cannot as I should!

BEN JONSON
(1573?–1637)

An Elegy upon the Death of Doctor Donne, Dean of Paul's

Can we not force from widowed poetry,
Now thou art dead, great Donne, one elegy
To crown thy hearse? Why yet did we not trust,
Though with unkneaded dough-baked prose, thy dust,
Such as th' unscissored lect'rer from the flower
Of fading rhet'ric, short-lived as his hour,

[95]

JOHN DONNE (1573-1631)

Dry as the sand that measures it, might lay
Upon the ashes, on the funeral day?
Have we nor tune nor voice? Didst thou dispense
Through all our language both the words and sense?
'Tis a sad truth. The pulpit may her plain
And sober Christian precepts still retain;
Doctrines it may, and wholesome uses, frame,
Grave homilies and lectures, but the flame
Of thy brave soul, that shot such heat and light
As burnt our earth and made our darkness bright,
Committed holy rapes upon the will,
Did through the eye the melting heart distil,
And the deep knowledge of dark truths so teach
As sense might judge where fancy could not reach,
Must be desired forever. So the fire
That fills with spirit and heat the Delphic choir,
Which, kindled first by thy Promethean breath,
Glowed here a while, lies quenched now in thy death.
The Muses' garden, with pedantic weeds
O'erspread, was purged by thee; the lazy seeds
Of servile imitation thrown away,
And fresh invention planted; thou didst pay
The debts of our penurious bankrupt age;
Licentious thefts, that make poetic rage
A mimic fury, when our souls must be
Possessed, or with Anacreon's ecstasy,
Or Pindar's, not their own; the subtle cheat
Of sly exchanges, and the juggling feat
Of two-edged words, or whatsoever wrong
By ours was done the Greek or Latin tongue,
Thou hast redeemed, and opened us a mine
Of rich and pregnant fancy; drawn a line
Of masculine expression, which had good
Old Orpheus seen, or all the ancient brood
Our superstitious fools admire, and hold
Their lead more precious than thy burnished gold,
Thou hadst been their exchequer, and no more
They each in other's dung had searched for ore.

JOHN DONNE (1573-1631)

Thou shalt yield no precedence, but of time
And the blind fate of language, whose tuned chime
More charms the outward sense; yet thou mayst claim
From so great disadvantage greater fame,
Since to the awe of thy imperious wit
Our troublesome language bends, made only fit
With her tough thick-ribbed hoops to gird about
Thy giant fancy, which had proved too stout
For their soft melting phrases. As in time
They had the start, so did they cull the prime
Buds of invention many a hundred year,
And left the rifled fields, besides the fear
To touch their harvest; yet from those bare lands
Of what was only thine, thy only hands,
And that their smallest work, have gleanëd more
Than all those times and tongues could reap before.
   But thou art gone, and thy strict laws will be
Too hard for libertines in poetry;
They will recall the goodly exiled train
Of gods and goddesses, which in thy just reign
Was banished nobler poems; now with these,
The silenced tales i' th' *Metamorphoses*,
Shall stuff their lines, and swell the windy page,
Till verse, refined by thee in this last age,
Turn ballad-rhyme, or those old idols be
Adored again with new apostasy.
   Oh, pardon me, that break with untuned verse
The reverend silence that attends thy hearse,
Whose solemn awful murmurs were to thee,
More than these rude lines, a loud elegy,
That did proclaim in a dumb eloquence
The death of all the arts; whose influence,
Grown feeble, in these panting numbers lies,
Gasping short-winded accents, and so dies.
So doth the swiftly turning wheel not stand
In th' instant we withdraw the moving hand,
But some short time retain a faint weak course,
By virtue of the first impulsive force;

JOHN DONNE (1573-1631)

And so, whilst I cast on thy funeral pile
Thy crown of bays, oh, let it crack awhile,
And spit disdain, till the devouring flashes
Suck all the moisture up, then turn to ashes.
  I will not draw the envy to engross
All thy perfections, or weep all the loss;
Those are too numerous for one elegy,
And this too great to be expressed by me.
Let others carve the rest; it shall suffice
I on thy grave this epitaph incise:
    Here lies a king that ruled as he thought fit
    The universal monarchy of wit;
    Here lies two flamens, and both those the best,
    Apollo's first, at last the true God's priest.

THOMAS CAREW
(1595?–?1645)

On Donne's Poetry

With Donne, whose muse on dromedary trots,
Wreathe iron pokers into true-love knots;
Rhyme's sturdy cripple, fancy's maze and clue,
Wit's forge and fire-blast, meaning's press and screw.

SAMUEL TAYLOR COLERIDGE
(1772–1834)

JOHN WEBSTER (1580?–?1625)

John Webster

Thunder: the flesh quails, and the soul bows down.
  Night: east, west, south, and northward, very night.
  Star upon struggling star strives into sight,
Star after shuddering star the deep storms drown.
The very throne of night, her very crown,
  A man lays hand on, and usurps her right.
  Song from the highest of heaven's imperious height

JOHN WEBSTER (1580?–?1625)

Shoots, as a fire to smite some towering town.
Rage, anguish, harrowing fear, heart-crazing crime,
Make monstrous all the murderous face of Time
  Shown in the spheral orbit of a glass
Revolving. Earth cries out from all her graves.
Frail, on frail rafts, across wide-wallowing waves,
  Shapes here and there of child and mother pass.

ALGERNON CHARLES SWINBURNE
(1837–1909)

Whispers of Immortality

Webster was much possessed by death
And saw the skull beneath the skin;
And breastless creatures under ground
Leaned backward with a lipless grin.

Daffodil bulbs instead of balls
Stared from the sockets of the eyes!
He knew that thought clings round dead limbs
Tightening its lusts and luxuries.

Donne, I suppose, was such another
Who found no substitute for sense;
To seize and clutch and penetrate,
Expert beyond experience,

He knew the anguish of the marrow
The ague of the skeleton;
No contact possible to flesh
Allayed the fever of the bone.

   . . . . .

Grishkin is nice: her Russian eye
Is underlined for emphasis;
Uncorseted, her friendly bust
Gives promise of pneumatic bliss.

The couched Brazilian jaguar
Compels the scampering marmoset
With subtle effluence of cat;
Grishkin has a maisonette;

JOHN WEBSTER (1580?–1625)

> The sleek Brazilian jaguar
> Does not in its aboreal gloom
> Distil so rank a feline smell
> As Grishkin in a drawing-room.
>
> And even the Abstract Entities
> Circumambulate her charm;
> But our lot crawls between dry ribs
> To keep our metaphysics warm.
>
> T. S. E<small>LIOT</small>
(1888–   )

PHILIP MASSINGER (1583–1640)

Philip Massinger

> Clouds here and there arisen an hour past noon
>   Chequered our English heaven with lengthening
>   bars
>   And shadow and sound of wheel-winged thunder-
>   cars
> Assembling strength to put forth tempest soon,
> When the clear still warm concord of thy tune
>   Rose under skies unscared by reddening Mars
>   Yet, like a sound of silver speech of stars,
> With full mild flame as of the mellowing moon.
> Grave and great-hearted Massinger, thy face
> High melancholy lights with loftier grace
>   Than gilds the brows of revel: sad and wise,
> The spirit of thought that moved thy deeper song,
> Sorrow serene in soft calm scorn of wrong,
>   Speaks patience yet from thy majestic eyes.
>
> A<small>LGERNON</small> C<small>HARLES</small> S<small>WINBURNE</small>
(1837–1909)

[100]

JOHN FORD (1586?–?1638)

To My Friend, Master John Ford

Unto this altar, rich with thine own spice,
I bring one grain to thy *Love's Sacrifice;*
And boast to see thy flames ascending, while
Perfumes enrich our air from thy sweet pile.
Look, here, thou that has malice to the stage,
And impudence enough for the whole age;
"Voluminously"—ignorant, be vext
To read this tragedy, and thy own be next.

JAMES SHIRLEY
(1596–1666)

To My Most Dearly-Loved Friend, Henry Reynolds, Esquire, of Poets and Poesy

[MISCELLANY]

My dearly lovéd friend, how oft have we
In winter evenings, meaning to be free,
To some well-chosen place used to retire,
And there with moderate meat, and wine, and fire,
Have passed the hours contentedly with chat;
Now talked of this, and then discoursed of that,
Spoke our own verses 'twixt ourselves; if not,
Other men's lines which we by chance had got,
Or some stage pieces famous long before,
Of which your happy memory had store;
And I remember you much pleaséd were
Of those who livéd long ago to hear,
As well as of those of these latter times
Who have enriched our language with their rhymes,
And in succession how still up they grew,
Which is the subject that I now pursue.
For from my cradle you must know that I
Was still inclined to noble poesy,
And when that once *Pueriles* I had read,

Pueriles] Latin primer used by schoolboys

[TO MY MOST DEARLY-LOVED FRIEND]

And newly had my Cato construéd,
In my small self I greatly marveled then,
Amongst all other, what strange kind of men
These poets were; and pleaséd with the name,
To my mild tutor merrily I came,
(For I was then a proper goodly page,
Much like a pigmy, scarce ten years of age)
Clasping my slender arms about his thigh,
O my dear master! cannot you, quoth I,
Make me a poet? Do it if you can,
And you shall see I'll quickly be a man.
Who me thus answered smiling: Boy, quoth he,
If you'll not play the wag, but I may see
You ply your learning, I will shortly read
Some poets to you. Phœbus be my speed,
To 't hard went I, when shortly he began
And first read to me honest Mantuan,
Then Virgil's *Eclogues;* being entered thus,
Methought I straight had mounted Pegasus,
And in his full career could make him stop
And bound upon Parnassus' bi-clift top.
I scorned your ballad then, though it were done
And had for finis, William Elderton.
But soft, in sporting with this childish jest
I from my subject have too long digressed;
Then to the matter that we took in hand,
Jove and Apollo for the Muses stand.
 Then noble Chaucer, in those former times
The first enriched our English with his rhymes,
And was the first of ours that ever brake
Into the Muses' treasure, and first spake
In weighty numbers, delving in the mine
Of perfect knowledge, which he could refine
And coin for current; and as much as then
The English language could express to men,
He made it do, and by his wondrous skill,
Gave us much light from his abundant quill.
 And honest Gower, who in respect of him
Had only sipped at Aganippe's brim,

[TO MY MOST DEARLY-LOVED FRIEND]

    And though in years this last was him before,
Yet fell he far short of the other's store.
    When after those, four ages very near,
They with the Muses which conversèd were:
That princely Surrey, early in the time
Of the eight Henry, who was then the prime
Of England's noble youth; with him there came
Wyatt, with reverence whom we still do name
Amongst our poets; Bryan had a share
With the two former, which accompted are
The time's best makers, and the authors were
Of those small poems which the title bear
Of *Songs and Sonnets*, wherein oft they hit
On many dainty passages of wit.
    Gascoigne and Churchyard after them again
In the beginning of Eliza's reign,
Accompted were great meterers many a day,
But not inspirèd with brave fire; had they
Lived but a little longer they had seen
Their works before them to have buried been.
    Grave moral Spenser after these came on,
Than whom I am persuaded there was none
Since the blind bard his *Iliads* up did make
Fitter a task like that to undertake,
To set down boldly, bravely to invent,
In all high knowledge surely excellent.
    The noble Sidney with this last arose,
That heroè for numbers and for prose,
That throughly paced our language as to show
The plenteous English hand in hand might go
With Greek or Latin; and did first reduce
Our tongue from Lyly's writing, then in use:
Talking of stones, stars, plants, of fishes, flies,
Playing with words and idle similes;
As th' English apes and very zanies be,
Of everything that they do hear and see,
So imitating his ridiculous tricks,

Songs and Sonnets] Tottel's famous miscellany

[TO MY MOST DEARLY-LOVED FRIEND]

    They spake and writ all like mere lunatics.
  Then Warner, though his lines were not so trimmed,
Nor yet his poem so exactly limned
And neatly jointed, but the critic may
Easily reprove him, yet this let me say
For my old friend: some passages there be
In him which I protest have taken me
With almost wonder, so fine, clear, and new
As yet they have been equalléd by few.
  Neat Marlowe, bathéd in the Thespian springs,
Had in him those brave translunary things
That the first poets had; his raptures were
All air and fire, which made his verses clear,
For that fine madness still he did retain
Which rightly should possess a poet's brain.
  And surely Nashe, though he a proser were,
A branch of laurel yet deserves to bear;
Sharply satiric was he, and that way
He went, since that his being to this day
Few have attempted, and I surely think
Those words shall hardly be set down with ink,
Shall scorch and blast so as his could, where he
Would inflict vengeance. And be it said of thee,
Shakespeare, thou hadst as smooth a comic vein,
Fitting the sock, and in thy natural brain
As strong conception and as clear a rage
As anyone that trafficked with the stage.
  Amongst these, Samuel Daniel, whom if I
May speak of, but to censure do deny,
Only have heard some wise men him rehearse
To be too much historian in verse;
His rhymes were smooth, his meters well did close,
But yet his manner better fitted prose.
Next these, learn'd Jonson in this list I bring,
Who had drunk deep of the Pierian spring,
Whose knowledge did him worthily prefer,
And long was lord here of the theater;
Who in opinion made our learn'st to stick,
Whether in poems rightly dramatic,

[TO MY MOST DEARLY-LOVED FRIEND]

    Strong Seneca or Plautus, he or they
Should bear the buskin or the sock away.
Others again here livéd in my days
That have of us deservéd no less praise
For their translations than the daintiest wit
That on Parnassus thinks he high'st doth sit,
And for a chair may 'mongst the muses call
As the most curious maker of them all;
As reverent Chapman, who hath brought to us
Musæus, Homer, and Hesiodus
Out of the Greek, and by his skill hath reared
Them to that height, and to our tongues endeared,
That were those poets at this day alive
To see their books thus with us to survive,
They would think, having neglected them so long,
They had been written in the English tongue.
    And Sylvester, whom from the French more weak
Made Bartas of his six days' labour speak
In natural English; who, had he there stayed
He had done well, and never had bewrayed
His own invention to have been so poor,
Who still wrote less in striving to write more.
    Then dainty Sandys, that hath to English done
Smooth sliding Ovid, and hath made him run
With so much sweetness and unusual grace,
As though the neatness of the English pace
Should tell the jetting Latin that it came
But slowly after, as though stiff and lame,
    So Scotland sent us hither, for our own,
That man whose name I ever would have known
To stand by mine, that most ingenious knight,
My Alexander, to whom in his right
I want extemely, yet in speaking thus
I do but show the love that was 'twixt us,
And not his numbers which were brave and high,
So like his mind was his clear poesy;
And my dear Drummond, to whom much I owe
For his much love, and proud I was to know

[TO MY MOST DEARLY-LOVED FRIEND]

His poesy; for which two worthy men,
I Menstry still shall love, and Hawthornden.
Then the two Beaumonts and my Browne arose,
My dear companions whom I freely chose
My bosom friends, and in their several ways
Rightly born poets, and in these last days
Men of much note and no less nobler parts,
Such as have freely told to me their hearts,
As I have mind to them; but if you shall
Say in your knowledge that these be not all
Have writ in numbers, be informed that I
Only myself to these few men do tie,
Whose works oft printed, set on every post,
To public censure subject have been most;
For such whose poems, be they ne'er so rare,
In private chambers that encloistered are,
And by transcription daintily must go,
As though the world unworthy were to know
Their rich composures, let those men that keep
These wondrous relics in their judgment deep,
And cry them up so, let such pieces be
Spoke of by those that shall come after me;
I pass not for them, nor do mean to run
In quest of these that them applause have won
Upon our stages in these latter days,
That are so many—let them have their bays
That do deserve it; let those wits that haunt
Those public circuits, let them freely chant
Their fine composures, and their praise pursue;
And so, my dear friend, for this time adieu.

MICHAEL DRAYTON
(1563–1631)

1627
Beaumonts] Sir John and Francis

Alexander's home was at Menstry, Drummond's at Hawthornden.

IV

ROBERT HERRICK (1591-1674)

For a Copy of Herrick

Many days have come and gone,
Many suns have set and shone,
HERRICK, since thou sang'st of Wake,
Morris-dance and Barley-break;—
Many men have ceased from care,
Many maidens have been fair,
Since thou sang'st of JULIA's eyes,
JULIA's lawns and tiffanies;—
Many things are past: but thou,
GOLDEN-MOUTH, art singing now,
Singing clearly as of old,
And thy numbers are of gold!

AUSTIN DOBSON
(1840-1921)

With a Copy of Herrick

Fresh with all airs of woodland brooks
    And scents of showers,
Take to your haunt of holy books
    This saint of flowers.

When meadows burn with budding May,
    And heaven is blue,
Before his shrine our prayers we say,—
    Saint Robin true.

Love crowned with thorns is on his staff,—
    Thorns of sweet briar;
His benediction is a laugh,
    Birds are his choir.

ROBERT HERRICK (1591–1674)

> His sacred robe of white and red
> Unction distils;
> He hath a nimbus round his head
> Of daffodils.
>
> Edmund Gosse
(1849–1928)

[MISCELLANY]

A Session of the Poets

A session was held the other day,
And Apollo himself was at it, they say;
The laurel that had been so long reserved
Was not to be given to him best deserved.
          And
Therefore the wits of the town came thither;
'Twas strange to see how they flocked together,
Each strongly confident of his own way,
Thought to gain the laurel away that day.

There was Selden, and he sat hard by the chair;
Wenman not far off, which was very fair;
Sandys with Townshend, for they kept no order;
Digby and Chillingworth a little further.
          And
There was Lucan's translator, too, and he
That makes God speak so big in 's poetry;
Selwin and Waller, and Bartlets both the brothers;
Jack Vaughan and Porter, and divers others.

The first that broke silence was good old Ben,
Prepared before with Canary wine,
And he told them plainly he deserved the bays,
For his were called Works, where others were but Plays.
          And
Bid them remember how he had purged the stage
Of errors that had lasted many an age;
And he hoped they did not think the *Silent Woman*,
The *Fox*, and the *Alchemist* outdone by no man.

[A SESSION OF THE POETS]

Apollo stopped him there, and bade him not go on,
'Twas merit, he said, and not presumption
Must carry 't, at which Ben turned about,
And in great choler offered to go out;
         But
Those that were there thought it not fit
To discontent so ancient a wit;
And therefore Apollo called him back again,
And made him mine host of his own *New Inn*.

Tom Carew was next, but he had a fault
That would not well stand with a laureate;
His muse was hard-bound, and th' issue of 's brain
Was seldom brought forth but with trouble and pain.
         And
All that were present there did agree,
A laureate muse should be easy and free;
Yet sure 'twas not that, but 'twas thought that, his grace
Considered, he was well he had a cup-bearer's place.

Will Davenant, ashamed of a foolish mischance
That he had got lately traveling in France,
Modestly hoped the handsomeness of 's muse
Might any deformity about him excuse.
         And
Surely the company would have been content,
If they could have found any precedent;
But in all their records, either in verse or prose,
There was not one laureate without a nose.

To Will Bartlet sure all the wits meant well,
But first they would see how his snow would sell;
Will smiled and swore in their judgments they went less
That concluded of merit upon success.

Suddenly taking his place again,
He gave way to Selwin, who straight stepped in;
But alas! he had been so lately a wit
That Apollo hardly knew him yet.

[A SESSION OF THE POETS]

Toby Mathews (pox on him, how came he there?)
Was whispering nothing in somebody's ear,
When he had the honor to be named in court;
But sir, you may thank my Lady Carlisle for 't,

For had not her care furnished you out
With something of handsome, without all doubt
You and your sorry lady muse had been
In the number of those that were not let in.

In haste from the court two or three came in,
And they brought letters, forsooth, from the queen;
'Twas discreetly done, too, for if th' had come
Without them, th' had scarce been let into the room.

Suckling next was called, but did not appear,
But straight one whispered Apollo i' th' ear,
That of all men living he cared not for 't;
He loved not the muses so well as his sport,

And prized black eyes, or a lucky hit
At bowls above all the trophies of wit;
But Apollo was angry, and publicly said,
'Twere fit that a fine were set upon 's head.

Wat Montague now stood forth to his trial,
And did not so much as suspect a denial;
But witty Apollo asked him first of all
If he understood his own pastoral.

For if he could do it, 'twould plainly appear
He understood more than any man there,
And did merit the bays above all the rest;
But the Monsieur was modest, and silence confessed.

During these troubles in the court was hid
One that Apollo soon missed, little Sid;
And having spied him, called him out of the throng,
And advised him in his ear not to write so strong.

[110]

[A SESSION OF THE POETS]

Then Murray was summoned, but 'twas urged that he
Was chief already of another company.

Hales, set by himself, most gravely did smile
To see them about nothing keep such a coil;
Apollo had spied him, but knowing his mind,
Passed by, and called Falkland that sat just behind.
                                                  But
He was of late so gone with divinity,
That he had almost forgot his poetry;
Though to say the truth, and Apollo did know it,
He might have been both his priest and his poet.

At length who but an alderman did appear,
At which Will Davenant began to swear;
But wiser Apollo bade him draw nigher,
And when he was mounted a little higher,

He openly declared that it was the best sign
Of good store of wit to have good store of coin;
And without a syllable more or less said,
He put the laurel on the alderman's head.

At this all the wits were in such a maze
That for a good while they did nothing but gaze
One upon another; not a man in the place
But had discontent writ in great in his face.

Only the small poets cheered up again,
Out of hope, as 'twas thought, of borrowing;
But sure they were out, for he forfeits his crown
When he lends any poets about the town.
                                        Sir John Suckling
                                          (1609–1642)

GEORGE HERBERT (1593-1633)

On Mr. G. Herbert's Book, entitled The Temple of Sacred Poems, sent to a gentlewoman

Know you, fair, on what you look:
Divinest love lies in this book,
Expecting fire from your eyes
To kindle this his sacrifice.
When your hands untie these strings,
Think you've an angel by the wings,
One that gladly will be nigh
To wait upon each morning sigh,
To flutter in the balmy air
Of your well-perfumëd prayer.
These white plumes of his he'll lend you,
Which every day to heaven will send you
To take acquaintance of the sphere
And all the smooth-faced kindred there.
  And though Herbert's name do owe
  These devotions, fairest, know
  That while I lay them on the shrine
  Of your white hand, they are mine.

RICHARD CRASHAW
(1613?–1649)

George Herbert

Wide pastures, thatch of turf, and ancient spire
  Replace soft elegance, the silk and sword—
  For music of the harp and clavichord,
At dusk and dawn he hears the throstles quire.
But in the coppice by the trampled byre
  The leaves proclaim the coming of a Lord,
  And for His rising, tree and hedge have stored
Pomanders of white hawthorn and rose-brier.
Like sap of Spring that swells the budding bough,
  Within his soul the sweet elixirs run,
    Flowering to bloom that will not fade nor fall:

GEORGE HERBERT (1593-1633)

> By the church door he waits with tranquil brow
>   Watching the swallows soar into the sun,
>   Desiring nothing, yet possessing all.
> THOMAS S. JONES, JR.
(1882-1932)

RICHARD CRASHAW (1613?-1649)

On the Death of Mr. Crashaw

Poet and *Saint!* to thee alone are given
  The two most sacred *Names* of *Earth* and *Heaven*.
The hard and rarest *Union* which can be
Next that of *Godhead* with *Humanitie*.
Long did the *Muses* banisht *Slaves* abide,
And built vain *Pyramids* to mortal pride;
Like *Moses* Thou (though Spells and Charms withstand)
Hast brought them nobly home back to their *Holy Land.*
  Ah wretched *We*, *Poets* of *Earth!* but *Thou*
Wert *Living* the same *Poet* which thou'rt *Now.*
Whilst *Angels* sing to thee their ayres divine,
And joy in an applause so great as *thine.*
Equal society with them to hold,
Thou need'st not make *new Songs*, but say the *Old.*
And they (kind Spirits!) shall all rejoyce to see
How little less then *They*, *Exalted Man* may be.
Still the old *Heathen Gods* in *Numbers* dwell,
The *Heav'enliest* thing on Earth still keeps up *Hell.*
Nor have we yet quite purg'd the *Christian Land;*
Still *Idols* here, like *Calves* at *Bethel* stand.
And though *Pans Death* long since all *Oracles* broke,
Yet still in Rhyme the *Fiend Apollo* spoke:
Nay with the worst of Heathen dotage We
(Vain men!) the *Monster Woman Deifie;*
Find *Stars*, and tye our *Fates* there in a *Face*,
And *Paradise* in them by whom we *lost* it, place.
What different faults corrupt our *Muses* thus?
Wanton as *Girles*, as old *Wives*, *Fabulous!*
  Thy spotless *Muse*, like *Mary*, did contain
The boundless *Godhead;* she did well disdain

[113]

RICHARD CRASHAW (1613?–1649)

That her *eternal Verse* employ'd should be
On a less subject then *Eternitie;*
And for a sacred *Mistress* scorn'd to take,
But her whom *God* himself scorn'd not his *Spouse* to make.
It (in a kind) *her Miracle* did do;
A fruitful *Mother* was, and *Virgin* too.
   How well (blest Swan) did Fate contrive thy death;
And made thee render up thy tuneful breath
In thy great *Mistress* Arms? thou most divine
And richest *Off'ering* of *Loretto's Shrine!*
Where like some holy *Sacrifice* t'expire,
A *Fever* burns thee, and *Love* lights the *Fire.*
Angels (they say) brought the fam'd *Chappel* there,
And bore the sacred Load in Triumph through the air.
'Tis surer much they brought thee there, and *They,*
And *Thou,* their charge, went *singing* all the way.
   Pardon, my *Mother Church,* if I consent
That *Angels* led him when from thee he went,
For even in *Error* sure no *Danger* is
When joyn'd with so much *Piety* as *His.*
Ah, mighty *God,* with shame I speak't, and grief,
Ah that our greatest *Faults* were in *Belief!*
And our weak *Reason* were ev'en weaker yet,
Rather then thus our *Wills* too strong for it.
His *Faith* perhaps in some nice Tenents might
Be wrong; his *Life,* I'm sure, was *in the right.*
And I my self a *Catholick* will be,
So far at least, great *Saint,* to *Pray* to thee.
   Hail, *Bard Triumphant!* and some care bestow
On *us,* the *Poets Militant* Below!
Oppos'ed by our old En'emy, adverse *Chance,*
Attacqu'ed by *Envy,* and by *Ignorance,*
Enchain'd by *Beauty,* tortur'd by *Desires,*
Expos'd by *Tyrant-Love* to savage *Beasts* and *Fires.*
Thou from low earth in nobler *Flames* didst rise,
And like *Elijah,* mount *Alive* the skies.
Elisha-like (but with a wish much less,
More fit thy *Greatness,* and my *Littleness*)
Lo here I beg (I whom thou once didst prove

RICHARD CRASHAW (1613?–1649)

So humble to *Esteem*, so Good to *Love*)
Not that thy *Spirit* might on me *Doubled* be,
I ask but *Half* thy mighty *Spirit* for Me.
And when my *Muse* soars with so strong a Wing,
'Twill learn of things *Divine*, and first of *Thee* to sing.
ABRAHAM COWLEY
(1618–1667)

Richard Crashaw

Great lamps of silver light his last retreat
  Where golden roses blossom without thorn
  And shining stoles and crowns of fir are worn
By saint and seraph kneeling at Love's feet:
There rises music mystical and sweet,
  Songs of ascension on grave chorals borne,—
  And in his flesh, by exaltation torn,
Bright ardors and unearthly passion meet.
Until the luster on the Lily wanes
  And throbbing organ tones no longer roll
    In vast progressions to the dome above,
Before the silver lamps he still remains,
  Feeling the Flame that pierced a seraph's soul,
    Consumed within the fiery Breath of Love.
THOMAS S. JONES, JR.
(1882–1932)

JOHN MILTON (1608–1674)

On Mr Milton's "Paradise Lost"

When I beheld the poet blind, yet bold,
In slender book his vast design unfold,
Messiah crown'd, Gods reconcil'd decree,
Rebelling angels, the forbidden tree,
Heav'n, hell, earth, chaos, all; the argument
Held me a while misdoubting his intent,
That he would ruine (for I saw him strong)
The sacred truths to fable and old song,
(So Sampson groap'd the temples posts in spight)
The world o'rewhelming to revenge his sight.

JOHN MILTON (1608-1674)

    Yet as I read, soon growing less severe,
I lik'd his project, the success did fear;
Through that wide field how he his way should find
O're which lame faith leads understanding blind;
Lest he perplext the things he would explain,
And what was easie he should render vain.
    Or if a work so infinite he spann'd,
Jealous I was that some less skilful hand
(Such as disquiet alwayes what is well,
And by ill imitating would excel)
Might hence presume the whole creations day
To change in scenes, and show it in a play.
    Pardon me, mighty poet, nor despise
My causeless, yet not impious, surmise.
But I am now convinc'd, and none will dare
Within thy labours to pretend a share.
Thou has not miss'd one thought that could be fit,
And all that was improper dost omit:
So that no room is here for writers left,
But to detect their ignorance or theft.
    That majesty which through thy work doth reign,
Draws the devout, deterring the profane.
And things divine thou treast of in such state
As them preserves, and thee, inviolate.
At once delight and horrour on us seize,
Thou singst with so much gravity and ease;
And above humane flight dost soar aloft,
With plume so strong, so equal, and so soft.
The bird nam'd from that paradise you sing
So never flags, but alwaies keeps on wing.
    Where couldst thou words of such a compass find?
Whence furnish such a vast expense of mind?
Just Heav'n thee, like Tiresias, to requite,
Rewards with prophesie thy loss of sight.
    Well mightst thou scorn thy readers to allure
With tinkling rhime, of thy own sense secure;
While the Town-Bays writes all the while and spells,
And like a pack-horse tires without his bells.

Town-Bays] Dryden was satirized under the name of Bays in Buckingham's *Rehearsal*.

JOHN MILTON (1608-1674)

Their fancies like our bushy points appear,
The poets tag them; we for fashion wear.
I too transported by the mode offend,
And while I mean to praise thee, must commend.
Thy verse created like thy theme sublime,
In number, weight, and measure, needs not rhime.
ANDREW MARVELL
(1621-1678)

Epigram on Milton

Three poets, in three distant ages born,
Greece, Italy, and England did adorn.
The first in loftiness of thought surpass'd,
The next in majesty, in both the last:
The force of Nature could no farther go;
To make a third, she join'd the former two.
JOHN DRYDEN
(1631-1700)

England, 1802

Milton! thou shouldst be living at this hour:
England hath need of thee: she is a fen
  Of stagnant waters: altar, sword, and pen,
Fireside, the heroic wealth of hall and bower,
Have forfeited their ancient English dower
  Of inward happiness. We are selfish men;
  O raise us up, return to us again,
And give us manners, virtue, freedom, power!
Thy soul was like a Star, and dwelt apart;
  Thou hadst a voice whose sound was like the sea:
  Pure as the naked heavens, majestic, free,
So didst thou travel on life's common way,
In cheerful godliness; and yet thy heart
  The lowliest duties on herself did lay.
WILLIAM WORDSWORTH
(1770-1850)

JOHN MILTON (1608–1674)

Milton

I pace the sounding sea-beach and behold
  How the voluminous billows roll and run,
  Upheaving and subsiding, while the sun
  Shines through their sheeted emerald far unrolled,
And the ninth wave, slow gathering fold by fold
  All its loose-flowing garments into one,
  Plunges upon the shore, and floods the dun
  Pale reach of sands, and changes them to gold.
So in majestic cadence rise and fall
  The mighty undulations of thy song,
  O sightless bard, England's Mæonides!
And ever and anon, high over all
  Uplifted, a ninth wave superb and strong,
  Floods all the soul with its melodious seas.

                HENRY WADSWORTH LONGFELLOW
                           (1807–1882)

Milton

(Alcaics)

O mighty-mouth'd inventor of harmonies,
O skill'd to sing of Time or Eternity,
  God-gifted organ-voice of England,
    Milton, a name to resound for ages;
Whose Titan angels, Gabriel, Abdiel,
Starr'd from Jehovah's gorgeous armouries,
  Tower, as the deep-domed empyrean
    Rings to the roar of an angel onset!
Me rather all that bowery loneliness,
The brooks of Eden mazily murmuring,
  And bloom profuse and cedar arches
    Charm, as a wanderer out in ocean,
Where some refulgent sunset of India
Streams o'er a rich ambrosial ocean isle,
  And crimson-hued the stately palm-woods
    Whisper in odorous heights of even.

                        ALFRED, LORD TENNYSON
                                (1809–1892)

ABRAHAM COWLEY (1618-1667)

On Mr. Abraham Cowley, His Death and Burial amongst the Ancient Poets

Old Chaucer, like the morning star,
To us discovers day from far;
His light those mists and clouds dissolved,
Which our dark nation long involved;
But he descending to the shades,
Darkness again the age invades.
Next like Aurora Spenser rose,
Whose purple blush the day foreshows;
The other three with his own fires
Phoebus, the poets' god, inspires:
By Shakespeare's, Jonson's, Fletcher's lines
Our stage's luster Rome's outshines.
These poets near our princes sleep,
And in one grave their mansion keep.
They lived to see so many days,
Till time had blasted all their bays;
But cursëd be the fatal hour
That plucked the fairest, sweetest flower
That in the Muses' garden grew,
And amongst withered laurels threw!
Time, which made them their fame outlive,
To Cowley scarce did ripeness give.
Old mother wit and nature gave
Shakespeare and Fletcher all they have;
In Spenser and in Jonson, art
Of slower nature got the start;
But both in him so equal are,
None knows which bears the happiest share;
To him no author was unknown,
Yet what he wrote was all his own.
He melted not the ancient gold,
Nor with Ben Jonson did make bold
To plunder all the Roman stores
Of poets and of orators;

ABRAHAM COWLEY (1618-1667)

    Horace his wit and Virgil's state
He did not steal, but emulate!
And when he would like them appear,
Their garb, but not their clothes, did wear.
He not from Rome alone, but Greece,
Like Jason brought the golden fleece;
To him that language, though to none
Of th' others, as his own was known.
On a stiff gale, as Flaccus sings,
The Theban swan extends his wings,
When through th' ethereal clouds he flies;
To the same pitch our swan doth rise—
Old Pindar's flights by him are reached,
When on that gale his wings are stretched.
His fancy and his judgment such,
Each to the other seemed too much,
His severe judgment, giving law,
His modest fancy kept in awe,
As rigid husbands jealous are
When they believe their wives too fair.
His English stream so pure did flow
As all that saw and tasted know;
But for his Latin vein so clear,
Strong, full, and high, it doth appear
That were immortal Virgil here,
Him, for his judge, he would not fear;
Of that great portraiture, so true
A copy pencil never drew.
My muse her song had ended here,
But both their genii straight appear;
Joy and amazement her did strike,
Two twins she never saw so like.
'Twas taught by wise Pythagoras,
One soul might through more bodies pass;

ABRAHAM COWLEY (1618–1667)

> Seeing such transmigration here,
> She thought it not a fable there—
> Such a resemblance of all parts,
> Life, death, age, fortune, nature, arts;
> Then lights her torch at theirs, to tell
> And show the world this parallel.
> Fixed and contemplative their looks
> Still turning over nature's books;
> Their works chaste, moral, and divine,
> Where profit and delight combine;
> They, gilding dirt, in noble verse
> Rustic philosophy rehearse.
> When heroes, gods, or god-like kings
> They praise, on their exalted wings
> To the celestial orbs they climb,
> And with the harmonious spheres keep time.
> Nor did their actions fall behind
> Their words, but with like candor shined;
> Each drew fair characters, yet none
> Of these they feigned, excels their own.
> Both by two generous princes loved,
> Who knew and judged what they approved;
> Yet having each the same desire,
> Both from the busy throng retire.
> Their bodies to their minds resigned,
> Cared not to propagate their kind;
> Yet though both fell before their hour,
> Time on their offspring hath no power;
> Nor fire nor fate their bays shall blast,
> Nor death's dark veil their day o'ercast.
>
> Sir John Denham
(1615–1669)

HENRY VAUGHAN (1622–1695)

At the Grave of Henry Vaughan

Above the voiceful windings of a river
An old green slab of simply graven stone
Shuns notice, overshadowed by a yew.
Here Vaughan lies dead, whose name flows on for ever
Through pastures of the spirit washed with dew
And starlit with eternities unknown.
Here sleeps the Silurist; the loved physician;
The face that left no portraiture behind;
The skull that housed white angels and had vision
Of daybreak through the gateways of the mind.
  Here faith and mercy, wisdom and humility
  (Whose influence shall prevail for evermore)
  Shine. And this lowly grave tells Heaven's tranquility.
  And here stand I, a suppliant at the door.
                          SIEGFRIED SASSOON
                              (1886–   )

Henry Vaughan

Something surrounds him when he walks alone
  Before the dawn has touched the ivied tower,
    Some burning faith that breathes through leaf and flower,
And leads the bird to branches winter-blown—
Some clarity the mountain peaks have known,
  The memory of high seraphic power
    His soul received as her immortal dower
In regions where the Sons of Morning shone.
Along the Vale of Usk he takes his way,
  While rushes murmur by the river bed
    And pale mist settles on the silver height,
To watch the edges of the East turn gray
  And hills above the purple valley-head
    Flame with the first great messages of Light.
                            THOMAS S. JONES, JR.
                              (1882–1932)

HENRY VAUGHAN (1622-1695)

The Age of Herbert & Vaughan

Then it was faith and fairness,
   White sun and western wind,
When every moment spoke
   The Holy to the mind,
And quickened saints' awareness.

In close and pregnant symbol
   Each primrosed morning showed
The triune God's patrol
   On every country road,
In bushy den and dimble.

And where young Prue was sweeping,
   Or giggling at the gate,
Or Tom was scaring crows
   Or the dog Sam licked the plate
Or ewe and lamb were sleeping,

The witness still recorded
   Glance, phrase or incident
That appertained to Christ
   And by these shows was meant
At once he stood rewarded!

EDMUND BLUNDEN
(1896–)

V

THOMAS SHADWELL (1642?–1692)

Mac Flecknoe

Or, a Satire Upon the True-Blue-Protestant Poet T. S.

All human things are subject to decay,
And when fate summons, monarchs must obey.
This Flecknoe found, who, like Augustus, young
Was call'd to empire, and had govern'd long;
In prose and verse, was own'd, without dispute,
Thro' all the realms of *Nonsense*, absolute.
This aged prince, now flourishing in peace,
And blest with issue of a large increase;
Worn out with business, did at length debate
To settle the succession of the State;
And, pond'ring which of all his sons was fit
To reign, and wage immortal war with wit,
Cried: " 'Tis resolv'd; for nature pleads, that he
Should only rule, who most resembles me.
Sh—— alone my perfect image bears,
Mature in dulness from his tender years:
Sh—— alone, of all my sons, is he
Who stands confirm'd in full stupidity.
The rest to some faint meaning make pretense,
But Sh—— never deviates into sense.
Some beams of wit on other souls may fall,
Strike thro', and make a lucid interval;
But Sh——'s genuine night admits no ray,
His rising fogs prevail upon the day.
Besides, his goodly fabric fills the eye,
And seems design'd for thoughtless majesty;

THOMAS SHADWELL (1642?–1692)

Thoughtless as monarch oaks that shade the plain,
And, spread in solemn state, supinely reign.
Heywood and Shirley were but types of thee,
Thou last great prophet of tautology.
Even I, a dunce of more renown than they,
Was sent before but to prepare thy way;
And, coarsely clad in Norwich drugget, came
To teach the nations in thy greater name.
My warbling lute, the lute I whilon strung,
When to King John of Portugal I sung,
Was but the prelude to that glorious day,
When thou on silver Thames didst cut thy way,
With well-tim'd oars before the royal barge,
Swell'd with the pride of thy celestial charge;
And big with hymn, commander of a host,
The like was ne'er in Epsom blankets toss'd.
Methinks I see the new Arion sail,
The lute still trembling underneath thy nail.
At thy well-sharpen'd thumb from shore to shore
The treble squeaks for fear, the basses roar;
Echoes from Pissing Alley Sh—— call,
And Sh—— they resound from Aston Hall.
About thy boat the little fishes throng,
As at the morning toast that floats along.
Sometimes, as prince of thy harmonious band,
Thou wield'st thy papers in thy threshing hand.
St. André's feet ne'er kept more equal time,
Not ev'n the feet of thy own *Psyche's* rhyme;
Tho' they in number as in sense excel:
So just, so like tautology, they fell,
That, pale with envy, Singleton forswore
The lute and sword, which he in triumph bore,
And bow'd he ne'er would act Villerius more."
Here stopp'd the good old sire, and wept for joy
In silent raptures of the hopeful boy.
All arguments, but most his plays, persuade,
That for anointed dulness he was made.
   Close to the walls which fair Augusta bind,
(The fair Augusta much to fears inclin'd,)

THOMAS SHADWELL (1642?-1692)

An ancient fabric rais'd t' inform the sight,
There stood of yore, and Barbican it hight:
A watchtower once; but now, so fate ordains,
Of all the pile an empty name remains.
From its old ruins brothel-houses rise,
Scenes of lewd loves, and of polluted joys,
Where their vast courts the mother-strumpets keep,
And, undisturb'd by watch, in silence sleep.
Near these a Nursery erects its head,
Where queens are form'd and future heroes bred;
Where unfledg'd actors learn to laugh and cry,
Where infant punks their tender voices try,
And little Maximins the gods defy.
Great Fletcher never treads in buskins here,
Nor greater Jonson dares in socks appear;
But gentle Simkin just reception finds
Amidst this monument of vanish'd minds:
Pure clinches the suburbian Muse affords,
And Panton waging harmless war with words.
Here Flecknoe, as a place to fame well known,
Ambitiously design'd his Sh——'s throne;
For ancient Dekker prophesied long since,
That in this pile should reign a mighty prince,
Born for a scourge of wit, and flail of sense;
To whom true dulness should some *Psyches* owe,
But worlds of *Misers* from his pen should flow;
Humorists and hypocrites it should produce,
Whole Raymond families, and tribes of Bruce.
  Now Empress Fame had publish'd the renown
Of Sh——'s coronation thro' the town.
Rous'd by report of Fame, the nations meet,
From near Bunhill, and distant Watling Street.
No Persian carpets spread th' imperial way,
But scatter'd limbs of mangled poets lay;
From dusty shops neglected authors come,
Martyrs of pies, and relics of the bum.
Much Heywood, Shirley, Ogleby there lay,
But loads of Sh—— almost chok'd the way.

THOMAS SHADWELL (1642?–1692)

Bilk'd stationers for yeomen stood prepar'd,
And Herringman was captain of the guard.
The hoary prince in majesty appear'd,
High on a throne of his own labors rear'd.
At his right hand our young Ascanius sate,
Rome's other hope, and pillar of the State.
His brows thick fogs, instead of glories, grace,
And lambent dulness play'd around his face.
As Hannibal did to the altars come,
Sworn by his sire a mortal foe to Rome;
So Sh—— swore, nor should his vow be vain,
That he till death true dulness would maintain;
And, in his father's right, and realm's defense,
Ne'er to have peace with wit, nor truce with sense.
The king himself the sacred unction made,
As king by office, and, as priest by trade.
In his sinister hand, instead of ball,
He plac'd a mighty mug of potent ale;
Love's Kingdom to his right he did convey,
At once his scepter, and his rule of sway;
Whose righteous lore the prince had practic'd young,
And from whose loins recorded *Psyche* sprung.
His temples, last, with poppies were o'erspread,
That nodding seem'd to consecrate his head.
Just at that point of time, if fame not lie,
On his left hand twelve reverend owls did fly.
So Romulus, 't is sung, by Tiber's brook,
Presage of sway from twice six vultures took.
Th'admiring throng loud acclamations make,
And omens of his future empire take.
The sire then shook the honors of his head,
And from his brows damps of oblivion shed
Full on the filial dulness: long he stood,
Repelling from his breast the raging god;
At length burst out in this prophetic mood:
  "Heavens bless my son, from Ireland let him reign
To far Barbadoes on the western main;
Of his dominion may no end be known,
And greater than his father's be his throne;

THOMAS SHADWELL (1642?–1692)

Beyond *Love's Kingdom* let him stretch his pen!"
He paus'd, and all the people cried, "Amen."
Then thus continued he: "My son, advance
Still in new impudence, new ignorance.
Success let others teach, learn thou from me
Pangs without birth, and fruitless industry.
Let *Virtuosos* in five years be writ;
Yet not one thought accuse thy toil of wit.
Let gentle George in triumph tread the stage,
Make Dorimant betray, and Loveit rage;
Let Cully, Cockwood, Fopling, charm the pit,
And in their folly shew the writer's wit.
Yet still thy fools shall stand in thy defense,
And justify their author's want of sense.
Let 'em be all by thy own model made
Of dulness, and desire no foreign aid;
That they to future ages may be known,
Not copies drawn, but issue of thy own.
Nay, let thy men of wit too be the same,
All full of thee, and differing but in name.
But let no alien S——dl——y interpose,
To lard with wit thy hungry *Epsom* prose.
And when false flowers of rhetoric thou wouldst cull,
Trust nature, do not labor to be dull;
But write thy best, and top; and, in each line,
Sir Formal's oratory will be thine:
Sir Formal, tho' unsought, attends thy quill,
And does thy northern dedications fill.
Nor let false friends seduce thy mind to fame,
By arrogating Jonson's hostile name.
Let father Flecknoe fire thy mind with praise,
And uncle Ogleby thy envy raise.
Thou art my blood, where Jonson has no part:
What share have we in nature, or in art?
Where did his wit on learning fix a brand,
And rail at arts he did not understand?
Where made he love in Prince Nicander's vein,
Or swept the dust in *Psyche's* humble strain?

THOMAS SHADWELL (1642?–1692)

Where sold he bargains, 'whip-stitch, kiss my arse,'
Promis'd a play and dwindled to a farce?
When did his Muse from Fletcher scenes purloin,
As thou whole Eth'rege dost transfuse to thine?
But so transfus'd, as oil on water's flow,
His always floats above, thine sinks below.
This is thy province, this thy wondrous way,
New humors to invent for each new play:
This is that boasted bias of thy mind,
By which one way, to dulness, 't is inclin'd;
Which makes thy writings lean on one side still,
And, in all changes, that way bends thy will.
Nor let thy mountain-belly make pretense
Of likeness; thine's a tympany of sense.
A tun of man in thy large bulk is writ,
But sure thou 'rt but a kilderkin of wit.
Like mine, thy gentle numbers feebly creep;
Thy tragic Muse gives smiles, thy comic sleep.
With whate'er gall thou sett'st thyself to write,
Thy inoffensive satires never bite.
In thy felonious heart tho' venom lies,
It does but touch thy Irish pen, and dies.
Thy genius calls thee not to purchase fame
In keen iambics, but mild anagram.
Leave writing plays, and choose for thy command
Some peaceful province in acrostic land.
There thou may'st wings display and altars raise,
And torture one poor word ten thousand ways.
Or, if thou wouldst thy diff'rent talents suit,
Set thy own songs, and sing them to thy lute."
   He said: but his last words were scarcely heard;
For Bruce and Longvil had a trap prepar'd,
And down they sent the yet declaiming bard.
Sinking he left his drugget robe behind,
Borne upwards by a subterranean wind.
The mantle fell to the young prophet's part,
With double portion of his father's art.

JOHN DRYDEN
(1631–1700)

[129]

JOHN OLDHAM (1653–1683)

To the Memory of Mr. Oldham

Farewell, too little, and too lately known,
Whom I began to think and call my own:
For sure our souls were near allied, and thine
Cast in the same poetic mold with mine.
One common note on either lyre did strike,
And knaves and fools we both abhorr'd alike.
To the same goal did both our studies drive;
The last set out the soonest did arrive.
Thus Nisus fell upon the slippery place,
While his young friend perform'd and won the race.
O early ripe! to thy abundant store
What could advancing age have added more?
It might (what nature never gives the young)
Have taught the numbers of thy native tongue.
But satire needs not those, and wit will shine
Thro' the harsh cadence of a rugged line:
A noble error, and but seldom made,
When poets are by too much force betray'd.
Thy generous fruits, tho' gather'd ere their prime,
Still shew'd a quickness; and maturing time
But mellows what we write to the dull sweets of rhyme.
Once more, hail and farewell; farewell, thou young,
But ah too short, Marcellus of our tongue;
Thy brows with ivy, and with laurels bound;
But fate and gloomy night encompass thee around.

JOHN DRYDEN
(1631–1700)

ANNE KILLIGREW (1660–1685)

To the Pious Memory of the accomplisht young lady, Mrs. Anne Killigrew, excellent in the two sister-arts of Poesy and Painting

Thou youngest virgin-daughter of the skies,
    Made in the last promotion of the blest;
Whose palms, new pluck'd from Paradise,
    In spreading branches more sublimely rise,

ANNE KILLIGREW (1660–1685)

Rich with immortal green above the rest:
Whether, adopted to some neighbouring star,
Thou roll'st above us, in thy wandering race,
   Or, in procession fix'd and regular,
   Moved with the heaven's majestic pace;
   Or, call'd to more superior bliss,
Thou tread'st with seraphims the vast abyss:
Whatever happy region be thy place,
Cease thy celestial song a little space;
Thou wilt have time enough for hymns divine,
   Since Heaven's eternal year is thine.
Hear, then, a mortal Muse thy praise rehearse,
   In no ignoble verse;
But such as thy own voice did practise here,
When thy first-fruits of Poesy were given,
To make thyself a welcome inmate there;
   While yet a young probationer,
   And candidate of heaven.

   If by traduction came thy mind,
   Our wonder is the less, to find
A soul so charming from a stock so good;
Thy father was transfused into thy blood:
So wert thou born into a tuneful strain,
An early, rich, and inexhausted vein.
   But if thy pre-existing soul
   Was form'd at first with myriads more,
It did through all the mighty poets roll
   Who Greek or Latin laurels wore,
And was that Sappho last, which once it was before.
   If so, then cease thy flight, O heaven-born mind!
Thou hast no dross to purge from thy rich ore:
   Nor can thy soul a fairer mansion find,
Than was the beauteous frame she left behind:
Return, to fill or mend the quire of thy celestial kind.

   May we presume to say, that, at thy birth,
New joy was sprung in heaven as well as here on earth?
   For sure the milder planets did combine
   On thy auspicious horoscope to shine,

ANNE KILLIGREW (1660-1685)

    And even the most malicious were in trine.
      Thy brother-angels at thy birth
      Strung each his lyre, and tuned it high,
      That all the people of the sky
    Might know a poetess was born on earth;
      And then, if ever, mortal ears
      Had heard the music of the spheres.
      And if no clustering swarm of bees
    On thy sweet mouth distill'd their golden dew,
      'Twas that such vulgar miracles
      Heaven had not leisure to renew:
    For all the blest fraternity of love
Solemnized there thy birth, and kept thy holiday above.

      O gracious God! how far have we
    Profaned thy heavenly gift of Poesy!
    Made prostitute and profligate the Muse,
    Debased to each obscene and impious use,
    Whose harmony was first ordain'd above,
    For tongues of angels and for hymns of love!
    O wretched we! why were we hurried down
      This lubrique and adulterate age
    (Nay, added fat pollutions of our own),
      To increase the streaming ordures of the stage?
    What can we say to excuse our second fall?
    Let this thy Vestal, Heaven, atone for all!
    Her Arethusian stream remains unsoil'd,
    Unmix'd with foreign filth, and undefiled;
Her wit was more than man, her innocence a child.

      Art she had none, yet wanted none,
        For Nature did that want supply:
      So rich in treasures of her own,
        She might our boasted stores defy:
    Such noble vigour did her verse adorn,
    That it seem'd borrow'd, where 'twas only born.
    Her morals, too, were in her bosom bred,
      By great examples daily fed,
What in the best of books, her father's life, she read.
    And to be read herself she need not fear;

ANNE KILLIGREW (1660–1685)

    Each test, and every light, her Muse will bear,
    Though Epictetus with his lamp were there.
    Even love (for love sometimes her Muse exprest)
Was but a lambent flame which play'd about her breast,
      Light as the vapours of a morning dream;
    So cold herself, whilst she such warmth exprest,
      'Twas Cupid bathing in Diana's stream. . . .

    Now all those charms, that blooming grace,
  The well-proportion'd shape, and beauteous face,
  Shall never more be seen by mortal eyes;
  In earth the much-lamented virgin lies.
  Not wit, nor piety could fate prevent;
    Nor was the cruel destiny content
    To finish all the murder at a blow,
  To sweep at once her life and beauty too;
  But, like a harden'd felon, took a pride
    To work more mischievously slow,
  And plunder'd first, and then destroy'd.
O double sacrilege on things divine,
  To rob the relic, and deface the shrine!
        But thus Orinda died:
Heaven, by the same disease did both translate;
As equal were their souls, so equal was their fate.

    Meantime, her warlike brother on the seas
    His waving streamers to the winds displays,
And vows for his return, with vain devotion, pays.
    Ah, generous youth! that wish forbear,
    The winds too soon will waft thee here!
    Slack all thy sails, and fear to come,
Alas, thou know'st not, thou art wreck'd at home!
No more shalt thou behold thy sister's face,
Thou hast already had her last embrace.
But look aloft, and if thou kenn'st from afar,
  Among the Pleiads a new kindled star,
  If any sparkles than the rest more bright,
  'Tis she that shines in that propitious light.

ANNE KILLIGREW (1660–1685)

When in mid-air the golden trump shall sound,
   To raise the nations under ground;
When, in the Valley of Jehoshaphat,
The judging God shall close the book of Fate,
   And there the last assizes keep
   For those who wake and those who sleep;
   When rattling bones together fly
   From the four corners of the sky;
When sinews o'er the skeletons are spread,
Those clothed with flesh, and life inspires the dead;
The sacred poets first shall hear the sound,
   And foremost from the tomb shall bound,
For they are cover'd with the lightest ground;
And straight, with inborn vigour, on the wing,
Like mounting larks, to the new morning sing.
There thou, sweet Saint, before the quire shall go,
   As harbinger of Heaven, the way to show,
The way which thou so well hast learn'd below.

                              JOHN DRYDEN
                                (1631–1700)

WILLIAM CONGREVE (1670–1729)

To My Dear Friend, Mr. Congreve, on His Comedy Call'd "The Double-Dealer"

Well then, the promis'd hour is come at last;
The present age of wit obscures the past:
Strong were our sires, and as they fought they writ,
Conqu'ring with force of arms, and dint of wit;
Theirs was the giant race, before the flood;
And thus, when Charles return'd, our empire stood.
Like Janus he the stubborn soil manur'd,
With rules of husbandry the rankness cur'd;
Tam'd us to manners, when the stage was rude;
And boist'rous English wit with art indued.
Our age was cultivated thus at length,
But what we gain'd in skill we lost in strength.
Our builders were with want of genius curst;
The second temple was not like the first:

WILLIAM CONGREVE (1670–1729)

Till you, the best Vitruvius, come at length;
Our beauties equal, but excel our strength.
Firm Doric pillars found your solid base;
The fair Corinthian crowns the higher space:
Thus all below is strength, and all above is grace.
In easy dialogue is Fletcher's praise;
He mov'd the mind, but had not power to raise.
Great Jonson did by strength of judgment please;
Yet, doubling Fletcher's force, he wants his ease.
In differing talents both adorn'd their age;
One for the study, t'other for the stage:
But both to Congreve justly shall submit,
One match'd in judgment, both o'er match'd in wit.
In him all beauties of this age we see,
Etherege his courtship, Southerne's purity,
The satire, wit, and strength of Manly Wycherley.
All this in blooming youth you have achiev'd,
Nor are your foil'd contemporaries griev'd.
So much the sweetness of your manners move,
We cannot envy you, because we love.
Fabius might joy in Scipio, when he saw
A beardless consul made against the law;
And join his suffrage to the votes of Rome,
Tho' he with Hannibal was overcome.
Thus old Romano bow'd to Raphael's fame,
And scholar to the youth he taught became.
  O that your brows my laurel had sustain'd;
Well had I been depos'd, if you had reign'd!
The father had descended for the son;
For only you are lineal to the throne.
Thus, when the state one Edward did depose,
A greater Edward in his room arose.
But now, not I, but poetry is curst;
For Tom the Second reigns like Tom the First.
But let 'em not mistake my patron's part,
Nor call his charity their own desert.
Yet this I prophesy: Thou shalt be seen
(Tho' with some short parenthesis between)
High on the throne of wit; and, seated there,
Not mine—that's little—but thy laurel wear.

WILLIAM CONGREVE (1670–1729)

Thy first attempt an early promise made;
That early promise this has more than paid.
So bold, yet so judiciously you dare,
That your least praise is to be regular.
Time, place, and action, may with pains be wrought;
But genius must be born, and never can be taught.
This is your portion; this your native store;
Heav'n, that but once was prodigal before,
To Shakespeare gave as much; she could not give him more.
  Maintain your post: that's all the fame you need;
For 't is impossible you should proceed.
Already I am worn with cares and age,
And just abandoning th' ungrateful stage;
Unprofitably kept at Heav'n's expense,
I live a rent-charge on his providence:
But you, whom ev'ry Muse and Grace adorn,
Whom I foresee to better fortune born,
Be kind to my remains; and O defend,
Against your judgment, your departed friend!
Let not the insulting foe my fame pursue,
But shade those laurels which descend to you;
And take for tribute what these lines express:
You merit more; nor could my love do less.

JOHN DRYDEN
(1631–1700)

JOHN DRYDEN (1631–1700)

From "An Account of the Greatest English Poets"

Since, dearest Harry, you will needs request
A short account of all the muse-possest,
That, down from Chaucer's days to Dryden's times,
Have spent their noble rage in British rhymes;
Without more preface, writ in formal length,
To speak the undertaker's want of strength,
I'll try to make their several beauties known,
And show their verses worth, tho' not my own.
  Long had our dull fore-fathers slept supine,
Nor felt the raptures of the tuneful Nine;

JOHN DRYDEN (1631–1700)

Till Chaucer first, a merry bard, arose,
And many a story told in rhyme and prose.
But age has rusted what the poet writ,
Worn out his language, and obscur'd his wit:
In vain he jests in his unpolish'd strain,
And tries to make his readers laugh in vain.
  Old Spenser next, warm'd with poetic rage,
In ancient tales amus'd a barb'rous age;
An age that yet uncultivate and rude,
Where'er the poet's fancy led, pursu'd
Through pathless fields, and unfrequented floods,
To dens of dragons, and enchanted woods.
But now the mystic tale, that pleas'd of yore,
Can charm an understanding age no more;
The long-spun allegories fulsome grow,
While the dull moral lies too plain below.
We view well-pleas'd at distance all the sights
Of arms and palfreys, battles, fields, and fights,
And damsels in distress, and courteous knights.
But when we look too near, the shades decay,
And all the pleasing landscape fades away.
  Great Cowley then (a mighty genius) wrote,
O'er-run with wit, and lavish of his thought:
His turns too closely on the reader press;
He more had pleas'd us, had he pleas'd us less.
One glittering thought no sooner strikes our eyes
With silent wonder, but new wonders rise.
As in the milky-way a shining white
O'er-flows the heav'ns with one continu'd light;
That not a single star can show his rays,
Whilst jointly all promote the common blaze.
Pardon, great poet, that I dare to name
Th' unnumber'd beauties of thy verse with blame;
Thy fault is only wit in its excess,
But wit like thine in any shape will please.
What Muse but thine can equal hints inspire,
And fit the deep-mouth'd Pindar to thy lyre:
Pindar, whom others in a labour'd strain,
And forc'd expression, imitate in vain?

JOHN DRYDEN (1631-1700)

Well-pleas'd in thee he soars with new delight,
And plays in more unbounded verse, and takes a nobler flight.
  Blest man! whose spotless life and charming lays
Employ'd the tuneful prelate in thy praise:
Blest man! who now shalt be forever known,
In Sprat's successful labours and thy own.
  But Milton next, with high and haughty stalks,
Unfetter'd in majestic numbers walks;
No vulgar hero can his Muse engage;
Nor earth's wide scene confine his hallow'd rage.
See! see, he upward springs, and tow'ring high
Spurns the dull province of mortality,
Shakes heav'n's eternal throne with dire alarms,
And sets th' Almighty Thunderer in arms.
Whate'er his pen describes I more than see,
Whilst ev'ry verse, array'd in majesty,
Bold, and sublime, my whole attention draws,
And seems above the critic's nicer laws.
How are you struck with terror and delight
When angel with arch-angel copes in fight!
When great Messiah's outspread banner shines,
How does the chariot rattle in his lines!
What sounds of brazen wheels, what thunder, scare,
And stun the reader with the din of war!
With fear my spirits and my blood retire,
To see the seraphs sunk in clouds of fire;
But when, with eager steps, from hence I rise,
And view the first gay scenes of Paradise;
What tongue, what words of rapture can express
A vision so profuse of pleasantness.
Oh had the poet ne'er profan'd his pen,
To varnish o'er the guilt of faithless men;
His other works might have deserv'd applause!
But now the language can't support the cause;
While the clean current, though serene and bright,
Betrays a bottom odious to the sight.
  But now, my Muse a softer strain rehearse,
Turn ev'ry line with art, and smooth thy verse;

JOHN DRYDEN (1631-1700)

The courtly Waller next commands thy lays:
Muse tune thy verse, with art, to Waller's praise.
While tender airs and lovely dames inspire
Soft melting thoughts, and propagate desire;
So long shall Waller's strains our passion move,
And Sacharissa's beauties kindle love.
Thy verse, harmonious bard, and flatt'ring song
Can make the vanquish'd great, the coward strong,
Thy verse can show ev'n Cromwell's innocence,
And compliment the storms that bore him hence.
Oh had thy Muse not come an age too soon,
But seen great Nassau on the British throne!
How had his triumphs glitter'd in thy page,
And warm'd thee to a more exalted rage!
What scenes of death and horror had we view'd,
And how had Boyne's wide current reek'd in blood!
Or if Maria's charms thou wouldst rehearse,
In smoother numbers and a softer verse;
Thy pen had well describ'd her graceful air,
And Gloriana would have seem'd more fair.
  Nor must Roscommon pass neglected by,
That makes ev'n rules a noble poetry:
Rules whose deep sense and heav'nly numbers show
The best of critics, and of poets too.
Nor, Denham, must we e'er forget thy strains,
While Cooper's Hill commands the neighb'ring plains.
  But see where artful Dryden next appears,
Grown old in rime, but charming ev'n in years.
Great Dryden next, whose tuneful Muse affords
The sweetest numbers, and the fittest words.
Whether in comic sounds or tragic airs
She forms her voice, she moves our smiles or tears.
If satire or heroic strains she writes,
Her hero pleases, and her satire bites.
From her no harsh unartful numbers fall,
She wears all dresses, and she charms in all.
How might we fear our English poetry,
That long has flourish'd, should decay with thee;

JOHN DRYDEN (1631–1700)

Did not the Muse's other hope appear,
Harmonious Congreve, and forbid our fear:
Congreve! whose fancy's unexhausted store
Has given already much, and promis'd more.
Congreve shall still preserve thy fame alive,
And Dryden's Muse shall in his friend survive.

JOSEPH ADDISON
(1672–1719)

from "The Progress of Poesy"

   Far from the sun and summer-gale,
In thy green lap was Nature's Darling laid,
What time, where lucid Avon stray'd,
To Him the mighty Mother did unveil
Her aweful face: The dauntless Child
Stretch'd forth his little arms, and smiled.
This pencil take (she said) whose colours clear
Richly paint the vernal year:
Thine too these golden keys, immortal Boy!
This can unlock the gates of Joy;
Of Horrour that, and thrilling Fears,
Or ope the sacred source of sympathetic Tears.

   Nor second He, that rode sublime
Upon the seraph-wings of Extasy,
The secrets of th' Abyss to spy.
He pass'd the flaming bounds of Place and Time:
The living Throne, the sapphire-blaze,
Where angels tremble, while they gaze,
He saw; but blasted with excess of light,
Closed his eyes in endless night.
Behold, where Dryden's less presumptuous car,
Wide o'er the fields of Glory bear
Two Coursers of ethereal race,
With necks in thunder cloath'd, and long-resounding pace.

   Hark, his hands the lyre explore!
Bright-eyed Fancy hov'ring o'er
Scatters from her pictur'd urn
Thoughts, that breath, and words, that burn.

JOHN DRYDEN (1631-1700)

    But ah! 'tis heard no more—
      Oh! Lyre divine, what daring Spirit
    Wakes thee now? tho' he inherit
    Nor the pride, nor ample pinion,
      That the Theban Eagle bear
    Sailing with supreme dominion
      Thro' the azure deep of air:
    Yet oft before his infant eyes would run
      Such forms, as glitter in the Muse's ray,
    With orient hues, unborrow'd of the Sun:
      Yet shall he mount, and keep his distant way
    Beyond the limits of a vulgar fate,
    Beneath the Good how far—but far above the Great.
                                 THOMAS GRAY
                                       (1716-1771)

JOSEPH ADDISON (1672-1719)

To the Earl of Warwick on the Death of Mr. Addison

If, dumb too long, the drooping Muse hath stay'd,
And left her debt to Addison unpaid;
Blame not her silence, Warwick, but bemoan,
And judge, oh judge, my bosom by your own.
What mourner ever felt poetic fires!
Slow comes the verse, that real woe inspires:
Grief unaffected suits but ill with art,
Or flowing numbers with a bleeding heart.
  Can I forget the dismal night, that gave
My soul's best part forever to the grave!
How silent did his old companions tread,
By midnight lamps, the mansions of the dead,
Through breathing statues, then unheeded things,
Through rows of warriors, and through walks of kings!
What awe did the slow solemn knell inspire;
The pealing organ, and the pausing choir;
The duties by the lawn-rob'd prelate paid;
And the last words, that dust to dust convey'd!

JOSEPH ADDISON (1672–1719)

   While speechless o'er thy closing grave we bend,
Accept these tears, thou dear departed friend,
Oh gone forever, take this long adieu;
And sleep in peace, next thy lov'd Montagu.
   To strew fresh laurels let the task be mine,
A frequent pilgrim, at thy sacred shrine;
Mine with true sighs thy absence to bemoan,
And grave with faithful epitaphs thy stone.
If e'er from me thy lov'd memorial part,
May shame afflict this alienated heart;
Of thee forgetful if I form a song,
My lyre be broken, and untun'd my tongue,
My griefs be doubled, from thy image free,
And mirth a torment, unchastis'd by thee.
   Oft let me range the gloomy aisles alone
(Sad luxury! to vulgar minds unknown)
Along the walls where speaking marbles show
What worthies form the hallow'd mold below:
Proud names, who once the reins of empire held;
In arms who triumph'd; or in arts excell'd;
Chiefs, grac'd with scars, and prodigal of blood;
Stern patriots, who for sacred freedom stood;
Just men, by whom impartial laws were given;
And saints, who taught, and led, the way to Heaven.
Ne'er to these chambers, where the mighty rest,
Since their foundation, came a nobler guest,
Nor e'er was to the bow'rs of bliss convey'd
A fairer spirit, or more welcome shade.
   In what new region, to the just assign'd,
What new employments please th' unbodied mind?
A winged Virtue, through th' ethereal sky,
From world to world unwearied does he fly?
Or curious trace the long laborious maze
Of Heav'n's decrees, where wond'ring angels gaze?
Does he delight to hear bold seraphs tell
How Michael battled, and the Dragon fell?
Or, mix'd with milder cherubim, to glow
In hymns of love, not ill essay'd below?

JOSEPH ADDISON (1672-1719)

Or dost thou warn poor mortals left behind,
A task well suited to thy gentle mind?
Oh, if sometimes thy spotless form descend,
To me thy aid, thou guardian Genius, lend!
When rage misguides me, or when fear alarms,
When pain distresses, or when pleasure charms,
In silent whisp'rings purer thoughts impart,
And turn from ill a frail and feeble heart;
Lead through the paths thy virtue trod before,
Till bliss shall join, nor death can part us more.
  That awful form (which, so ye heav'ns decree,
Must still be lov'd and still deplor'd by me)
In nightly visions seldom fails to rise,
Or, rous'd by fancy, meets my waking eyes.
If bus'ness calls, or crowded courts invite,
Th' unblemish'd statesman seems to strike my sight;
If in the stage I seek to soothe my care,
I meet his soul, which breathes in Cato there;
If pensive to the rural shades I rove,
His shape o'ertakes me in the lonely grove:
'Twas there of just and good he reason'd strong,
Clear'd some great truth, or rais'd some serious song;
There patient show'd us the wise course to steer,
A candid censor, and a friend severe;
There taught us how to live; and (oh! too high
The price for knowledge) taught us how to die.
  Thou hill, whose brow the antique structures grace,
Rear'd by bold chiefs of Warwick's noble race,
Why, once so lov'd, whene'er thy bow'r appears,
O'er my dim eyeballs glance the sudden tears!
How sweet were once thy prospects fresh and fair,
Thy sloping walks, and unpolluted air!
How sweet the glooms beneath thy aged trees,
Thy noon-tide shadow, and thy ev'ning breeze!
His image thy forsaken bow'rs restore;
Thy walks and airy prospects charm no more,
No more the summer in thy glooms allay'd,
Thy ev'ning breezes, and thy noon-day shade.

JOSEPH ADDISON (1672–1719)

From other ills, however fortune frown'd,
Some refuge in the Muse's art I found:
Reluctant now I touch the trembling string,
Bereft of him, who taught me how to sing,
And these sad accents, murmur'd o'er his urn,
Betray that absence, they attempt to mourn.
Oh! must I then (now fresh my bosom bleeds,
And Craggs in death to Addison succeeds)
The verse, begun to one lost friend, prolong,
And weep a second in th' unfinish'd song!
  These works divine, which on his deathbed laid
To thee, O Craggs, th' expiring sage convey'd,
Great, but ill-omen'd monument of fame,
Nor he surviv'd to give, nor thou to claim.
Swift after him thy social spirit flies,
And close to his, how soon! thy coffin lies.
Blest pair! whose union future bards shall tell
In future tongues: each other's boast! farewell.
Farewell! whom join'd in fame, in friendship tried,
No chance could sever, nor the grave divide.

THOMAS TICKELL
(1686–1740)

JONATHAN SWIFT (1667–1745)

Swift's Epitaph

Swift has sailed into his rest;
Savage indignation there
Cannot lacerate his breast.
Imitate him if you dare,
World-besotted traveler; he
Served human liberty.

WILLIAM BUTLER YEATS
(1865–1939)

THOMAS PARNELL (1679-1718)

Epitaph on Dr. Parnell

This tomb inscribed to gentle PARNELL's name,
May speak our gratitude, but not his fame.
What heart but feels his sweetly moral lay,
That leads to truth through Pleasure's flowery way?
Celestial themes confess'd his tuneful aid;
And Heaven, that lent him genius, was repaid.
Needless to him the tribute we bestow,
The transitory breath of fame below:
More lasting rapture from his works shall rise,
While converts thank their poet in the skies.

OLIVER GOLDSMITH
(1728-1774)

JOHN GAY (1685-1732)

On Mr. Gay

In Westminster Abbey, 1732

Of manners gentle, of affections mild;
In wit, a man; simplicity, a child:
With native humour temp'ring virtuous rage,
Form'd to delight at once and lash the age:
Above temptation in a low estate,
And uncorrupted, ev'n among the great:
A safe companion, and an easy friend,
Unblam'd through life, lamented in thy end.
These are thy honours! not that here thy bust
Is mix'd with heroes, or with kings thy dust;
But that the worthy and the good shall say,
Striking their pensive bosoms—*Here* lies GAY.

ALEXANDER POPE
(1688-1744)

JOHN GAY (1685-1732)

From "Epistle to Dr. Arbuthnot"

Bless'd be the great! for those they take away,
And those they left me—for they left me Gay;
Left me to see neglected Genius bloom,
Neglected die, and tell it on his tomb:
Of all thy blameless life the sole return
My Verse, and Queensb'ry weeping o'er thy urn!
  Oh let me live my own, and die so too
(To live and die is all I have to do)!
Maintain a poet's dignity and ease,
And see what friends, and read what books I please.

ALEXANDER POPE
(1688-1744)

[MISCELLANY]

The First Epistle of the Second Book of Horace

To AUGUSTUS
[*George II*]

While you, great Patron of Mankind! sustain
The balanced world, and open all the main;
Your country, chief, in Arms abroad defend,
At home with Morals, Arts, and Laws amend;
How shall the Muse, from such a monarch, steal
An hour, and not defraud the public weal?
  Edward and Henry, now the boast of Fame,
And virtuous Alfred, a more sacred name,
After a life of gen'rous toils endured,—
The Gaul's subdued, or property secured,
Ambition humbled, mighty cities storm'd,
Or laws establish'd, and the world reform'd—
Closed their long glories with a sigh, to find
Th' unwilling gratitude of base Mankind!
All human Virtue, to its latest breath,
Finds Envy never conquer'd but by Death.
The great Alcides, ev'ry labour past,
Had still this monster to subdue at last:

[THE FIRST EPISTLE]

Sure fate of all, beneath whose rising ray
Each star of meaner merit fades away!
Oppress'd we feel the beam directly beat;
Those suns of glory please not till they set.
   To thee the World its present homage pays,
The harvest early, but mature the praise:
Great friend of Liberty! in Kings a name
Above all Greek, above all Roman fame;
Whose word is truth, as sacred and revered
As Heav'n's own oracles from altars heard.
Wonder of Kings! like whom to mortal eyes
None e'er has risen, and none e'er shall rise.
   Just in one instance, be it yet confest
Your people, sir, are partial in the rest;
Foes to all living worth except your own,
And advocates for folly dead and gone.
Authors, like coins, grow dear as they grow old;
It is the Rust we value, not the Gold.
Chaucer's worst ribaldry is learn'd by rote,
And beastly Skelton heads of houses quote;
One likes no language but the Faery Queen;
A Scot will fight for Christ's Kirk o' the Green;
And each true Briton is to Ben so civil,
He swears the Muses met him at the Devil.
Tho' justly Greece her eldest sons admires,
Why should not we be wiser than our sires?
In every public virtue we excel,
We build, we paint, we sing, we dance, as well;
And learned Athens to our art must stoop,
Could she behold us tumbling thro' a hoop.
   If time improve our Wit as well as Wine,
Say at what age a poet grows divine?
Shall we, or shall we not, account him so
Who died, perhaps, a hundred years ago?
End all dispute; and fix the year precise
When British bards begin t' immortalize?
   'Who lasts a century can have no flaw;
I hold that Wit a classic, good in law.'

[THE FIRST EPISTLE]

    Suppose he wants a year, will you compound?
And shall we deem him ancient, right, and sound,
Or damn to all eternity at once
At ninety-nine a modern and a dunce?
'We shall not quarrel for a year or two;
By courtesy of England he may do.'
    Then by the rule that made the horsetail bare,
I pluck out year by year, as hair by hair,
And melt down Ancients like a heap of snow,
While you, to measure merits, look in Stowe,
And estimating authors by the year,
Bestow a garland only on a bier.
    Shakespeare (whom you and every playhouse bill
Style the divine! the matchless! what you will)
For Gain, not Glory, wing'd his roving flight,
And grew immortal in his own despite.
Ben, old and poor, as little seem'd to heed
The life to come in every poet's creed.
Who now reads Cowley? if he pleases yet,
His Moral pleases, not his pointed Wit:
Forgot his Epic, nay, Pindaric art,
But still I love the language of his heart.
    'Yet surely, surely these were famous men!
What boy but hears the sayings of old Ben?
In all debates where Critics bear a part,
Not one but nods, and talks of Jonson's Art,
Of Shakespeare's Nature, and of Cowley's Wit;
How Beaumont's judgment check'd what Fletcher writ;
How Shadwell hasty, Wycherley was slow;
But for the passions, Southern sure, and Rowe!
These, only these, support the crowded stage,
From eldest Heywood down to Cibber's age.'
All this may be; the People's voice is odd;
It is, and it is not, the voice of God.
To Gammer Gurton if it give the bays,
And yet deny the Careless Husband praise,
Or say our fathers never broke a rule;
Why then, I say, the Public is a fool.

[THE FIRST EPISTLE]

> But let them own that greater faults than we
> They had, and greater virtues, I'll agree
> Spenser himself affects the obsolete,
> And Sidney's verse halts ill on Roman feet;
> Milton's strong pinion now not Heav'n can bound,
> Now, serpent-like, in prose he sweeps the ground.
> In quibbles Angel and Archangel join,
> And God the Father turns a School-divine.
> Not that I'd lop the beauties from his book,
> Like slashing Bentley with his desp'rate hook;
> Or damn all Shakespeare, like th' affected fool
> At Court, who hates whate'er he read at School.
>   But for the Wits of either Charles's days,
> The mob of gentlemen who wrote with ease;
> Sprat, Carew, Sedley, and a hundred more
> (Like twinkling stars the Miscellanies o'er),
> One simile that solitary shines
> In the dry Desert of a thousand lines,
> Or lenthen'd thought, that gleams thro' many a page,
> Has sanctified whole poems for an age.
> I lose my patience, and I own it too,
> When works are censured not as bad, but new;
> While, if our elders break all Reason's laws,
> These fools demand not pardon, but applause.
>   On Avon's bank, where flowers eternal blow,
> If I but ask if any weed can grow,
> One tragic sentence if I dare deride,
> Which Betterton's grave action dignified,
> Or well-mouth'd Booth with emphasis proclaims,
> (Tho' but perhaps a muster-roll of names),
> How will our fathers rise up in a rage,
> And swear all shame is lost in GEORGE's age!
> You'd think no fools disgraced the former reign,
> Did not some grave examples yet remain,
> Who scorn a lad should teach his father skill,
> And having once been wrong, will be so still.
> He who, to seem more deep than you or I,
> Extols old bards, or Merlin's prophecy,

[THE FIRST EPISTLE]

    Mistake him not; he envies, not admires,
And to debase the sons exalts the sires.
Had ancient times conspired to disallow
What then was new, what had been ancient now?
Or what remain'd, so worthy to be read
By learned critics of the mighty dead?
    In days of ease, when now the weary sword
Was sheath'd, and luxury with Charles restor'd,
In every taste of foreign courts improv'd,
'All by the King's example liv'd and lov'd,'
Then peers grew proud in horsemanship t' excel;
Newmarket's glory rose, as Britain's fell;
The soldier breathed the gallantries of France,
And ev'ry flowery Courtier writ Romance.
Then marble, soften'd into life, grew warm,
And yielding metal flow'd to human form;
Lely on animated canvas stole
The sleepy eye, that spoke the melting soul.
No wonder then, when all was love and sport,
The willing Muses were debauch'd at court;
On each enervate string they taught the note
To pant, or tremble thro' a Eunuch's throat.
    But Britain, changeful as a child at play,
Now calls in princes, and now turns away.
Now Whig, now Tory, what we loved we hate;
Now all for Pleasure, now for Church and State;
Now for Prerogatives, and now for laws;
Effects unhappy, from a noble cause.
    Time was, a sober Englishman would knock
His servants up, and rise by five o'clock;
Instruct his family in ev'ry rule,
And send his wife to church, his son to school.
To worship like his fathers was his care;
To teach their frugal virtues to his heir;
To prove that Luxury could never hold,
And place on good security his gold.
Now times are changed, and one poetic itch
Has seized the Court and City, Poor and Rich;

[THE FIRST EPISTLE]

    Sons, sires, and grandsires, all will wear the bays;
Our wives read Milton, and our daughters plays;
To theatres and to rehearsals throng,
And all our grace at table is a song.
I, who so oft renounce the Muses, lie:
Not **'s self e'er tells more fibs than I.
When sick of Muse, our follies we deplore,
And promise our best friends to rhyme no more,
We wake next morning in a raging fit,
And call for pen and ink to show our wit.
    He served a 'prenticeship who sets up shop;
Ward tried on puppies and the poor his drop;
Ev'n Radcliff's doctors travel first to France,
Nor dare to practise till they've learn'd to dance.
Who builds a bridge that never drove a pile?
(Should Ripley venture, all the world would smile),
But those who cannot write, and those who can,
All rhyme, and scrawl, and scribble, to a man.
    Yet, Sir, reflect; the mischief is not great;
These madmen never hurt the Church or State:
Sometimes the folly benefits mankind,
And rarely av'rice taints the tuneful mind.
Allow him but his plaything of a Pen,
He ne'er rebels, or plots, like other men:
Flight of cashiers, or mobs, he'll never mind,
And knows no losses while the Muse is kind.
To cheat a friend or ward, he leaves to Peter;
The good man heaps up nothing but mere metre,
Enjoys his Garden and his Book in quiet;
And then—a perfect hermit in his diet.
    Of little use the man you may suppose
Who says in verse what others say in prose;
Yet let me show a Poet's of some weight,
And (tho' no soldier) useful to the State.
What will a child learn sooner than a song?
What better teach a foreigner the tongue—
What's long or short, each accent where to place,
And speak in public with some sort of grace?

[THE FIRST EPISTLE]

I scare can think him such a worthless thing,
Unless he praise some monster of a King;
Or virtue or religion turn to sport,
To please a lewd or unbelieving Court.
Unhappy Dryden!—In all Charles's days
Roscommon only boasts unspotted bays;
And in our own (excuse some courtly stains)
No whiter page than Addison remains.
He from the taste obscene reclaims our youth,
And sets the passions on the side of Truth,
Forms the soft bosom with the gentlest Art,
And pours each human virtue in the heart.
Let Ireland tell how wit upheld her cause,
Her trade supported, and supplied her laws;
And leave on Swift this grateful verse engraved,
'The rights a Court attack'd, a Poet saved.'
Behold the hand that wrought a Nation's cure,
Stretch'd to relieve the idiot and the poor;
Proud vice to brand, or injured worth adorn,
And stretch the ray to ages yet unborn.
Not but there are, who merit other palms;
Hopkins and Sternhold glad the heart with psalms;
The boys and girls whom charity maintains
Implore your help in these pathetic strains:
How could Devotion touch the country pews
Unless the Gods bestow'd a proper Muse?
Verse cheers their leisure, verse assists their work,
Verse prays for peace, or sings down pope and Turk.
The silenced preacher yields to potent strain,
And feels that Grace his prayer besought in vain;
The blessing thrills thro' all the lab'ring throng,
And Heav'n is won by violence of song.
  Our rural ancestors, with little blest,
Patient of labour when the end was rest,
Indulged the day that housed their annual grain
With feasts, and off'rings, and a thankful strain.
The joy their wives, their sons, and servants share,
Ease of their toil, and partners of their care:
The Laugh, the Jest, attendants on the bowl,
Smooth'd ev'ry brow, and open'd ev'ry soul:

[THE FIRST EPISTLE]

With growing years the pleasing license grew,
And taunts alternate innocently flew.
But Times corrupt, and Nature, ill inclin'd,
Produced the point that left a sting behind;
Till friend with friend, and families at strife,
Triumphant malice raged thro' private life.
Who felt the wrong, or fear'd it, took th' alarm,
Appeal'd to law, and Justice lent her arm.
At length by wholesome dread of statutes bound,
The poets learn'd to please, and not to wound:
Most warp'd to Flatt'ry's side; but some more nice,
Preserv'd the freedom, and forbore the vice.
Hence Satire rose, that just the medium hit,
And heals with morals what it hurts with wit.
We conquer'd France, but felt our captive's charms,
Her arts victorious triumph'd o'er our arms;
Britain to soft refinements less a foe,
Wit grew polite, and numbers learn'd to flow.
Waller was smooth; but Dryden taught to join
The varying verse, the full resounding line,
The long majestic march, and energy divine:
Tho' still some traces of our rustic vein
And splay-foot verse remain'd, and will remain.
Late, very late, correctness grew our care,
When the tired nation breathed from civil war
Exact Racine and Corneille's noble fire
Show'd us that France had something to admire.
Not but the tragic spirit was our own,
And full in Shakespeare, fair in Otway, shone;
But Otway fail'd to polish or refine,
And fluent Shakespeare scarce effaced a line.
Ev'n copious Dryden wanted, or forgot,
The last and greatest art—the art to blot.
  Some doubt if equal pains or equal fire
The humbler Muse of Comedy require.
But in known images of life I guess
The labour greater, as th' indulgence less.
Observe how seldom ev'n the best succeed:
Tell me if Congreve's fools are fools indeed?

[THE FIRST EPISTLE]

What pert low dialogue has Farquhar writ!
How Van wants grace, who never wanted wit:
The stage how loosely does Astrea tread,
Who fairly puts all characters to bed!
And idle Cibber, how he breaks the laws,
To make poor Pinkey eat with vast applause!
But fill their purse, our poet's work is done,
Alike to them by pathos or by pun.
 O you! whom Vanity's light bark conveys
On Fame's made voyage by the wind of praise,
With what a shifting gale your course you ply,
For ever sunk too low, or borne too high.
Who pants for glory finds but short repose;
A breath revives him, or a breath o'erthrows.
Farewell the Stage! if just as thrives the play
The silly bard grows fat or falls away.
 There still remains, to mortify a Wit,
The many-headed monster of the pit;
A senseless, worthless, and unhonour'd crowd,
Who, to disturb their betters, mighty proud,
Clatt'ring their sticks before ten lines are spoke,
Call for the Farce, the Bear, or the Blackjoke.
What dear delight to Britons farce affords!
Ever the taste of Mobs, but now of Lords:
(Taste! that eternal wanderer, which flies
From heads to ears, and now from ears to eyes.)
The play stands still; damn action and discourse!
Back fly the scenes, and enter foot and horse;
Pageants on pageants, in long order drawn,
Peers, heralds, bishops, ermine, gold, and lawn;
The Champion too! and, to complete the jest,
Old Edward's armour beams on Cibber's breast.
With laughter sure Democritus had died,
Had he beheld an audience gape so wide.
Let bear or elephant be e'er so white,
The people sure, the people are the sight!
Ah, luckless Poet! stretch thy lungs and roar,
That bear or elephant shall heed thee more;

[THE FIRST EPISTLE]

While all its throats the gallery extends,
And all the thunder of the pit ascends!
Loud as the wolves on Orcas' stormy steep
Howl to the roarings of the northern deep,
Such is the shout, the long applauding note,
At Quin's high plume, or Oldfield's petticoat;
Or when from court a birthday suit bestow'd,
Sinks the lost actor in the tawdry load.
Booth enters—hark! the universal peal!
'But has he spoken?'—Not a syllable.
'What shook the stage, and made the people stare?'
Cato's long wig, flower'd gown, and lacker'd chair.
   Yes, lest you think I rally more than teach,
Or praise malignly arts I cannot reach,
Let me for once presume t' instruct the times,
To know the Poet from the man of rhymes:
'T is he who gives my breast a thousand pains,
Can make me feel each passion that he feigns,
Enrage, compose, with more than magic art,
With pity and with terror tear my heart,
And snatch me o'er the earth, or thro' the air,
To Thebes, to Athens, when he will, and where.
   But not this part of the poetic state
Alone deserves the favour of the great.
Think of those authors, Sir, who would rely
More on a reader's sense than gazer's eye.
Or who shall wander where the Muses sing?
Who climb their mountain, or who taste their spring?
How shall we fill a library with Wit,
When Merlin's Cave is half unfurnish'd yet?
   My liege! why writers little claim your thought
I guess, and, with their leave, will tell the fault.
We Poets are (upon a poet's word)
Of all mankind the creatures most absurd:
The season when to come, and when to go,
To sing, or cease to sing, we never know;
And if we will recite nine hours in ten,
You lose your patience just like other men.

[THE FIRST EPISTLE]

Then, too, we hurt ourselves when, to defend
A single verse, we quarrel with a friend;
Repeat, unask'd; lament, the wit's too fine
For vulgar eyes, and point out every line:
But most when straining with too weak a wing
We needs will write epistles to the King;
And from the moment we oblige the town,
Expect a Place or Pension from the Crown;
Or dubb'd historians by express command,
T' enrol your triumphs o'er the seas and land,
Be call'd to Court to plan some work divine,
As once for Louis, Boileau and Racine.
   Yet think, great Sir! (so many virtues shown)
Ah! think what poet best may make them known;
Or choose at least some minister of grace,
Fit to bestow the Laureate's weighty place.
   Charles, to late times to be transmitted fair,
Assign'd his figure to Bernini's care;
And great Nassau to Kneller's hand decreed
To fix him graceful on the bounding steed:
So well in paint and stone they judg'd of merit;
But Kings in Wit may want discerning spirit.
The hero William, and the martyr Charles,
One knighted Blackmore, and one pension'd Quarles,
Which made old Ben and surly Bennis swear
'No Lord's anointed, but a Russian bear.'
   Not with such majesty, such bold relief,
The forms august of King, or conquering Chief,
E'er swell'd on marble, as in verse have shined
(In polish'd verse) the manners and the mind.
O! could I mount on the Maeonian wing,
Your arms, your actions, your repose, to sing!
What seas you travers'd, and what fields you fought!
Your country's peace how oft, how dearly bought!
How barb'rous rage subsided at your word,
And nations wonder'd while they dropp'd the sword!
How, when you nodded, o'er the land and deep,
Peace stole her wing, and wrapt the world in sleep,

[THE FIRST EPISTLE]

Till earth's extremes your mediation own,
And Asia's tyrants tremble at your throne!
But verse, alas! your Majesty disdains;
And I'm not used to panegyric strains.
The zeal of fools offends at any time,
But most of all the zeal of fools in rhyme.
Besides, a Fate attends on all I write,
That when I aim at praise they say I bite.
A vile encomium doubly ridicules:
There's nothing blackens like the ink of fools.
If true, a woful likeness; and, if lies,
'Praise undeserv'd is scandal in disguise.'
Well may he blush who gives it, or receives;
And when I flatter, let my dirty leaves
(Like Journals, Odes, and such forgotten things,
As Eusden, Philips, Settle, writ of Kings)
Clothe spice, line trunk, or, flutt'ring in a row,
Befringe the rails of Bedlam and Soho.

ALEXANDER POPE
(1688–1744)

1737

ALEXANDER POPE (1688–1744)

To Mr. Pope

To praise, yet still with due respect to praise,
A bard triumphant in immortal bays,
The learn'd to show, the sensible to commend,
Yet still preserve the province of the friend—
What life, what vigour, must the lines require,
What music tune them, what affection fire!
  Oh! might thy genius in my bosom shine,
Thou shouldst not fail of numbers worthy thine;
The brightest ancients might at once agree
To sing within my lays, and sing of thee.
  Horace himself would own thou dost excel
In candid arts, to play the critic well.
  Ovid himself might wish to sing the dame
Whom Windsor Forest sees a gliding stream;

ALEXANDER POPE (1688-1744)

On silver feet, with annual osier crown'd,
She runs forever through poetic ground.
  How flame the glories of Belinda's hair,
Made by thy Muse the envy of the fair!
Less shone the tresses Egypt's princess wore,
Which sweet Callimachus so sung before;
Here courtly trifles set the world at odds,
Belles war with beaux, and whims descend for gods;
The new machines in names of ridicule,
Mock the grave frenzy of the chemic fool.
But know, ye fair, a point conceal'd with art,
The sylphs and gnomes are but a woman's heart;
The Graces stand in sight; a satyr train
Peep o'er their heads, and laugh behind the scene.
  In Fame's fair temple, o'er the boldest wits
Enshrin'd on high, the sacred Virgil sits,
And sits in measures, such as Virgil's Muse
To place thee near him might be fond to choose.
How might he tune th' alternate reed with thee,
Perhaps a Strephon thou, a Daphnis he,
While some old Damon, o'er the vulgar wise,
Thinks he deserves, and thou deserv'st the prize!
Rapt with the thought, my fancy seeks the plains,
And turns me shepherd while I hear the strains.
Indulgent nurse of ev'ry tender gale,
Parent of flow'rets, old Arcadia, hail!
Here in the cool my limbs at ease I spread,
Here let thy poplars whisper o'er my head,
Still slide thy waters soft among the trees,
Thy aspen quiver in a breathing breeze,
Smile all thy valleys in eternal spring,
Be hush'd, ye winds! while Pope and Virgil sing.
  In English lays, and all sublimely great,
Thy Homer warms with all his ancient heat;
He shines in council, thunders in the fight,
And flames with ev'ry sense of great delight.
Long has that poet reign'd, and long unknown,
Like monarchs sparkling on a distant throne,

ALEXANDER POPE (1688-1744)

In all the majesty of Greek retir'd,
Himself unknown, his mighty name admir'd;
His language, failing, wrapp'd him round with night;
Thine, rais'd by thee, recalls the work to light.
So wealthy mines, that ages long before
Fed the large realms around with golden ore,
When chok'd by sinking banks, no more appear,
And shepherds only say, "The mines were here":
Should some rich youth (if nature warm his heart,
And all his projects stand inform'd with art)
Here clear the caves, there ope the leading vein;
The mines, detected, flame with gold again.
  How vast, how copious are thy new designs!
How ev'ry music varies in thy lines!
Still as I read, I feel my bosom beat,
And rise in raptures by another's heat.
Thus in the wood, when summer dress'd the days,
When Windsor lent us tuneful hours of ease,
Our ears the lark, the thrush, the turtle blest,
And Philomela sweetest o'er the rest:
The shades resound with song—oh, softly tread!
While a whole season warbles round my head.
  This to my friend—and when a friend inspires,
My silent harp its master's hand requires,
Shakes off the dust, and makes these rocks resound;
For fortune plac'd me in unfertile ground,
Far from the joys that with my soul agree,
From wit, from learning—far, oh far from thee!
Here moss-grown trees expand the smallest leaf,
Here half an acre's corn is half a sheaf;
Here hills with naked heads the tempest meet,
Rocks at their side, and torrents at their feet,
Or lazy lakes, unconscious of a flood,
Whose dull brown naiads ever sleep in mud.
  Yet here content can dwell, and learnéd ease,
A friend delight me, and an author please;
Ev'n here I sing, while Pope supplies the theme,—
Show my own love, though not increase his fame.
              THOMAS PARNELL
                (1679-1718)

ALEXANDER POPE (1688-1744)

From "Mr. Pope's Welcome from Greece"

Upon his having finished his translation of Homer's Iliad

Long hast thou, friend! been absent from thy soil,
    Like patient Ithacus at siege of Troy;
I have been witness of thy six years' toil,
    Thy daily labours, and thy night's annoy,
Lost to thy native land, with great turmoil,
    On the wide sea, oft threat'ning to destroy:
Methinks with thee I've trod Sigæan ground,
And heard the shores of Hellespont resound.

Did I not see thee when thou first sett'st sail
    To seek adventures fair in Homer's land?
Did I not see thy sinking spirits fail,
    And wish thy bark had never left the strand?
Ev'n in mid ocean often didst thou quail,
    And oft lift up thy holy eye and hand,
Praying the Virgin dear, and saintly choir,
Back to the port to bring thy bark entire.

Cheer up, my friend, thy dangers now are o'er;
    Methinks—nay, sure the rising coasts appear;
Hark how the gun salute from either shore,
    As thy trim vessel cuts the Thames so fair:
Shouts answ'ring shouts, from Kent and Essex roar,
    And bells break loud thro' every gust of air:
Bonfires do blaze, and bones and cleavers ring,
As at the coming of some mighty king.

Now pass we Gravesend with a friendly wind,
    And Tilbury's white fort, and long Blackwall;
Greenwich, where dwells the friend of human kind,
    More visited than or her park or hall,
Withers the good, and (with him ever join'd)
    Facetious Disney, greet thee first of all:
I see his chimney smoke, and hear him say,
Duke! that's the room for Pope, and that for Gay.

ALEXANDER POPE (1688-1744)

Come in, my friends, here shall ye dine and lie,
  And here shall breakfast, and here dine again;
And sup, and breakfast on, (if ye comply)
  For I have still some dozens of champagne:
His voice still lessens as the ship sails by;
  He waves his hand to bring us back in vain;
For now I see, I see proud London's spires;
Greenwich is lost, and Deptford dock retires.

Oh, what a concourse swarms on yonder key!
  The sky re-echoes with new shouts of joy:
By all this show, I ween, 'tis Lord May'r's day,
  I hear the voice of trumpet and hautboy.—
No, now I see them near—oh, these are they
  Who come in crowds to welcome thee from Troy.
Hail to the bard whom long as lost we mourn'd,
From siege, from battle, and from storm return'd!

* * * * *

See generous Burlington, with goodly Bruce,
  (But Bruce comes wafted in a soft sedan)
Dan Prior next, belov'd by every muse,
  And friendly Congreve, unreproachful man!
(Oxford by Cunningham hath sent excuse)
  See hearty Watkins comes with cup and can;
And Lewis, who has never friend forsaken;
And Laughton whisp'ring asks—Is Troy town taken?

Earl Warwick comes, of free and honest mind;
  Bold, gen'rous Craggs, whose heart was ne'er disguis'd:
Ah why, sweet St. John, cannot I thee find?
  St. John for ev'ry social virtue priz'd.—
Alas! to foreign climates he's confin'd,
  Or else to see thee here I well surmiz'd:
Thou too, my Swift, dost breathe Bœotian air;
When wilt thou bring back wit and humour here?

Harcourt I see for eloquence renown'd,
  The mouth of justice, oracle of law!
Another Simon is beside him found,
  Another Simon, like as straw to straw.

ALEXANDER POPE (1688–1744)

How Lansdowne smiles, with lasting laurel crown'd!
   What mitred prelate there commands our awe?
See Rochester approving nods his head,
And ranks one modern with the mighty dead.

Carlton and Chandos thy arrival grace;
   Hanmer, whose eloquence th' unbiass'd sways;
Harley, whose goodness opens in his face,
   And shews his heart the seat where virtue stays.
Ned Blount advances next, with busy pace,
   In haste, but saunt'ring, hearty in his ways:
I see the friendly Carylls come by dozens,
Their wives, their uncles, daughters, sons, and cousins.

Arbuthnot there I see, in physic's art,
   As Galen learn'd, or famed Hippocrate;
Whose company drives sorrow from the heart,
   As all disease his medicines dissipate:
Kneller amid the triumph bears his part,
   Who could (were mankind lost) a new create:
What can th' extent of his vast soul confine?
A painter, critic, engineer, divine!

Thee Jervas hails, robust and debonair,
   Now have we conquer'd Homer, friends, he cries:
Dartneuf, grave joker, joyous Ford is there,
   And wond'ring Maine, so fat with laughing eyes:
(Gay, Maine, and Cheney, boon companions dear,
   Gay fat, Maine fatter, Cheney huge of size)
Yea Dennis, Gildon, (hearing thou hast riches)
And honest, hatless Cromwell, with red breeches.

O Wanley, whence com'st thou with shorten'd hair,
   And visage from thy shelves with dust besprent?
'Forsooth (quoth he) from placing Homer there,
   For ancients to compyle is myne entente:
Of ancients only hath Lord Harley care;
   But hither me hath my meeke lady sent:—
In manuscript of Greeke rede we thilke same,
But book yprint best plesyth myn gude dame.'

ALEXANDER POPE (1688-1744)

Yonder I see, among th' expecting crowd,
  Evans with laugh jocose, and tragic Young;
High-buskin'd Booth, grave Mawbert, wand'ring Frowd,
  And Titcomb's belly waddles slow along.
See Digby faints at Southern talking loud,
  Yea Steele and Tickell mingle in the throngs;
Tickell whose skiff (in partnership they say)
  Set forth for Greece, but founder'd in the way.

* * * * *

How lov'd! how honour'd thou! yet be not vain;
  And sure thou art not, for I hear thee say,
All this, my friends, I owe to Homer's strain,
  On whose strong pinions I exalt my lay.
What from contending cities did he gain;
  And what rewards his grateful country pay?
None, none were paid—why then all this for me?
These honours, Homer, had been just to thee.

JOHN GAY
(1685-1732)

From "Table Talk"

In front of these came Addison. In him
Humour in holiday and sightly trim,
Sublimity and Attic taste, combin'd,
To polish, furnish, and delight, the mind.
Then Pope, as harmony itself exact,
In verse well-disciplin'd, complete, compact,
Gave virtue and morality a grace,
That, quite eclipsing pleasure's painted face,
Levied a tax of wonder and applause,
Even on the fools that trampled on their laws.
But he (his musical finesse was such,
So nice his ear, so delicate his touch)
Made poetry a mere mechanic art;
And ev'ry warbler has his tune by heart.
Nature imparting her satiric gift,
Her serious mirth, to Arbuthnot and Swift,

ALEXANDER POPE (1688-1744)

> With droll sobriety they rais'd a smile
> At folly's cost, themselves unmov'd the while.
> That constellation set, the world in vain
> Must hope to look upon their like again. . . .
> WILLIAM COWPER
(1731-1800)

Pope at Twickenham

Beyond a hundred years and more,
A garden lattice like a door
   Stands open in the sun,
Admitting fitful winds that set
Astir the fragrant mignonette
   In waves of speckled dun:

Sweet waves, above whose odorous flow
Red roses bud, red roses blow,
   In beds that gem the lawn—
Enamell'd rings and stars of flowers,
By summer beams and vernal showers
   From earth nutritious drawn.

Within the broad bay-window, there,
Lo! huddled in his easy-chair,
   One hand upon his knee,
A hand so thin, so wan, so frail,
It tells of pains and griefs a tale,
   A small bent form I see.

The day is fair, the hour is noon,
From neighboring thicket thrills the boon
   The nuthatch yields in song:
All drench'd with recent rains, the leaves
Are dripping—drip the sheltering eaves,
   The dropping notes among.

And twinkling diamonds in the grass
Show where the flitting zephyrs pass,
   That shake the green blades dry;

ALEXANDER POPE (1688–1744)

And golden radiance fills the air
And gilds the floating gossamer
   That glints and trembles by.

Yet, blind to each familiar grace,
Strange anguish on his pallid face,
   And eyes of dreamful hue,
That lonely man sits brooding there,
Still huddled in his easy-chair,
   With memories life will rue.

Where bay might crown that honor'd head,
A homely crumpled nightcap spread
   Half veils the careworn brows;
In morning-gown of rare brocade
His puny shrunken shape array'd
   His sorrowing soul avows:

Avows in every dropping line
Dejection words not thus define
   So eloquent of woe;
Yet never to those mournful eyes,
The heart's full-brimming fountains, rise
   Sweet tears to overflow.

No token here of studied grief,
But plainest signs that win belief,
   A simple scene and true.
Beside the mourner's chair display'd,
The matin meal's slight comforts laid
   Trimly the board bestrew.

'Mid silvery sheen of burnish'd plate,
The chill'd and tarnish'd chocolate
   On snow-white damask stands;
Untouch'd the trivial lures remain
In dainty pink-tinged porcelain,
   Still ranged by usual hands.

ALEXANDER POPE (1688–1744)

A drowsy bee above the cream
Hums loitering in the sunny gleam
   That tips each rim with gold;
A checker'd maze of light and gloom
Floats in the quaintly-litter'd room
   With varying charms untold.

Why sits that silent watcher there,
Still brooding with that face of care,
   That gaze of tearless pain?
What bonds of woe his spirit bind,
What treasure lost can leave behind
   Such stings within his brain?

He dreams of one who lies above,
He never more in life can love—
   That mother newly dead;
He waits the artist-friend whose skill
Shall catch the angel-beauty still
   Upon her features spread.

A reverent sorrow fills the air,
And makes a throne of grief the chair
   Where filial genius mourns:
Death proving still, at direst need,
Life's sceptre-wand—a broken reed,
   Love's wreath—a crown of thorns.

                              CHARLES KENT
                              (1823–1902)

Mr. Pope

When Alexander Pope strolled in the city
Strict was the glint of pearl and gold sedans;
Ladies leaned out, more out of fear than pity,
For Pope's tight back was rather a goat's than man's.

Often one thinks the urn should have more bones
Than skeletons provide for speedy dust,
The urn gets hollow, cobwebs brittle as stones
Weave to the funeral shell a frivolous rust.

ALEXANDER POPE (1688–1744)

    And he who dribbled couplets like a snake
    Coiled to a lithe precision in the sun,
    Is missing. The jar is empty; you may break
    It only to find that Mr. Pope is gone.

    What requisitions of a verity
    Prompted the wit and rage between his teeth
    One cannot say; around a crooked tree
    A moral climbs whose name should be a wreath.
                                ALLEN TATE
                                       (1899–   )

JOHN DYER (1700?–1758)

To the Poet, John Dyer

Bard of the Fleece, whose skilful genius made
That work a living landscape fair and bright;
Nor hallowed less with musical delight
Than those soft scenes through which thy childhood strayed,
Those southern tracts of Cambria, "deep embayed,
With green hills fenced, with ocean's murmur lulled;"
Though hasty Fame hath many a chaplet culled
For worthless brows, while in the pensive shade
Of cold neglect she leaves thy head ungraced,
Yet pure and powerful minds, hearts meek and still,
A grateful few, shall love thy modest Lay,
Long as the shepherd's bleating flock shall stray
O'er naked Snowdon's wide aërial waste;
Long as the thrush shall pipe on Grongar Hill!
                              WILLIAM WORDSWORTH
                                   (1770–1850)

JAMES THOMSON (1700–1748)

Ode on the Death of Mr. Thomson

(The scene of the following stanzas is suppos'd to lie on the Thames near Richmond.)

I

In yonder grave a Druid lies
  Where slowly winds the stealing wave!
The year's best sweets shall duteous rise
  To deck its Poet's sylvan grave!

II

In yon deep bed of whisp'ring reeds
  His airy harp shall now be laid,
That he, whose heart in sorrow bleeds
  May love thro' life the soothing shade.

III

Then maids and youths shall linger here,
  And while its sounds at distance swell,
Shall sadly seem in Pity's ear
  To hear the Woodland Pilgrim's knell.

IV

Remembrance oft shall haunt the shore
  When Thames in summer-wreaths is drest,
And oft suspend the dashing oar
  To bid his gentle spirit rest!

V

And oft as Ease and Health retire
  To breezy lawn, or forest deep,
The friend shall view yon whit'ning spire
  And 'mid the varied landscape weep.

VI

But thou, who own'st that earthy bed,
  Ah! what will ev'ry dirge avail?
Or tears, which Love and Pity shed
  That mourn beneath the gliding sail!

JAMES THOMSON (1700-1748)

VII

Yet lives there one, whose heedless eye
   Shall scorn thy pale shrine glimm'ring near?
With him, sweet bard, may Fancy die,
   And Joy desert the blooming year.

VIII

But thou, lorn Stream, whose sullen tide
   No sedge-crown'd Sisters now attend,
Now waft me from the green hill's side
   Whose cold turf hides the buried friend!

IX

And see, the fairy valleys fade,
   Dun Night has veil'd the solemn view!
—Yet once again, dear parted Shade
   Meek Nature's child again adieu!

X

The genial meads assign'd to bless
   Thy life, shall mourn thy early doom,
Their hinds, and shepherd-girls shall dress
   With simple hands thy rural tomb.

XI

Long, long, thy stone and pointed clay
   Shall melt the musing Briton's eyes,
O! Vales, and Wild Woods, shall he say
   In yonder grave Your Druid lies!

                                WILLIAM COLLINS
                                  (1721-1759)

WILLIAM COLLINS (1721-1759)

Remembrance of Collins

Composed upon the Thames near Richmond

   Glide gently, thus for ever glide,
   O Thames! that other bards may see
   As lovely visions by thy side
   As now, fair river! come to me.

WILLIAM COLLINS (1721–1759)

O glide, fair stream! for ever so,
Thy quiet soul on all bestowing,
Till all our minds for ever flow
As thy deep waters now are flowing.

Vain thought!—Yet be as now thou art,
That in thy waters may be seen
The image of a poet's heart,
How bright, how solemn, how serene!
Such as did once the Poet bless,
Who murmuring here a later ditty,
Could find no refuge from distress
But in the milder grief of pity.

Now let us, as we float along,
For *him* suspend the dashing oar;
And pray that never child of song
May know that Poet's sorrows more.
How calm! how still! the only sound,
The dripping of the oar suspended!
—The evening darkness gathers round
By virtue's holiest Powers attended.

WILLIAM WORDSWORTH
(1770–1850)

SAMUEL JOHNSON (1709–1784)

Epitaph on Dr. Johnson

Here Johnson lies, a sage by all allowed,
Whom to have bred may well make England proud;
Whose prose was eloquence, by wisdom taught,
The graceful vehicle of virtuous thought;
Whose verse may claim, grave, masculine, and strong,
Superior praise to the mere poet's song;
Who many a noble gift from Heaven possessed.
And faith at last, alone worth all the rest.
O man, immortal by a double prize,
By fame on earth, by glory in the skies!

WILLIAM COWPER
(1731–1800)

THOMAS GRAY (1716-1771)

To Mr. Gray

Not that her blooms are mark'd with beauty's hue,
My rustic Muse her votive chaplet brings;
Unseen, unheard, O Gray, to thee she sings!—
While slowly pacing through the churchyard dew,
At curfew-time, beneath the dark-green yew,
Thy pensive genius strikes the moral strings;
Or borne sublime on Inspiration's wings,
Hears Cambria's bards devote the dreadful clue
Of Edward's race, with murthers foul defil'd;
Can aught my pipe to reach thine ear essay?
No, bard divine! For many a care beguil'd
By the sweet magic of thy soothing lay,
For many a raptur'd thought, and vision wild,
To thee this strain of gratitude I pay.
THOMAS WARTON, JR.
(1728-1790)

JOSEPH WARTON (1722-1800)
THOMAS WARTON, JR. (1728-1790)

The Wartons

And Other Early Romantic Landscape-Poets

Mild hearts! and modest as the evening bell
    That rings so often through your meadow rhyme,
May there be elms and belfries where you dwell,
    And the last streaks of day still gild old time!

In the new heaven and true Jerusalem
    Can such things be? That can they! where you rove
The glow-worm shall not hide his elvish gem,
    The owl with ghostly wing shall tour the grove.

And when the charms and fairies of the night
    Are changed to sparkling dew and morning's choir,
Gazing the vale farms, from some sheep-strown height,
    How will you welcome Phoebus' dancing fire!

JOSEPH WARTON (1722-1800)
THOMAS WARTON, JR. (1728-1790)

>   On ancient arches shall your primrose peep,
>   On diamond lattices your sunbeam play,
>   Across shy brooks your little peasants leap,
>   And peace and innocence divide the day.
>
>   Nor shall the shades of poets not be seen
>   Whom you have loved. Milton in his young prime,
>   Spenser and Chaucer on the daisied green
>   Shall join with you and hear May-morning chime.
>
>   EDMUND BLUNDEN
>   (1896–   )

CHRISTOPHER SMART (1722-1771)

From "Parleyings with Certain People of Importance"

With Christopher Smart

I

It seems as if .... or did the actual chance
Startle me and perplex?   Let truth be said!
How might this happen?   Dreaming, blindfold led
By visionary hand, did soul's advance
Precede my body's, gain inheritance
Of fact by fancy—so that when I read
At length with waking eyes your Song, instead
Of mere bewilderment, with me first glance
Was but full recognition that in trance
Or merely thought's adventure some old day
Of dim and done-with boyishness, or—well,
Why might it not have been, the miracle
Broke on me as I took my sober way
Through veritable regions of our earth
And made discovery, many a wondrous one?

II

Anyhow, fact or fancy, such its birth:
I was exploring some huge house, had gone
Through room and room complacently, no dearth

CHRISTOPHER SMART (1722-1771)

Anywhere of the signs of decent taste,
Adequate culture: wealth had run to waste
Nowise, nor penury was proved by stint:
All showed the Golden Mean without a hint
Of brave extravagance that breaks the rule.
The master of the mansion was no fool
Assuredly, no genius just as sure!
Safe mediocrity had scorned the lure
Of now too much and now too little cost,
And satisfied me sight was never lost
Of moderate design's accomplishment
In calm completeness. On and on I went
With no more hope than fear of what came next,
Till lo, I push a door, sudden uplift
A hanging, enter, chance upon a shift
Indeed of scene! So—thus it is thou deck'st
High heaven, our low earth's brick-and-mortar work?

III

It was the Chapel. That a star, from murk
Which hid, should flashingly emerge at last,
Were small surprise: but from broad day I passed
Into a presence that turned shine to shade.
There fronted me the Rafael Mother-Maid,
Never to whom knelt votarist in shrine
By Nature's bounty helped, by Art's divine
More varied—beauty with magnificence—
Than this: from floor to roof one evidence
Of how far earth may rival heaven. No niche
Where glory was not prisoned to enrich
Man's gaze with gold and gems, no space but glowed
With color, gleamed with carving—hues which owed
Their outburst to a brush the painter fed
With rainbow-substance—rare shapes never wed
To actual flesh and blood, which, brain-born once,
Became the sculptor's dowry, Art's response
To earth's despair. And all seemed old yet new:
Youth,—in the marble's curve, the canvas' hue,

[173]

CHRISTOPHER SMART (1722-1771)

Apparent,—wanted not the crowning thrill
Of age the consecrator. Hands long still
Had worked here—could it be, what lent them skill
Retained a power to supervise, protect,
Enforce new lessons with the old, connect
Our life with theirs? No merely modern touch
Told me that here the artist, doing much,
Elsewhere did more, perchance does better, lives—
So needs must learn.

IV

Well, these provocatives
Having fulfilled their office, forth I went
Big with anticipation—well-nigh fear—
Of what next room and next for startled eyes
Might have in store, surprise beyond surprise.
Next room and next and next—what followed here?
Why, nothing! not one object to arrest
My passage—everywhere too manifest
The previous decent null and void of best
And worst, mere ordinary right and fit,
Calm commonplace which neither missed, nor hit
Inch-high, inch-low, the placid mark proposed.

V

Armed with this instance, have I diagnosed
Your case, my Christopher? The man was sound
And sane at starting: all at once the ground
Gave way beneath his step, a certain smoke
Curled up and caught him, or perhaps down broke
A fireball wrapping flesh and spirit both
In conflagration. Then—as heaven were loth
To linger—let earth understand too well
How heaven at need can operate—off fell
The flame-robe, and the untransfigured man
Resumed sobriety,—as he began,
So did he end nor alter pace, not he!

CHRISTOPHER SMART (1722-1771)
VI

Now, what I fain would know is—could it be
That he—whoe'er he was that furnished forth
The Chapel, making thus, from South to North,
Rafael touch Leighton, Michelagnolo
Join Watts, was found but once combining so
The elder and the younger, taking stand
On Art's supreme,—or that yourself who sang
A Song where flute-breath silvers trumpet-clang,
And stations you for once on either hand
With Milton and with Keats, empowered to claim
Affinity on just one point—(or blame
Or praise my judgment, thus it fronts you full)—
How came it you resume the void and null,
Subside to insignificance,—live, die
—Proved plainly two mere mortals who drew nigh
One moment—that, to Art's best hierarchy,
This, to the superhuman poet-pair?
What if, in one point only, then and there
The otherwise all-unapproachable
Allowed impingement? Does the sphere pretend
To span the cube's breadth, cover end to end
The plane with its embrace? No, surely! Still,
Contact is contact, sphere's touch no whit less
Than cube's superimposure. Such success
Befell Smart only out of throngs between
Milton and Keats that donned the singing-dress—
Smart, solely of such songmen, pierced the screen
'Twixt thing and word, lit language straight from soul,—
Left no fine film-flake on the naked coal
Live from the censer—shapely or uncouth,
Fire-suffused through and through, one blaze of truth
Undeadened by a lie,—(you have my mind)—
For, think! this blaze outleapt with black behind
And blank before, when Hayley and the rest . . .
But let the dead successors worst and best
Bury their dead: with life be my concern—
Yours with the fire-flame: what I fain would learn

CHRISTOPHER SMART (1722-1771)

Is just—(suppose me haply ignorant
Down to the common knowledge, doctors vaunt)
Just this—why only once the fire-flame was:
No matter if the marvel came to pass
The way folk judged—if power too long suppressed
Broke loose and maddened, as the vulgar guessed
Or simply brain-disorder (doctors said),
A turmoil of the particles disturbed,
Brain's workaday performance in your head,
Spurred spirit to wild action health had curbed,
And so verse issued in a cataract
Whence prose, before and after, unperturbed
Was wont to wend its way. Concede the fact
That here a poet was who always could—
Never before did—never after would—
Achieve the feat: how were such fact explained?

VII

Was it that when, by rarest chance, there fell
Disguise from Nature, so that Truth remained
Naked, and whoso saw for once could tell
Us others of her majesty and might
In large, her lovelinesses infinite
In little,—straight you used the power wherewith
Sense, penetrating as through rind to pith
Each object, thoroughly revealed might view
And comprehend the old things thus made new,
So that while eye saw, soul to tongue could trust
Thing which struck word out, and once more adjust
Real vision to right language, till heaven's vault
Pompous with sunset, storm-stirred sea's assault
On the swilled rock-ridge, earth's embosomed brood
Of tree and flower and weed, with all the life
That flies or swims or crawls, in peace or strife,
Above, below,—each had its note and name
For Man to know by,—Man who, now—the same
As erst in Eden, needs that all he sees
Be named him ere he note by what degrees

CHRISTOPHER SMART (1722-1771)

Of strength and beauty to its end Design
Ever thus operates—(your thought and mine,
No matter for the many dissident)—
So did you sing your Song, so truth found vent
In words for once with you?

VIII

Then—back was furled
The robe thus thrown aside, and straight the world
Darkened into the old oft-catalogued
Repository of things that sky, wave, land,
Or show or hide, clear late, accretion-clogged
Now, just as long ago, by tellings and
Re-tellings to satiety, which strike
Muffled upon the ear's drum. Very like
None was so startled as yourself when friends
Came, hailed your fast-returning wits: "Health mends
Importantly, for—to be plain with you—
This scribble on the wall was done—in lieu
Of pen and paper—with—ha, ha!—your key
Denting it on the wainscot! Do you see
How wise our caution was? Thus much we stopped
Of babble that had else grown print: and lopped
From your trim bay-tree this unsightly bough—
Smart's who translated Horace! Write us now" . . .
Why, what Smart did write—never afterward
One line to show that he, who paced the sward,
Had reached the zenith from his madhouse cell.

IX

Was it because you judged (I know full well
You never had the fancy)—judged—as some—
That who makes poetry must reproduce
Thus ever and thus only, as they come,
Each strength, each beauty, everywhere diffuse
Throughout creation, so that eye and ear,
Seeing and hearing, straight shall recognize,
At touch of just a trait, the strength appear,—

CHRISTOPHER SMART (1722-1771)

Suggested by a line's lapse see arise
All evident the beauty,—fresh surprise
Startling at fresh achievement? "So, indeed,
Wallows the whale's bulk in the waste of brine,
Nor otherwise its feather-tufts make fine
Wild Virgin's Bower when stars faint off to seed!"
(My prose—your poetry I dare not give,
Purpling too much my mere gray argument.)
—Was it because you judged—when fugitive
Was glory found, and wholly gone and spent
Such power of startling up deaf ear, blind eye,
At truth's appearance,—that you humbly bent
The head and, bidding vivid work good-by,
Doffed lyric dress and trod the world once more
A drab-clothed decent proseman as before?
Strengths, beauties, by one word's flash thus laid bare
—That was effectual service: made aware
Of strengths and beauties, Man but hears the text,
Awaits your teaching. Nature? What comes next?
Why all the strength and beauty?—to be shown
Thus in one word's flash, thenceforth let alone
By Man who needs must deal with aught that's known
Never so lately and so little? Friend,
First give us knowledge, then appoint its use!
Strength, beauty are the means: ignore their end?
As well you stopped at proving how profuse
Stones, sticks, nay stubble lie to left and right
Ready to help the builder,—careless quite
If he should take, or leave the same to strew
Earth idly,—as by word's flash bring in view
Strength, beauty, then bid who beholds the same
Go on beholding. Why gains unemployed?
Nature was made to be by Man enjoyed
First; followed duly by enjoyment's fruit,
Instruction—haply leaving joy behind:
And you, the instructor, would you slack pursuit
Of the main prize, as poet help mankind
Just to enjoy, there leave them? Play the fool,
Abjuring a superior privilege?

CHRISTOPHER SMART (1722–1771)

Please simply when your function is to rule—
By thoughts incite to deed? From edge to edge
Of earth's round, strength and beauty everywhere
Pullulate—and must you particularize
All, each and every apparition? Spare
Yourself and us the trouble! Ears and eyes
Want so much strength and beauty, and no less
Nor more, to learn life's lesson by. Oh, yes—
The other method's favored in our day!
The end ere the beginning: as you may
Master the heavens before you study earth,
Make you familiar with the meteor's birth
Ere you descend to scrutinize the rose!
I say, o'erstep no least one of the rows
That lead man from the bottom where he plants
Foot first of all, to life's last ladder-top:
Arrived there, vain enough will seem the vaunts
Of those who say—"We scale the skies, then drop
To earth—to find, how all things there are loth
To answer heavenly law: we understand
The meteor's course, and lo, the rose's growth—
How other than should be by law's command!"
Would not you tell such—"Friends, beware lest fume
Offuscate sense: learn earth first ere presume
To teach heaven legislation. Law must be
Active in earth or nowhere: earth you see,—
Or there or not at all, Will, Power and Love
Admit discovery,—as below, above
Seek next law's confirmation! But reverse
The order, where's the wonder things grow worse
Than, by the law your fancy formulates,
They should be? Cease from anger at the fates
Which thwart themselves so madly. Live and learn,
Not first learn and then live, is our concern.
                                    ROBERT BROWNING
                                      (1812–1889)

SIR WILLIAM JONES (1746-1794)

On the Ingenious Mr. Jones's elegant Translations and Imitations of Eastern Poetry, and his Resolution to decline translating the Persian Poets

The Asian Muse, a stranger fair!
Becomes at length Britannia's care;
And Hafiz' lays, and Sadi's strains,
Resound along our Thames's plains.
They sing not all of streams and bowers,
Or banquet scenes, or social hours;
Nor all of Beauty's blooming charms,
Or War's rude fields, or feats of arms;
But Freedom's lofty notes sincere,
And Virtue's moral lore severe,
But ah! they sing for us no more!
The scarcely-tasted pleasure's o'er!
For he, the bard whose tuneful art
Can best their vary'd themes impart—
For he, alas! the task declines;
And Taste, at loss irreparable, repines.

JOHN SCOTT
(1730–1783)

WILLIAM COWPER (1731-1800)

Cowper

Cowper, the poet of the fields
  Who found the muse on common ground—
The homesteads that each cottage shields
  He loved—and made them classic ground.

The lonely house, the rural walk
  He sang so musically true,
E'en now they share the people's talk
  Who love the poet Cowper too.

WILLIAM COWPER (1731-1800)

> Who has not read the 'Winter Storm,'
>   And does not feel the falling snow
> And woodmen keeping noses warm
>   With pipes wherever forests grow?
>
> The 'Winter's Walk' and 'Summer's Noon'—
>   We meet together by the fire
> And think the walks are o'er too soon
>   When books are read and we retire.
>
> Who travels o'er those sweet fields now
>   And brings not Cowper to his mind?
> Birds sing his name in every bough,
>   Nature repeats it in the wind.
>
> And every place the poet trod
>   And every place the poet sung
> Are like the Holy Land of God,
>   In every mouth, on every tongue.

JOHN CLARE
(1793–1864)

Cowper's Grave

I

It is a place where poets crowned may feel the heart's decaying;
It is a place where happy saints may weep amid their praying;
Yet let the grief and humbleness as low as silence languish:
Earth surely now may give her calm to whom she gave her anguish.

II

O poets, from a maniac's tongue was poured the deathless singing!
O Christians, at your cross of hope a hopeless hand was clinging!
O men, this man in brotherhood your weary paths beguiling,
Groaned inly while he taught you peace, and died while ye were smiling!

III

And now, what time ye all may read through dimming tears his story,
How discord on the music fell and darkness on the glory,

WILLIAM COWPER (1731-1800)

And how when, one by one, sweet sounds and wandering lights departed,
He wore no less a loving face because so broken-hearted,

IV

He shall be strong to sanctify the poet's high vocation,
And bow the meekest Christian down in meeker adoration;
Nor ever shall he be, in praise, by wise or good forsaken,
Named softly as the household name of one whom God hath taken.

V

With quiet sadness and no gloom I learn to think upon him,
With meekness that is gratefulness to God whose heaven hath won him,
Who suffered once the madness-cloud to His own love to blind him,
But gently led the blind along where breath and bird could find him;

VI

And wrought within his shattered brain such quick poetic senses
As hills have language for, and stars, harmonious influences:
The pulse of dew upon the grass kept his within its number,
And silent shadows from the trees refreshed him like a slumber.

VII

Wild timid hares were drawn from woods to share his home-caresses,
Uplooking to his human eyes with sylvan tendernesses:
The very world, by God's constraint, from falsehood's ways removing,
Its women and its men became, beside him, true and loving.

VIII

And though, in blindness, he remained unconscious of that guiding,
And things provided came without the sweet sense of providing,
He testified this solemn truth, while frenzy desolated,
—Nor man nor nature satisfies whom only God created.

IX

Like a sick child that knoweth not his mother while she blesses
And drops upon his burning brow the coolness of her kisses,—

WILLIAM COWPER (1731-1800)

That turns his fevered eyes around,—"My mother! where's my mother?"—
As if such tender words and deeds could come from any other!—

X

The fever gone, with leaps of heart he sees her bending o'er him,
Her face all pale from watchful love,—the unweary love she bore him!—
Thus woke the poet from the dream his life's long fever gave him,
Beneath those deep pathetic Eyes which closed in death to save him;

XI

Thus? oh, not *thus!* no type of earth can image that awaking,
Wherein he scarcely heard the chant of seraphs, round him breaking,
Or felt the new immortal throb of soul from body parted,
But felt those eyes alone, and knew—"*My* Saviour! *not* deserted!"

XII

Deserted! Who hath dreamt that when the cross in darkness rested,
Upon the Victim's hidden face no love was manifested?
What frantic hands outstretched have e'er the atoning drops averted?
What tears have washed them from the soul, that *one* should be deserted?

XIII

Deserted! God could separate from his own essence rather;
And Adam's sins *have* swept between the righteous Son and Father:
Yea, once Immanuel's orphaned cry his universe hath shaken—
It went up single, echoless, "My God, I am forsaken!"

XIV

It went up from the Holy's lips amid his lost creation,
That, of the lost, no son should use those words of desolation!
That earth's worst frenzies, marring hope, should mar not hope's fruition,
And I, on Cowper's grave, should see his rapture in a vision.

ELIZABETH BARRETT BROWNING
(1806-1861)

VI

THOMAS CHATTERTON (1752–1770)

Monody on the Death of Chatterton

    Now prompts the Muse poetic lays,
    And high my bosom beats with love of Praise!
    But, Chatterton! methinks I hear thy name,
For cold my Fancy grows, and dead each Hope of Fame.

    When Want and cold Neglect had chill'd thy soul,
Athirst for Death I see thee drench the bowl!
      Thy corpse of many a livid hue
      On the bare ground I view,
    Whilst various passions all my mind engage;
      Now is my breast distended with a sigh,
      And now a flash of Rage
Darts through the tear, that glistens in my eye.

    Is this the land of liberal Hearts!
    Is this the land, where Genius ne'er in vain
Pour'd forth her soul-enchanting strain?
    Ah me! yet Butler 'gainst the bigot foe
      Well-skill'd to aim keen Humour's dart,
      Yet Butler felt Want's poignant sting;
      And Otway, Master of the Tragic art,
      Whom Pity's self had taught to sing,
    Sank beneath a load of Woe;
This ever can the generous Briton hear,
And starts not in his eye th' indignant Tear?

    Elate of Heart and confident of Fame,
From vales where Avon sports, the Minstrel came,
      Gay as the Poet hastes along
      He meditates the future song,

THOMAS CHATTERTON (1752-1770)

How Ælla battled with his country's foes,
   And whilst Fancy in the air
   Paints him many a vision fair
His eyes dance rapture and his bosom glows.
With generous joy he views th' ideal gold:
   He listens to many a Widow's prayers,
   And many an Orphan's thanks he hears;
     He soothes to peace the care-worn breast,
     He bids the Debtor's eyes know rest,
   And Liberty and Bliss behold:
And now he punishes the heart of steel,
And her own iron rod he makes Oppression feel.

Fated to heave sad Disappointment's sigh,
To feel the Hope now rais'd, and now deprest,
To feel the burnings of an injur'd breast,
   From all thy Fate's deep sorrow keen
   In vain, O Youth, I turn th' affrighted eye;
   For powerful Fancy evernigh
The hateful picture forces on my sight.
   There, Death of every dear delight,
   Frowns Poverty of Giant mien!
In vain I seek the charms of youthful grace,
Thy sunken eye, thy haggard cheeks it shews,
The quick emotions struggling in the Face
   Faint index of thy mental Throes,
When each strong Passion spurn'd controll,
And not a Friend was nigh to calm thy stormy soul.

Such was the sad and gloomy hour
When anguish'd Care of sullen brow
Prepared the Poison's death-cold power.
Already to thy lips was rais'd the bowl,
   When filial Pity stood thee by,
   Thy fixéd eyes she bade thee roll
On scenes that well might melt thy soul—
   Thy native cot she held to view,
   Thy native cot, where Peace ere long
   Had listen'd to thy evening song;

THOMAS CHATTERTON (1752–1770)

Thy sister's shrieks she bade thee hear,
And mark thy mother's thrilling tear,
She made thee feel her deep-drawn sigh,
And all her silent agony of Woe.

And from *thy* Fate shall such distress ensue?
Ah! dash the poison'd chalice from thy hand!
And thou had'st dash'd it at her soft command;
But that Despair and Indignation rose,
And told again the story of thy Woes,
Told the keen insult of th' unfeeling Heart,
The dread dependence on the low-born mind,
Told every Woe, for which thy breast might smart,
Neglect and grinning scorn and Want combin'd—
    Recoiling back, thou sent'st the friend of Pain
To roll a tide of Death thro' every freezing vein.

    O Spirit blest!
Whether th' eternal Throne around,
Amidst the blaze of Cherubim,
Thou pourest forth the grateful hymn,
Or, soaring through the blest Domain,
Enraptur'st Angels with thy strain,—
Grant me, like thee, the lyre to sound,
Like thee, with fire divine to glow—
But ah! when rage the Waves of Woe,
Grant me with firmer breast t'oppose their hate,
And soar beyond the storms with upright eye elate!

                             SAMUEL TAYLOR COLERIDGE
                                    (1772–1834)

THOMAS CHATTERTON (1752-1770)

From "Resolution and Independence"

I thought of Chatterton, the marvellous Boy,
The sleepless Soul that perished in his pride;
Of Him who walked in glory and in joy
Following his plough, along the mountain-side:
By our own spirits are we deified:
We Poets in our youth begin in gladness;
But thereof come in the end despondency and madness.
WILLIAM WORDSWORTH
(1770–1850)

To Chatterton

O Chatterton! how very sad thy fate!
   Dear child of sorrow—son of misery!
   How soon the film of death obscur'd that eye,
Whence Genius mildly flash'd, and high debate.
How soon that voice, majestic and elate,
   Melted in dying numbers! Oh! how nigh
   Was night to thy fair morning. Thou didst die
A half-blown flow'ret which cold blasts amate.
But this is past: thou art among the stars
   Of highest Heaven: to the rolling spheres
Thou sweetly singest: nought thy hymning mars,
   Above the ingrate world and human fears.
On earth the good man base detraction bars
   From thy fair name, and waters it with tears.
JOHN KEATS
(1795–1821)

Thomas Chatterton

With Shakspeare's manhood at a boy's wild heart,—
   Through Hamlet's doubt to Shakspeare near allied,
   And kin to Milton through his Satan's pride,—
At Death's sole door he stooped, and craved a dart;
And to the dear new bower of England's art,—
   Even to that shrine Time else had deified,
   The unuttered heart that soared against his side,—

THOMAS CHATTERTON (1752-1770)

Drove the fell point, and smote life's seals apart.
Thy nested home-loves, noble Chatterton;
  The angel-trodden stair thy soul could trace
  Up Redcliffe's spire; and in the world's armed space
Thy gallant sword-play:—these to many an one
Are sweet for ever; as thy grave unknown
  And love-dream of thine unrecorded face.
DANTE GABRIEL ROSSETTI
(1828-1882)

GEORGE CRABBE (1754-1832)

From "English Bards and Scotch Reviewers"

There be who say, in these enlighten'd days,
That splendid lies are all the poet's praise;
That strain'd invention, ever on the wing,
Alone impels the modern bard to sing.
'T is true that all who rhyme—nay, all who write,
Shrink from that fatal word to genius—trite;
Yet Truth sometimes will lend her noblest fires,
And decorate the verse herself inspires:
This fact in Virtue's name let Crabbe attest;
Though nature's sternest painter, yet her best.
LORD BYRON
(1788-1824)

George Crabbe

Give him the darkest inch your shelf allows,
Hide him in lonely garrets, if you will,—
But his hard, human pulse is throbbing still
With the sure strength that fearless truth endows.
In spite of all fine science disavows,
Of his plain excellence and stubborn skill
There yet remains what fashion cannot kill,
Though years have thinned the laurel from his brows.
Whether or not we read him, we can feel
From time to time the vigor of his name
Against us like a finger for the shame

GEORGE CRABBE (1754-1832)

And emptiness of what our souls reveal
In books that are as altars where we kneel
To consecrate the flicker, not the flame.
EDWIN ARLINGTON ROBINSON
(1869-1935)

FRIEDRICH VON SCHILLER (1759-1805)

To the Author of "The Robbers"

Schiller! that hour I would have wish'd to die.
If through the shuddering midnight I had sent
From the dark dungeon of the Tower time-rent
That fearful voice, a famish'd Father's cry—
Lest in some after moment aught more mean
Might stamp me mortal! A triumphant shout
Black Horror scream'd, and all her goblin rout
Diminish'd shrunk from the more withering scene!
Ah! Bard tremendous in sublimity!
Could I behold thee in thy loftier mood
Wandering at eve with finely frenzied eye
Beneath some vast old tempest-swinging wood!
Awhile with mute awe gazing I would brood:
Then weep aloud in a wild ecstasy.
SAMUEL TAYLOR COLERIDGE
(1772-1834)

WILLIAM BLAKE (1757-1827)

William Blake

(To Frederick Shields, on His Sketch of Blake's Workroom and Death-room, 3, Fountain Court, Strand.)

This is the place. Even here the dauntless soul,
  The unflinching hand, wrought on; till in that nook,
  As on that very bed, his life partook
New birth, and passed. Yon river's dusky shoal,
  Whereto the close-built coiling lanes unroll,
    Faced his work-window, whence his eyes would stare,
    Thought-wandering, unto nought that met them there,

WILLIAM BLAKE (1757–1827)

> But to the unfettered irreversible goal.
> This cupboard, Holy of Holies, held the cloud
>   Of his soul writ and limned; this other one,
> His true wife's charge, full oft to their abode
>   Yielded for daily bread the martyr's stone,
>   Ere yet their food might be that Bread alone,
> The words now home-speech of the mouth of God.

DANTE GABRIEL ROSSETTI
(1828–1882)

William Blake

He came to the desert of London town
  Grey miles long;
He wandered up and he wandered down,
  Singing a quiet song.

He came to the desert of London town,
  Mirk miles broad;
He wandered up and he wandered down,
  Ever alone with God.

There were thousands and thousands of human kind
  In this desert of brick and stone:
But some were deaf and some were blind,
  And he was there alone.

At length the good hour came; he died
  As he had lived, alone:
He was not missed from the desert wide,
  Perhaps he was found at the Throne

JAMES THOMSON
(1834–1882)

ROBERT BURNS (1759-1796)

At the Grave of Burns
1803

Seven Years after His Death

I shiver, Spirit fierce and bold,
At thought of what I now behold:
As vapours breathed from dungeons cold
    Strike pleasure dead,
So sadness comes from out the mould
    Where Burns is laid.

And have I then thy bones so near,
And thou forbidden to appear?
As if it were thyself that's here
    I shrink with pain;
And both my wishes and my fear
    Alike are vain.

Off weight—nor press on weight!—away
Dark thoughts!—they came, but not to stay;
With chastened feelings would I pay
    The tribute due
To him, and aught that hides his clay
    From mortal view.

Fresh as the flower, whose modest worth
He sang, his genius "glinted" forth,
Rose like a star that touching earth,
    For so it seems,
Doth glorify its humble birth
    With matchless beams.

The piercing eye, the thoughtful brow,
The struggling heart, where be they now?—
Full soon the Aspirant of the plough,
    The prompt, the brave,
Slept, with the obscurest, in the low
    And silent grave.

ROBERT BURNS (1759-1796)

I mourned with thousands, but as one
More deeply grieved, for He was gone
Whose light I hailed when first it shone.
    And showed my youth
How Verse may build a princely throne
    On humble truth.

Alas! where er the current tends,
Regret pursues and with it blends,—
Huge Criffel's hoary top ascends
    By Skiddaw seen,—
Neighbours we were, and loving friends
    We might have been;

True friends though diversely inclined;
But heart with heart and mind with mind,
Where the main fibres are entwined,
    Through Nature's skill,
May even by contraries be joined
    More closely still.

The tear will start, and let it flow;
Thou "poor Inhabitant below,"
At this dread moment—even so—
    Might we together
Have sate and talked where gowans blow,
    Or on wild heather.

What treasures would have then been placed
Within my reach; of knowledge graced
By fancy what a rich repast!
    But why go on?—
Oh! spare to sweep, thou mournful blast,
    His grave grass-grown.

There, too, a Son, his joy and pride,
(Not three weeks past the Stripling died,)
Lies gathered to his Father's side,
    Soul-moving sight!
Yet one to which is not denied
    Some sad delight:

ROBERT BURNS (1759–1796)

> For *he* is safe, a quiet bed
> Hath early found among the dead,
> Harboured where none can be misled,
> > Wronged, or distrest;
> And surely here it may be said
> > That such are blest.
>
> And oh for Thee, by pitying grace
> Checked oft-times in a devious race,
> May He who halloweth the place
> > Where Man is laid
> Receive thy Spirit in the embrace
> > For which it prayed!
>
> Sighing I turned away; but ere
> Night fell I heard, or seemed to hear,
> Music that sorrow comes not near.
> > A ritual hymn,
> Chaunted in love that casts out fear
> > By Seraphim.
>
> WILLIAM WORDSWORTH
(1770–1850)

Robert Burns

> I see amid the fields of Ayr
> A ploughman, who, in foul and fair,
> > Sings at his task
> So clear, we know not if it is
> The laverock's song we hear, or his,
> > Nor care to ask.
>
> For him the ploughing of those fields
> A more ethereal harvest yields
> > Than sheaves of grain;
> Songs flush with purple bloom the rye,
> The plover's call, the curlew's cry,
> > Sing in his brain.
>
> Touched by his hand, the wayside weed
> Becomes a flower; the lowliest reed
> > Beside the stream

ROBERT BURNS (1759–1796)

    Is clothed with beauty; gorse and grass
    And heather, where his footsteps pass,
        The brighter seem.

    He sings of love, whose flame illumes
    The darkness of lone cottage rooms;
        He feels the force,
    The treacherous undertow and stress
    Of wayward passions, and no less
        The keen remorse.

    At moments, wrestling with his fate,
    His voice is harsh, but not with hate;
        The brush-wood, hung
    Above the tavern door, lets fall
    Its bitter leaf, its drop of gall
        Upon his tongue.

    But still the music of his song
    Rises o'er all, elate and strong;
        Its master-chords
    Are Manhood, Freedom, Brotherhood,
    Its discords but an interlude
        Between the words.

    And then to die so young and leave
    Unfinished what he might achieve!
        Yet better sure
    Is this, than wandering up and down,
    An old man in a country town,
        Infirm and poor.

    For now he haunts his native land
    As an immortal youth; his hand
        Guides every plough;
    He sits beside each ingle-nook,
    His voice is in each rushing brook,
        Each rustling bough.

ROBERT BURNS (1759–1796)

> His presence haunts this room to-night,
> A form of mingled mist and light
>   From that far coast.
> Welcome beneath this roof of mine!
> Welcome! this vacant chair is thine,
>   Dear guest and ghost!
>   HENRY WADSWORTH LONGFELLOW
>   (1807–1882)

Burns

On Receiving a Sprig of Heather in Blossom

No more these simple flowers belong
  To Scottish maid and lover;
Sown in the common soil of song,
  They bloom the wide world over.

In smiles and tears, in sun and showers,
  The minstrel and the heather,
The deathless singer and the flowers
  He sang of live together.

Wild heather-bells and Robert Burns!
  The moorland flower and peasant!
How, at their mention, memory turns
  Her pages old and pleasant!

The gray sky wears again its gold
  And purple of adorning,
And manhood's noonday shadows hold
  The dews of boyhood's morning.

The dews that washed the dust and soil
  From off the wings of pleasure,
The sky, that flecked the ground of toil
  With golden threads of leisure.

ROBERT BURNS (1759–1796)

I call to mind the summer day,
   The early harvest mowing,
The sky with sun and clouds at play,
   And flowers with breezes blowing.

I hear the blackbird in the corn,
   The locust in the haying;
And, like the fabled hunter's horn,
   Old tunes my heart is playing.

How oft that day, with fond delay,
   I sought the maple's shadow,
And sang with Burns the hours away,
   Forgetful of the meadow!

Bees hummed, birds twittered, overhead
   I heard the squirrels leaping,
The good dog listened while I read,
   And wagged his tail in keeping.

I watched him while in sportive mood
   I read *"The Twa Dogs"* story,
And half believed he understood
   The poet's allegory.

Sweet day, sweet songs!—The golden hours
   Grew brighter for that singing,
From brook and bird and meadow flowers
   A dearer welcome bringing.

New light on home-seen Nature beamed,
   New glory over Woman;
And daily life and duty seemed
   No longer poor and common.

I woke to find the simple truth
   Of fact and feeling better
Than all the dreams that held my youth
   A still repining debtor:

ROBERT BURNS (1759-1796)

    That Nature gives her handmaid, Art,
      The themes of sweet discoursing;
    The tender idyls of the heart
      In every tongue rehearsing.

    Why dream of lands of gold and pearl,
      Of loving knight and lady,
    When farmer boy and barefoot girl
      Were wandering there already?

    I saw through all familiar things
      The romance underlying;
    The joys and griefs that plume the wings
      Of Fancy skyward flying.

    I saw the same blithe day return,
      The same sweet fall of even,
    That rose on wooded Craigie-burn,
      And sank on crystal Devon.

    I matched with Scotland's heathery hills
      The sweetbrier and the clover;
    With Ayr and Doon, my native rills,
      Their wood-hymns chanting over.

    O'er rank and pomp, as he had seen,
      I saw the Man uprising;
    No longer common or unclean,
      The child of God's baptizing!

    With clearer eyes I saw the worth
      Of life among the lowly;
    The Bible at his Cotter's hearth
      Had made my own more holy.

    And if at times an evil strain,
      To lawless love appealing,
    Broke in upon the sweet refrain
      Of pure and healthful feeling,

ROBERT BURNS (1759-1796)

It died upon the eye and ear,
    No inward answer gaining;
No heart had I to see or hear
    The discord and the staining.

Let those who never erred forget
    His worth, in vain bewailings;
Sweet Soul of Song!—I own my debt
    Uncancelled by his failings!

Lament who will the ribald line
    Which tells his lapse from duty
How kissed the maddening lips of wine
    Or wanton ones of beauty;

But think, while falls that shade between
    The erring one and Heaven,
That he who loved like Magdalen,
    Like her may be forgiven.

Not his the song whose thunderous chime
    Eternal echoes render,—
The mournful Tuscan's haunted rhyme,
    And Milton's starry splendor!

But who his human heart has laid
    To Nature's bosom nearer?
Who sweetened toil like him, or paid
    To love a tribute dearer?

Through all his tuneful art, how strong
    The human feeling gushes!
The very moonlight of his song
    Is warm with smiles and blushes!

Give lettered pomp to teeth of Time,
    So "Bonnie Doon" but tarry;
Blot out the Epic's stately rhyme,
    But spare his Highland Mary!
        JOHN GREENLEAF WHITTIER
            (1807-1892)

FRIEDRICH HÖLDERLIN (1770–1843)

Hölderlin's Journey

When Hölderlin started from Bordeaux
   He was not mad but lost in mind,
For time and space had fled away
   With her he had to find.

"The morning bells rang over France
   From tower to tower. At noon I came
Into a maze of little hills,
   Head-high and every hill the same.

"A little world of emerald hills,
   And at their heart a faint bell tolled;
Wedding or burial, who could say?
   For death, unseen, is bold.

"Too small to climb, too tall to show
   More than themselves, the hills lay round.
Nearer to her, or farther? They
   Might have stretched to the world's bound.

"A shallow candour was their all,
   And the mean riddle, How to tally
Reality with such appearance?
   When in the nearest valley

"Perhaps already she I sought,
   She, sought and seeker, had gone by,
And each of us in turn was trapped
   By simple treachery.

"The evening brought a field, a wood.
   I left behind the hills of lies, .
And watched beside a mouldering gate
   A deer with its rock-crystal eyes.

"On either pillar of the gate
   A deer's head watched within the stone.
The living deer with quiet look
   Seemed to be gazing on

FRIEDRICH HÖLDERLIN (1770–1843)

"It's pictured death—and suddenly
    I knew, Diotima was dead,
As if a single thought had sprung
    From the cold and the living head.

"That image held me and I saw
    All moving things so still and sad,
But till I came into the mountains
    I know I was not mad.

"What made the change? The hills and towers
    Stood otherwise than they should stand,
And without fear the lawless roads
    Ran wrong through all the land.

"Upon the swarming towns of iron
    The bells hailed down their iron peals,
Above the iron bell the swallows
    Glided on iron wheels.

"And there I watched in one confounded
    The living and the unliving head.
Why should it be? For now I know
    Diotima was dead

"Before I left the starting place;
    Empty the course, the garland gone,
And all that race as motionless
    As these two heads of stone."

So Hölderlin mused for thirty years
    On a green hill by Tübingen,
Dragging in pain a broken mind
    And giving thanks to God and men.

                      EDWIN MUIR
                      (1887–   )

WILLIAM WORDSWORTH (1770-1850)

To William Wordsworth

*Composed on the Night After His Recitation
of a Poem on the Growth of an Individual Mind*

Friend of the wise! and Teacher of the Good!
Into my heart have I received that Lay
More than historic, that prophetic Lay
Wherein (high theme by thee first sung aright)
Of the foundations and the building up
Of a Human Spirit thou hast dared to tell
What may be told, to the understanding mind
Revealable; and what within the mind
By vital breathings secret as the soul
Of vernal growth, oft quickens in the heart
Thoughts all too deep for words!—

                              Theme hard as high!
Of smiles spontaneous, and mysterious fears
(The first-born they of Reason and twin-birth),
Of tides obedient to external force,
And currents self-determined, as might seem,
Or by some inner Power; of moments awful,
Now in thy inner life, and now abroad,
When power streamed from thee, and thy soul received
The light reflected, as a light bestowed—
Of fancies fair, and milder hours of youth,
Hyblean murmurs of poetic thought
Industrious in its joy, in vales and glens
Native or outland, lakes and famous hills!
Or on the lonely high-road, when the stars
Were rising; or by secret mountain-streams,
The guides and the companions of thy way!

Of more than Fancy, of the Social Sense
Distending wide, and man beloved as man,
Where France in all her towns lay vibrating
Like some becalmèd bark beneath the burst
Of Heaven's immediate thunder, when no cloud
Is visible, or shadow on the main.

WILLIAM WORDSWORTH (1770–1850)

For thou wert there, thine own brows garlanded,
Amid the tremor of a realm aglow,
Amid a mighty nation jubilant,
When from the general heart of human kind
Hope sprang forth like a full-born Deity!
—Of that dear Hope afflicted and struck down,
So summoned homeward, thenceforth calm and sure
From the dread watch-tower of man's absolute self,
With light unwaning on her eyes, to look
Far on—herself a glory to behold,
The Angel of the vision! Then (last strain)
Of Duty, chosen Laws controlling choice,
Action and joy!—An Orphic song indeed,
A song divine of high and passionate thoughts
To their own music chaunted!

       O great Bard!
Ere yet that last strain dying awed the air,
With stedfast eye I viewed thee in the choir
Of ever-enduring men. The truly great
Have all one age, and from one visible space
Shed influence! They, both in power and act,
Are permanent, and Time is not with them,
Save as it worketh for them, they in it.
Nor less a sacred Roll, than those of old,
And to be placed, as they, with gradual fame
Among the archives of mankind, thy work
Makes audible a linkèd lay of Truth,
Of Truth profound a sweet continuous lay,
Not learnt, but native, her own natural notes!
Ah! as I listened with a heart forlorn,
The pulses of my being beat anew:
And even as Life returns upon the drowned,
Life's joy rekindling roused a throng of pains—
Keen pangs of Love, awakening as a babe
Turbulent, with an outcry in the heart;
And fears self-willed, that shunned the eye of Hope;
And Hope that scarce would know itself from Fear;

WILLIAM WORDSWORTH (1770–1850)

 Sense of past Youth, and Manhood come in vain,
And Genius given, and Knowledge won in vain;
And all which I had culled in wood-walks wild,
And all which patient toil had reared, and all,
Commune with thee had opened out—but flowers
Strewed on my corse, and borne upon my bier
In the same coffin, for the self-same grave!
 That way no more! and ill beseems it me,
Who came a welcomer in herald's guise,
Singing of Glory, and Futurity,
To wander back on such unhealthful road,
Plucking the poisons of self-harm! And ill
Such intertwine beseems triumphal wreaths
Strew'd before thy advancing!

       Nor do thou,
Sage Bard! impair the memory of that hour
Of thy communion with my nobler mind
By pity or grief, already felt too long!
Nor let my words import more blame than needs.
The tumult rose and ceased: for Peace is nigh
Where Wisdom's voice has found a listening heart.
Amid the howl of more than wintry storms,
The Halcyon hears the voice of vernal hours
Already on the wing.

      Eve following eve,
Dear tranquil time, when the sweet sense of Home
Is sweetest! moments for their own sake hailed
And more desired, more precious, for thy song,
In silence listening, like a devout child,
My soul lay passive, by thy various strain
Driven as in surges now beneath the stars,
With momentary stars of my own birth,
Fair constellated foam, still darting off
Into the darkness; now a tranquil sea,
Outspread and bright, yet swelling to the moon.

WILLIAM WORDSWORTH (1770–1850)

    And when—O Friend! my comforter and guide!
    Strong in thyself, and powerful to give strength!—
    Thy long sustainéd Song finally closed,
    And thy deep voice had ceased—yet thou thyself
    Wert still before my eyes, and round us both
    That happy vision of belovéd faces—
    Scarce conscious, and yet conscious of its close
    I sate, my being blended in one thought
    (Thought was it? or aspiration? or resolve?)
    Absorbed, yet hanging still upon the sound—
    And when I rose, I found myself in prayer.
                           SAMUEL TAYLOR COLERIDGE
                                    (1772–1834)

January, 1807

To Wordsworth

    Poet of Nature, thou hast wept to know
      That things depart which never may return;
      Childhood and youth, friendship and love's first glow,
      Have fled like sweet dreams, leaving thee to mourn.
    These common woes I feel. One loss is mine,
      Which thou too feel'st, yet I alone deplore;
      Thou wert as a lone star whose light did shine
      On some frail bark in winter's midnight roar;
    Thou hast like to a rock-built refuge stood
      Above the blind and battling multitude;
      In honored poverty thy voice did weave
    Songs consecrate to truth and liberty,—
      Deserting these, thou leavest me to grieve,
      Thus having been, that thou shouldst cease to be.
                                    PERCY BYSSHE SHELLEY
                                          (1792–1822)

WILLIAM WORDSWORTH (1770–1850)
The Lost Leader

Just for a handful of silver he left us,
   Just for a riband to stick in his coat—
Found the one gift of which fortune bereft us,
   Lost all the others she lets us devote;
They, with the gold to give, doled him out silver,
   So much was theirs who so little allowed:
How all our copper had gone for his service!
   Rags—were they purple, his heart had been proud!
We that loved him so, followed him, honored him,
   Lived in his mild and magnificent eye,
Learned his great language, caught his clear accents,
   Made him our pattern to live and to die!
Shakespeare was of us, Milton was for us,
   Burns, Shelley, were with us,—they watch from their graves!
He alone breaks from the van and the freemen,
   —He alone sinks to the rear and the slaves!

We shall march prospering,—not through his presence;
   Songs may inspirit us,—not from his lyre;
Deeds will be done,—while he boasts his quiescence,
   Still bidding crouch whom the rest bade aspire:
Blot out his name, then, record one lost soul more,
   One task more declined, one more footpath untrod,
One more devils'-triumph and sorrow for angels,
   One wrong more to man, one more insult to God!
Life's night begins: let him never come back to us!
   There would be doubt, hesitation and pain,
Forced praise on our part—the glimmer of twilight,
   Never glad confident morning again!
Best fight on well, for we taught him—strike gallantly,
   Menace our heart ere we master his own;
Then let him receive the new knowledge and wait us,
   Pardoned in heaven, the first by the throne!

                                            Robert Browning
                                              (1812–1889)

WILLIAM WORDSWORTH (1770–1850)

On a Portrait of Wordsworth by B. R. Haydon

Wordsworth upon Helvellyn! Let the cloud
Ebb audibly along the mountain-wind,
Then break against the rock, and show behind
The lowland valleys floating up to crowd
The sense with beauty. He with forehead bowed
And humble-lidded eyes, as one inclined
Before the sovran thought of his own mind,
And very meek with inspirations proud,
Takes here his rightful place as poet-priest
By the high altar, singing prayer and prayer
To the higher Heavens. A noble vision free
Our Haydon's hand has flung out from the mist:
No portrait this, with Academic air!
This is the poet and his poetry.

ELIZABETH BARRETT BROWNING
(1806–1861)

William Wordsworth

1845

Gentle and grave, in simple dress,
And features by keen mountain air
Moulded to solemn ruggedness,
The man we came to see sat there:
Not apt for speech, nor quickly stirr'd
Unless when heart to heart replied;
A bearing equally remov'd
From vain display or sullen pride.

The sinewy frame yet spoke of one
Known to the hillsides: on his head
Some five-and-seventy winters gone
Their crown of perfect white had shed:—
As snow-tipp'd summits toward the sun

WILLIAM WORDSWORTH (1770–1850)

In calm of lonely radiance press,
Touch'd by the broadening light of death
With a serener pensiveness.

O crown of venerable age!
O brighter crown of well-spent years!
The bard, the patriot, and the sage,
The heart that never bow'd to fears!
That was an age of soaring souls;
Yet none with a more liberal scope
Survey'd the sphere of human things;
None with such manliness of hope.

Others, perchance, as keenly felt,
As musically sang as he;
To Nature as devoutly knelt,
Or toil'd to serve humanity:
But none with those ethereal notes,
That star-like sweep of self-control;
The insight into worlds unseen,
The lucid sanity of soul.

The fever of our fretful life,
The autumn poison of the air,
The soul with its own self at strife,
He saw and felt, but could not share:
With eye made clear by pureness, pierced
The life of Man and Nature through;
And read the heart of common things,
Till new seem'd old, and old was new.

To his own self not always just,
Bound in the bonds that all men share,—
Confess the failings as we must,
The lion's mark is always there!
Nor any song so pure, so great
Since his, who closed the sightless eyes,
Our Homer of the war in Heaven,
To wake in his own Paradise.

WILLIAM WORDSWORTH (1770–1850)

    O blaring trumpets of the world!
    O glories, in their budding sere!
    O flaunting roll of Fame unfurl'd!
    Here was the king—the hero here!
    It was a strength and joy for life
    In that great presence once to be;
    That on the boy he gently smil'd,
    That those white hands were laid on me.
              FRANCIS TURNER PALGRAVE
                      (1824–1897)

From "Stanzas in Memory of the Author of 'Obermann'"

By England's lakes, in grey old age,
His quiet home one keeps;
And one, the strong much-toiling Sage,
In German Weimar sleeps.

But Wordworth's eyes avert their ken
From half of human fate;
And Goethe's course few sons of men
May think to emulate.

For he pursued a lonely road,
His eyes on Nature's plan;
Neither made man too much a God,
Nor God too much a man.

Strong was he, with a spirit free
From mists, and sane, and clear;
Clearer, how much! than ours: yet we
Have a worse course to steer.

For though his manhood bore the blast
Of Europe's stormiest time,
Yet in a tranquil world was pass'd
His tender youthful prime.

WILLIAM WORDSWORTH (1770–1850)

But we, brought forth and rear'd in hours
Of change, alarm, surprise—
What shelter to grow ripe is ours?
What leisure to grow wise?

Like children bathing on the shore,
Buried a wave beneath,
The second wave succeeds, before
We have had time to breathe.

Too fast we live, too much are tried,
Too harass'd, to attain
Wordsworth's sweet calm, or Goethe's wide
And luminous view to gain.

MATTHEW ARNOLD
(1822–1888)

Memorial Verses

April, 1850

Goethe in Weimar sleeps, and Greece,
Long since, saw Byron's struggle cease.
But one such death remain'd to come;
The last poetic voice is dumb—
We stand to-day by Wordsworth's tomb.

When Byron's eyes were shut in death,
We bow'd our head and held our breath.
He taught us little; but our soul
Had *felt* him like the thunder's roll.
With shivering heart the strife we saw
Of passion with eternal law;
And yet with reverential awe
We watch'd the fount of fiery life
Which served for that Titanic strife.

When Goethe's death was told, we said:
Sunk, then, is Europe's sagest head.
Physician of the iron age,
Goethe has done his pilgrimage.

WILLIAM WORDSWORTH (1770-1850)

He took the suffering human race,
He read each wound, each weakness clear;
And struck his finger on the place,
And said: *Thou ailest here, and here!*
He look'd on Europe's dying hour
Of fitful dream and feverish power;
His eye plunged down the weltering strife,
The turmoil of expiring life—
He said: *The end is everywhere,
Art still has truth, take refuge there!*
And he was happy, if to know
Causes of things, and far below
His feet to see the lurid flow
Of terror, and insane distress,
And headlong fate, be happiness.

And Wordsworth!—Ah, pale ghosts, rejoice!
For never has such soothing voice
Been to your shadowy world convey'd,
Since erst, at morn, some wandering shade
Heard the clear song of Orpheus come
Through Hades, and the mournful gloom.
Wordsworth has gone from us—and ye,
Ah, may ye feel his voice as we!
He too upon a wintry clime
Had fallen—on this iron time
Of doubts, disputes, distractions, fears.
He found us when the age had bound
Our souls in its benumbing round;
He spoke, and loosed our heart in tears.
He laid us as we lay at birth
On the cool flowery lap of earth,
Smiles broke from us and we had ease;
The hills were round us, and the breeze
Went o'er the sun-lit fields again;
Our foreheads felt the wind and rain.
Our youth return'd; for there was shed
On spirits that had long been dead,
Spirits dried up and closely furl'd,
The freshness of the early world.

WILLIAM WORDSWORTH (1770-1850)

Ah! since dark days still bring to light
Man's prudence and man's fiery might,
Time may restore us in his course
Goethe's sage mind and Byron's force;
But where will Europe's latter hour
Again find Wordsworth's healing power?
Others will teach us how to dare,
And against fear our breast to steel,
Others will strengthen us to bear—
But who, ah! who, will make us feel?
The cloud of mortal destiny,
Others will front it fearlessly—
But who, like him, will put it by?

Keep fresh the grass upon his grave,
O Rotha, with thy living wave!
Sing him thy best! for few or none
Hears thy voice right, now he is gone.

MATTHEW ARNOLD
(1822-1888)

SAMUEL TAYLOR COLERIDGE (1772-1834)

From "The Prelude"
Book VI

* * * * *

I, too, have been a wanderer; but, alas!
How different the fate of different men.
Though mutually unknown, yea, nursed and reared
As if in several elements, we were framed
To bend at last to the same discipline,
Predestined, if two beings ever were,
To seek the same delights, and have one health,
One happiness. Throughout this narrative,
Else sooner ended, I have borne in mind
For whom it registers the birth, and marks the growth,
Of gentleness, simplicity, and truth,
And joyous loves, that hallow innocent days
Of peace and self-command. Of rivers, fields,
And groves I speak to thee, my Friend! to thee,

SAMUEL TAYLOR COLERIDGE (1772–1834)

Who, yet a liveried schoolboy, in the depths
Of the huge city, on the leaded roof
Of that wide edifice, thy school and home,
Wert used to lie and gaze upon the clouds
Moving in heaven; or, of that pleasure tired,
To shut thine eyes, and by internal light
See trees, and meadows, and thy native stream,
Far distant, thus beheld from year to year
Of a long exile. Nor could I forget,
In this late portion of my argument,
That scarcely, as my term of pupilage
Ceased, had I left those academic bowers
When thou wert thither guided. From the heart
Of London, and from cloisters there, thou camest,
And didst sit down in temperance and peace,
A rigorous student. What a stormy course
Then followed. Oh! it is a pang that calls
For utterance, to think what easy change
Of circumstances might to thee have spared
A world of pain, ripened a thousand hopes,
For ever withered. Through this retrospect
Of my collegiate life I still have had
Thy after-sojourn in the self-same place
Present before my eyes, have played with times
And accidents as children do with cards,
Or as a man, who, when his house is built,
A frame locked up in wood and stone, doth still,
As impotent fancy prompts, by his fireside,
Rebuild it to his liking. I have thought
Of thee, thy learning, gorgeous eloquence,
And all the strength and plumage of thy youth,
Thy subtle speculations, toils abstruse
Among the schoolmen, and Platonic forms
Of wild ideal pageantry, shaped out
From things well-matched or ill, and words for things,
The self-created sustenance of a mind
Debarred from Nature's living images
Compelled to be a life unto herself,
And unrelentingly possessed by thirst

SAMUEL TAYLOR COLERIDGE (1772–1834)

    Of greatness, love, and beauty. Not alone,
Ah! surely not in singleness of heart
Should I have seen the light of evening fade
From smooth Cam's silent waters: had we met,
Even at that early time, needs must I trust
In the belief, that my maturer age,
My calmer habits, and more steady voice,
Would with an influence benign have soothed,
Or chased away, the airy wretchedness
That battened on thy youth. But thou hast trod
A march of glory, which doth put to shame
These vain regrets; health suffers in thee, else
Such grief for thee would be the weakest thought
That ever harboured in the breast of man.

          *   *   *   *   *

WILLIAM WORDSWORTH
(1770–1850)

Samuel Taylor Coleridge

His Soul fared forth (as from the deep home-grove
  The father-songster plies the hour-long quest,)
  To feed his soul-brood hungering in the nest;
But his warm Heart, the mother-bird, above
Their callow fledgling progeny still hove
  With tented roof of wings and fostering breast
  Till the Soul fed the soul-brood. Richly blest
From Heaven their growth, whose food was Human Love.
Yet ah! Like desert pools that show the stars
  Once in long leagues,—even such the scarce-snatched hours
  Which deepening pain left to his lordliest powers:—
Heaven lost through spider-trammelled prison-bars.
  Six years, from sixty saved! Yet kindling skies
  Own them, a beacon to our centuries.

DANTE GABRIEL ROSSETTI
(1828–1882)

SAMUEL TAYLOR COLERIDGE (1772–1834)

Coleridge

I see thee pine like her in golden story
Who, in her prison, woke and saw, one day,
The gates thrown open—saw the sunbeams play,
With only a web 'tween her and summer's glory;
Who, when that web—so frail, so transitory
It broke before her breath—had fallen away,
Saw other webs and others rise for aye
Which kept her prison'd till her hair was hoary.
Those songs half-sung that yet were all-divine—
That woke Romance, the queen, to reign afresh—
Had been but preludes from that lyre of thine,
Could thy rare spirit's wings have pierced the mesh
Spun by the wizard who compels the flesh,
But lets the poet see how heav'n can shine.

WALTER THEODORE WATTS–DUNTON
(1832–1914)

ROBERT SOUTHEY (1774–1843)

From "Don Juan"

Dedication

Bob Southey! You're a poet—Poet-laureate,
    And representative of all the race;
Although 'tis true that you turned out a Tory at
    Last—yours has lately been a common case;
And now, my Epic Renegade! what are ye at?
    With all the Lakers, in and out of place?
A nest of tuneful persons, to my eye
Like "four and twenty Blackbirds in a pye;

"Which pye being opened they began to sing"
    (This old song and new simile holds good),
"A dainty dish to set before the King,"
    Or Regent, who admires such kind of food;—
And Coleridge, too, has lately taken wing,
    But like a hawk encumbered with his hood—
Explaining metaphysics to the nation—
I wish he would explain his Explanation.

ROBERT SOUTHEY (1774-1843)

You, Bob! are rather insolent, you know,
  At being disappointed in your wish
To supersede all warblers here below,
  And be the only Blackbird in the dish;
And then you overstrain yourself, or so,
  And tumble downward like the flying fish
Gasping on deck, because you soar too high, Bob
And fall for lack of moisture quite a-dry, Bob!

And Wordsworth, in a rather long "Excursion"
  (I think the quarto holds five hundred pages),
Has given a sample from the vasty version
  Of his new system to perplex the sages;
'Tis poetry—at least by his assertion,
  And may appear so when the dog-star rages—
And he who understands it would be able
To add a story to the Tower of Babel.

* * * * *

Your bays may hide the baldness of your brows—
  Perhaps some virtuous blushes;—let me go—
To you I envy neither fruit nor boughs—
  And for the fame you would engross below,
The field is universal, and allows
  Scope to all such as feel the inherent glow;
Scott, Rogers, Campbell, Moore, and Crabbe will try
'Gainst you the question with posterity.

* * * * *

If, fallen in evils days on evil tongues,
  Milton appealed to the Avenger, Time,
If Time, the Avenger, execrates his wrongs,
  And makes the word "*Miltonic*" mean "*sublime*,"
He deigned not to belie his soul in songs,
  Nor turn his very talent to a crime;
He did not loathe the Sire to laud the Son,
But closed the tyrant-hater he begun.

Think'st thou, could he—the blind Old Man—arise,
  Like Samuel from the grave, to freeze once more
The blood of monarchs with his prophecies,
  Or be alive again—again all hoar

ROBERT SOUTHEY (1774-1843)

With time and trials, and those helpless eyes,
　　And heartless daughters—worn—and pale—and poor;
Would *he* adore a sultan? *he* obey
The intellectual eunuch Castlereagh?

　　　　　*　　*　　*　　*　　*

Meantime, Sir Laureate, I proceed to dedicate,
　　In honest simple verse, this song to you.
And, if in flattering strains I do not predicate,
　　'Tis that I still retain my "buff and blue";
My politics as yet are all to educate:
　　Apostasy's so fashionable, too,
To keep *one* creed's a task grown quite Herculean:
Is it not so, my Tory, Ultra-Julian?

　　　　　　　　　　　　LORD BYRON
　　　　　　　　　　　　(1788-1824)

To Southey, 1833

Indweller of a peaceful vale,
Ravaged erewhile by white-hair'd Dane;
Rare architect of many a wondrous tale,
Which, till Helvellyn's head lie prostrate, shall remain!

From Arno's side I hear thy Derwent flow,
And see methinks the lake below
Reflect thy graceful progeny, more fair
And radiant than the purest waters are,
Even when gurgling in their joy among
The bright and blessed throng
Whom, on her arm recline,
The beauteous Proserpine
With tenderest regretful gaze,
Thinking of Enna's yellow field, surveys.

　　Alas! that snows are shed
　　Upon thy laurel's head,
Hurtled by many cares and many wrongs!
　　Malignity lets none
　　Approach the Delphic throne;
A hundred lane-fed curs bark down Fame's hundred tongues.

ROBERT SOUTHEY (1774-1843)

But this is in the night, when men are slow
    To raise their eyes, when high and low,
The scarlet and the colourless, are one:
    Soon Sleep unbars his noiseless prison,
    And active minds again are risen;
Where are the curs? dream-bound, and whimpering in the sun.

At fife's or lyre's or tabor's sound
The dance of youth, O Southey, runs not round,
But closes at the bottom of the room
Amid the falling dust and deepening gloom,
    Where the weary sit them down,
And Beauty too unbraids, and waits a lovelier crown.

We hurry to the river we must cross,
    And swifter downward every footstep wends;
Happy, who reach it ere they count the loss
    Of half their faculties and half their friends!
    When we are come to it, the stream
    Is not so dreary as they deem
    Who look on it from haunts too dear;
The weak from Pleasure's baths feel most its chilling air!

No firmer breast than thine hath Heaven
    To poet, sage, or hero given:
No heart more tender, none more just
    To that He largely placed in trust:
Therefore shalt thou, whatever date
Of years be thine, with soul elate
Rise up before the Eternal throne,
And hear, in God's own voice, "Well done."

    Not, were that submarine
    Gem-lighted city mine,
Wherein my name, engraven by thy hand,
Above the royal gleam of blazonry shall stand;
    Not, were all Syracuse
    Pour'd forth before my Muse,

ROBERT SOUTHEY (1774-1843)

With Hiero's cars and steeds, and Pindar's lyre
Brightening the path with more than solar fire,
Could I, as would beseem, requite the praise
Showered upon my low head from thy most lofty lays.
WALTER SAVAGE LANDOR
(1775-1864)

WALTER SAVAGE LANDOR (1775-1864)

Landor

Like crown'd athlete that in a race has run,
And points his finger at those left behind,
And follows on his way as now inclin'd,
With song and laughter in the glowing sun;
And joys at that which he hath joyous done,
And, like a child, will wanton with the wind,
And pluck the flowers his radiant brows to bind—
Re-crown himself as conscious he hath won;
And still regardless of his fellow-men
He follows on his road intent and fain
To please himself, and caring not to gain
The world's applause which he might seek in vain:
A soldier, yet would, careless, sport and play
And leave the reckoning for a distant day.
ALEXANDER HAY JAPP
(1837-1905)

In Memory of Walter Savage Landor

 Back to the flower-town, side by side,
  The bright months bring,
 New-born, the bridegroom and the bride,
  Freedom and spring.

 The sweet land laughs from sea to sea,
  Filled full of sun;
 All things come back to her, being free;
  All things but one.

WALTER SAVAGE LANDOR (1775-1864)

In many a tender wheaten plot
    Flowers that were dead
Live, and old suns revive; but not
    That holier head.

By this white wandering waste of sea,
    Far north, I hear
One face shall never turn to me
    As once this year:

Shall never smile and turn and rest
    On mine as there,
Nor one most sacred hand be prest
    Upon my hair.

I came as one whose thoughts half linger,
    Half run before;
The youngest to the oldest singer
    That England bore.

I found him whom I shall not find
    Till all grief end,
In holiest age our mightiest mind,
    Father and friend.

But thou, if anything endure,
    If hope there be,
O spirit that man's life left pure,
    Man's death set free,

Not with disdain of days that were
    Look earthward now;
Let dreams revive the reverend hair,
    The imperial brow;

Come back in sleep, for in the life
    Where thou art not
We find none like thee. Time and strife
    And the world's lot

WALTER SAVAGE LANDOR (1775-1864)

> Move thee no more; but love at least
>   And reverent heart
> May move thee, royal and released,
>   Soul, as thou art.
>
> And thou, his Florence, to thy trust
>   Receive and keep,
> Keep safe his dedicated dust,
>   His sacred sleep.
>
> So shall thy lovers, come from far,
>   Mix with thy name
> As morning-star with evening-star
>   His faultless fame.

ALGERNON CHARLES SWINBURNE
(1837-1909)

THOMAS MOORE (1779-1852)

To Thomas Moore

> What are you doing now,
>   Oh Thomas Moore?
> What are you doing now,
>   Oh Thomas Moore?
> Sighing or suing now,
> Rhyming or wooing now,
> Billing or cooing now,
>   Which, Thomas Moore?
>
> But the Carnival's coming,
>   Oh Thomas Moore!
> The Carnival's coming,
>   Oh Thomas Moore!
> Masking and humming,
> Fifing and drumming,
> Guitarring and strumming,
>   Oh Thomas Moore!

December 24, 1816

LORD BYRON
(1788-1824)

THOMAS MOORE (1779-1852)

To Thomas Moore

My boat is on the shore,
    And my bark is on the sea;
But, before I go, Tom Moore,
    Here's a double health to thee!

Here's a sigh to those who love me,
    And a smile to those who hate;
And, whatever sky's above me,
    Here's a heart for every fate.

Though the ocean roar around me,
    Yet it still shall bear me on;
Though a desert should surround me,
    It hath springs that may be won.

Were't the last drop in the well,
    As I gasp'd upon the brink,
Ere my fainting spirit fell,
    'Tis to thee that I would drink.

With that water, as this wine,
    The libation I would pour
Should be—peace with thine and mine,
    And a health to thee, Tom Moore.

July, 1817

LORD BYRON
(1788-1824)

GEORGE GORDON, LORD BYRON (1788-1824)

To [Byron]

O mighty mind, in whose deep stream this age
Shakes like a reed in the unheeding storm,
Why dost thou curb not thine own sacred rage?

PERCY BYSSHE SHELLEY
(1792-1822)

GEORGE GORDON, LORD BYRON (1788-1824)

Sonnet to Byron

(I am afraid these verses will not please you, but)

If I esteemed you less, Envy would kill
  Pleasure, and leave to Wonder and Despair
  The ministration of the thoughts that fill
  The mind which, like a worm whose life may share
A portion of the unapproachable,
  Marks your creations rise as fast and fair
  As perfect worlds at the Creator's will.
  But such is my regard that nor your power
To soar above the heights where others (climb),
  Nor fame, that shadow of the unborn hour
  Cast from the envious future on the time,
Move one regret for his unhonoured name
  Who dares these words:—the worm beneath the sod
  May lift itself in homage of the God.

PERCY BYSSHE SHELLEY
(1792–1822)

To Byron

Byron! how sweetly sad thy melody!
  Attuning still the soul to tenderness,
  As if soft Pity, with unusual stress,
  Had touch'd her plaintive lute, and thou, being by,
  Hadst caught the tones, nor suffer'd them to die.
  O'er shadowing sorrow doth not make thee less
  Delightful: thou thy griefs dost dress
With a bright halo, shining beamily,
As when a cloud the golden moon doth veil,
  Its sides are ting'd with a resplendent glow,
  Through the dark robe oft amber rays prevail,
  And like fair veins in sable marble flow;
Still warble, dying swan! still tell the tale,
  The enchanting tale, the tale of pleasing woe.

JOHN KEATS
(1795–1821)

GEORGE GORDON, LORD BYRON (1788–1824)

From "Stanzas from the Grande Chartreuse"

What helps it now, that Byron bore,
With haughty scorn which mock'd the smart,
Through Europe to the Ætolian shore
The pageant of his bleeding heart?
That thousands counted every groan,
And Europe made his woe her own?

What boots it, Shelley! that the breeze
Carried thy lovely wail away,
Musical through Italian trees
Which fringe thy soft blue Spezzian bay?
Inheritors of thy distress
Have restless hearts one throb the less?

Or are we easier, to have read,
O Obermann! the sad, stern page,
Which tells us how thou hidd'st thy head
From the fierce tempest of thine age
In the lone brakes of Fontainebleau,
Or chalets near the Alpine snow?

Ye slumber in your silent grave!—
The world, which for an idle day
Grace to your mood of sadness gave,
Long since hath flung her weeds away.
The eternal trifler breaks your spell;
But we—we learnt your lore too well!

MATTHEW ARNOLD
(1822–1888)

From "Letter to Lord Byron"

I like your muse because she's gay and witty,
    Because she's neither prostitute nor frump,
The daughter of a European city,
    And country houses long before the slump;
    I like her voice that does not make me jump:
And you I find sympatisch, a good townee,
Neither a preacher, ninny, bore, nor Brownie.

GEORGE GORDON, LORD BYRON (1788-1824)

A poet, swimmer, peer, and man of action,
    —It beats Roy Campbell's record by a mile—
You offer every possible attraction.
    By looking into your poetic style,
    And love-life on the chance that both were vile,
Several have earned a decent livelihood,
Whose lives were uncreative but were good.

You've had your packet from the critics, though:
    They grant you warmth of heart, but at your head
Their moral and aesthetic brickbats throw.
    A 'vulgar genius' so George Eliot said,
    Which doesn't matter as George Eliot's dead,
But T.S. Eliot, I am sad to find,
Damns you with: 'an uninteresting mind.'

A statement which I must say I'm ashamed at;
    A poet must be judged by his intention,
And serious thought you never said you aimed at.
    I think a serious critic ought to mention
    That one verse style was really your invention,
A style whose meaning does not need a spanner,
You are the master of the airy manner.

By all means let us touch our humble caps to
    La poésie pure, the epic narrative;
But comedy shall get its round of claps, too.
    According to his powers, each may give;
    Only on varied diet can we live.
The pious fable and the dirty story
Share in the total literary glory.

                                      W. H. AUDEN
                                      (1907–   )

PERCY BYSSHE SHELLEY (1792–1822)

From "Pauline"

I ne'er had ventured e'en to hope for this,
Had not the glow I felt at His award,
Assured me all was not extinct within:
His whom all honor, whose renown springs up
Like sunlight which will visit all the world,
So that e'en they who sneered at him at first,
Come out to it, as some dark spider crawls
From his foul nets which some lit torch invades,
Yet spinning still new films for his retreat.
Thou didst smile, poet, but can we forgive?

Sun-treader, life and light be thine forever!
Thou art gone from us; years go by and spring
Gladdens and the young earth is beautiful,
Yet thy songs come not, other bards arise,
But none like thee: they stand, thy majesties,
Like mighty works which tell some spirit there
Hath sat regardless of neglect and scorn,
Till, its long task completed, it hath risen
And left us, never to return, and all
Rush in to peer and praise when all in vain.
The air seems bright with thy past presence yet,
But thou art still for me as thou hast been
When I have stood with thee as on a throne
With all thy dim creations gathered round
Like mountains, and I felt of mould like them,
And with them creatures of my own were mixed,
Like things half-lived, catching and giving life.
But thou art still for me who have adored
Though single, panting but to hear thy name
Which I believed a spell to me alone,
Scarce deeming thou wast as a star to men!
As one should worship long a sacred spring
Scarce worth a moth's flitting, which long grasses cross,
And one small tree embowers droopingly—
Joying to see some wandering insect won

PERCY BYSSHE SHELLEY (1792–1822)

To live in its few rushes, or some locust
To pasture on its boughs, or some wild bird
Stoop for its freshness from the trackless air:
And then should find it but the fountain-head,
Long lost, of some great river washing towns
And towers, and seeing old woods which will live
But by its banks untrod of human foot,
Which, when the great sun sinks, lie quivering
In light as some thing lieth half of life
Before God's foot, waiting a wondrous change;
Then girt with rocks which seek to turn or stay
Its course in vain, for it does ever spread
Like a sea's arm as it goes rolling on,
Being the pulse of some great country—so
Wast thou to me, and art thou to the world!
And I, perchance, half feel a strange regret
That I am not what I have been to thee:
Like a girl one has silently loved long
In her first loneliness in some retreat,
When, late emerged, all gaze and glow to view
Her fresh eyes and soft hair and lips which bloom
Like a mountain berry: doubtless it is sweet
To see her thus adored, but there have been
Moments when all the world was in our praise,
Sweeter than any pride of after hours.
Yet, sun-treader, all hail! From my heart's heart
I bid thee hail! E'en in my wildest dreams,
I proudly feel I would have thrown to dust
The wreaths of fame which seemed o'erhanging me,
To see thee for a moment as thou art.
And if thou livest, if thou lovest, spirit!
Remember me who set this final seal
To wandering thought—that one so pure as thou
Could never die. Remember me who flung
All honor from my soul, yet paused and said,
"There is one spark of love remaining yet,
For I have naught in common with him, shapes
Which followed him avoid me, and foul forms

PERCY BYSSHE SHELLEY (1792-1822)

Seek me, which ne'er could fasten on his mind;
And though I feel how low I am to him,
Yet I aim not even to catch a tone
Of harmonies he called profusely up;
So, one gleam still remains, although the last."
Remember me who praise thee e'en with tears,
For never more shall I walk calm with thee;
Thy sweet imaginings are as an air,
A melody some wondrous singer sings,
Which, though it haunt men oft in the still eve,
They dream not to essay; yet it no less
But more is honored. I was thine in shame,
And now when all thy proud renown is out,
I am a watcher whose eyes have grown dim
With looking for some star which breaks on him
Altered and worn and weak and full of tears.

ROBERT BROWNING
(1812-1889)

Memorabilia

I

Ah, did you once see Shelley plain,
    And did he stop and speak to you,
And did you speak to him again?
    How strange it seems and new!

II

But you were living before that,
    And also you are living after;
And the memory I started at—
    My starting moves your laughter!

III

I crossed a moor, with a name of its own
    And a certain use in the world no doubt,
Yet a hand's-breadth of it shines alone
    'Mid the blank miles round about:

PERCY BYSSHE SHELLEY (1792–1822)

IV

For there I picked up on the heather,
And there I put inside my breast
A moulted feather, an eagle-feather!
Well, I forget the rest.

ROBERT BROWNING
(1812–1889)

Percy Bysshe Shelley

*(Inscription for the Couch, Still Preserved, on Which
He Passed the Last Night of His Life.)*

'Twixt those twin worlds,—the world of Sleep, which gave
  No dream to warn,—the tidal world of Death,
  Which the earth's sea, as the earth, replenisheth,—
Shelley, Song's orient sun, to breast the wave,
Rose from this couch that morn. Ah! did he brave
  Only the sea?—or did man's deed of hell
Engulph his bark 'mid mists impenetrable? . . .
No eye discerned, nor any power might save.
When that mist cleared, O Shelley? what dread veil
  Was rent for thee, to whom far-darkling Truth
  Reigned sovereign guide through thy brief ageless youth?
Was the Truth *thy* Truth, Shelley!—Hush? All-Hail,
  Past doubt, thou gav'st it; and in Truth's bright sphere
Art first of praisers, being most praisèd here.

DANTE GABRIEL ROSSETTI
(1828–1882)

Shelley's Skylark

(The neighbourhood of Leghorn: March 1887)

Somewhere afield here something lies
In Earth's oblivious eyeless trust
That moved a poet to prophecies—
A pinch of unseen, unguarded dust:

PERCY BYSSHE SHELLEY (1792–1822)

The dust of the lark that Shelley heard,
And made immortal through times to be;—
Though it only lived like another bird,
And knew not its immortality:

Lived its meek life; then, one day, fell—
A little ball of feather and bone;
And how it perished, when piped farewell,
And where it wastes, are alike unknown.

Maybe it rests in the loam I view,
Maybe it throbs in a myrtle's green,
Maybe it sleeps in the coming hue
Of a grape on the slopes of yon inland scene.

Go find it, faeries, go and find
That tiny pinch of priceless dust,
And bring a casket silver-lined,
And framed of gold that gems encrust;

And we will lay it safe therein,
And consecrate it to endless time;
For it inspired a bard to win
Ecstatic heights in thought and rhyme.

THOMAS HARDY
(1840–1928)

A Red Carpet for Shelley

I

But this is nothing; an eccentric joke,
The legendary patchwork of a year
Flung into muddiness, like Raleigh's cloak,
To ask the honour of your step, my dear.
Your path is printed on the atmosphere
Forever as a flame against the smoke
Of obscure vision, and I must invoke
Your magnanimity to make it clear.

[229]

PERCY BYSSHE SHELLEY (1792–1822)

If I might spread soft words like living grass
Laid smooth beneath the heavy wheels of Time;
If I might loose the river of a rhyme
Or build a pavement out of gold and glass
Providing Heaven for you to walk upon,
It would be well; it would be better done.

II

The only engine which can fabricate
Language from spirit is the heart of each;
Industrious blood has braided into speech
The airy filaments of love and hate.
I have the labour of my own estate,
A pitiful machine which shall not reach
A single stellar thread; I cannot teach
Its narrow nerves the virtue to be great.

If my devout affection had been given
Commensurate power, which doubt nor custom dulls;
If I possessed the pure and fiery pulse
By true divinity informed and driven,
I would unroll the rounded moon and sun
And knit them up for you to walk upon.

III

The little sum of my experience
Remains the sole contrivance I produce
To weave this mesh, to colour and confuse
These ragged syllables with soul and sense.
I have been put to one supreme expense;
This was the noblest tincture I could use,
This the most subtle grain; I cannot choose
The dye to turn the lacklustre intense.

I have the proper scarlet of my veins,
The clean involved precision of my mind,
And you, who are so excellently kind,
Will not reject the tissue of my pains,
Stained by mortality's vermilion
To make a world for you to walk upon.

PERCY BYSSHE SHELLEY (1792-1822)

IV

Forgive the savage texture of the spoil
Tinted so barbarously by the clay
The rusty iron and the ocean-spray
Which lifted up my body from the soil.
Forgive the complicated brittle coil
Of my infirm invention, which I lay
Where you may pause, and pass, and never stay.
Here are the shocks of maize, the honey and oil,

The fruits like harvest moons, the fabulous land,
The crystal hills, the veiled prismatic plain;
And you will come, and you will not remain,
Nor leave a trace along the gilded sand.
So presently you will be come and gone;
Here's a strange road for you to walk upon.

ELINOR WYLIE
(1885-1928)

JOHN KEATS (1795-1821)

To John Keats

'Tis well you think me truly one of those,
Whose sense discerns the loveliness of things;
For surely as I feel the bird that sings
Behind the leaves, or dawn as up it grows,
Or the rich bee rejoicing as he goes,
Or the glad issue of emerging springs,
Or overhead the glide of a dove's wings,
Or turf, or trees, or, midst of all, repose.
And surely as I feel things lovelier still,
The human look, and the harmonious form
Containing woman, and the smile in ill,
And such as heart as Charles's, wise and warm,—
As surely as all this, I see, ev'n now,
Young Keats, a flowering laurel on your brow.

LEIGH HUNT
(1784-1859)

JOHN KEATS (1795-1821)

Adonais

An Elegy on the Death of John Keats

I

I weep for Adonais—he is dead!
Oh, weep for Adonais! though our tears
Thaw not the frost which binds so dear a head!
And thou, sad Hour, selected from all years
To mourn our loss, rouse thy obscure compeers,
And teach them thine own sorrow! Say: 'With me
Died Adonais; till the Future dares
Forget the Past, his fate and fame shall be
An echo and a light unto eternity!'

II

Where wert thou, mighty Mother, when he lay,
When thy Son lay, pierced by the shaft which flies
In darkness? where was lorn Urania
When Adonais died? With veilèd eyes,
'Mid listening Echoes, in her Paradise
She sate, while one, with soft enamoured breath,
Rekindled all the fading melodies,
With which, like flowers that mock the corse beneath,
He had adorned and hid the coming bulk of death.

III

Oh, weep for Adonais—he is dead!
Wake, melancholy Mother, wake and weep!
Yet wherefore? Quench within their burning bed
Thy fiery tears, and let thy loud heart keep
Like his a mute and uncomplaining sleep;
For he is gone where all things wise and fair
Descend. Oh, dream not that the amorous Deep
Will yet restore him to the vital air;
Death feeds on his mute voice, and laughs at our despair.

IV

Most musical of mourners, weep again!
Lament anew, Urania!—He died,
Who was the sire of an immortal strain,
Blind, old, and lonely, when his country's pride

JOHN KEATS (1795-1821)

    The priest, the slave, and the liberticide
    Trampled and mocked with many a loathèd rite
    Of lust and blood; he went, unterrified,
    Into the gulf of death; but his clear Sprite
Yet reigns o'er earth; the third among the sons of light.

V

    Most musical of mourners, weep anew!
    Not all to that bright station dared to climb;
    And happier they their happiness who knew,
    Whose tapers yet burn through that night of time
    In which suns perished; others more sublime,
    Struck by the envious wrath of man or God,
    Have sunk, extinct in their refulgent prime;
    And some yet live, treading the thorny road,
Which leads, through toil and hate, to Fame's serene abode.

VI

    But now, thy youngest, dearest one has perished,
    The nursling of thy widowhood, who grew,
    Like a pale flower by some sad maiden cherished
    And fed with true-love tears instead of dew;
    Most musical of mourners, weep anew!
    Thy extreme hope, the loveliest and the last,
    The bloom, whose petals, nipped before they blew,
    Died on the promise of the fruit, is waste;
The broken lily lies—the storm is overpast.

VII

    To that high Capital, where kingly Death
    Keeps his pale court in beauty and decay,
    He came; and bought, with price of purest breath,
    A grave among the eternal.—Come away!
    Haste, while the vault of blue Italian day
    Is yet his fitting charnel-roof! while still
    He lies, as if in dewy sleep he lay;
    Awake him not! surely he takes his fill
Of deep and liquid rest, forgetful of all ill.

JOHN KEATS (1795-1821)

VIII

He will awake no more, oh, never more!
Within the twilight chamber spreads apace
The shadow of white Death, and at the door
Invisible Corruption waits to trace
His extreme way to her dim dwelling-place;
The eternal Hunger sits, but pity and awe
Soothe her pale rage, nor dares she to deface
So fair a prey, till darkness and the law
  Of change shall o'er his sleep the mortal curtain draw.

IX

Oh, weep for Adonais!—The quick Dreams,
The passion-wingèd ministers of thought,
Who were his flocks, whom near the living streams
Of his young spirit he fed, and whom he taught
The love which was its music, wander not,—
Wander no more, from kindling brain to brain,
But droop there, whence they sprung; and mourn their lot
Round the cold heart, where, after their sweet pain,
  They ne'er will gather strength, or find a home again.

X

And one with trembling hand clasps his cold head,
And fans him with her moonlight wings, and cries,
'Our love, our hope, our sorrow, is not dead;
See, on the silken fringe of his faint eyes,
Like dew upon a sleeping flower, there lies
A tear some Dream has loosened from his brain.'
Lost Angel of a ruined Paradise!
She knew not 't was her own; as with no stain
  She faded, like a cloud which had outwept its rain.

XI

One from a lucid urn of starry dew
Washed his light limbs, as if embalming them;
Another clipped her profuse locks, and threw
The wreath upon him, like an anadem,

JOHN KEATS (1795-1821)

Which frozen tears instead of pearls begem;
Another in her wilful grief would break
Her bow and wingèd reeds, as if to stem
A greater loss with one which was more weak;
And dull the barbèd fire against his frozen cheek.

XII

Another Splendor on his mouth alit,
That mouth whence it was wont to draw the breath
Which gave it strength to pierce the guarded wit,
And pass into the panting heart beneath
With lightning and with music; the damp death
Quenched its caress upon his icy lips;
And, as a dying meteor stains a wreath
Of moonlight vapor, which the cold night clips,
It flushed through his pale limbs, and passed to its eclipse.

XIII

And others came—Desires and Adorations,
Wingèd Persuasions and veiled Destinies,
Splendors, and Glooms, and glimmering Incarnations
Of hopes and fears, and twilight Fantasies;
And Sorrow, with her family of Sighs,
And Pleasure, blind with tears, led by the gleam
Of her own dying smile instead of eyes,
Came in slow pomp;—the moving pomp might seem
Like pageantry of mist on an autumnal stream.

XIV

All he had loved, and moulded into thought
From shape, and hue, and odor, and sweet sound,
Lamented Adonais. Morning sought
Her eastern watch tower, and her hair unbound,
Wet with the tears which should adorn the ground,
Dimmed the aërial eyes that kindle day;
Afar the melancholy thunder moaned,
Pale Ocean in unquiet slumber lay,
And the wild winds flew round, sobbing in their dismay.

JOHN KEATS (1795-1821)

XV

Lost Echo sits amid the voiceless mountains,
And feeds her grief with his remembered lay,
And will no more reply to winds or fountains,
Or amorous birds perched on the young green spray,
Or herdsman's horn, or bell at closing day;
Since she can mimic not his lips, more dear
Than those for whose disdain she pined away
Into a shadow of all sounds:—a drear
Murmur, between their songs, is all the woodmen hear.

XVI

Grief made the young Spring wild, and she threw down
Her kindling buds, as if she Autumn were,
Or they dead leaves; since her delight is flown,
For whom should she have waked the sullen year?
To Phœbus was not Hyacinth so dear,
Nor to himself Narcissus, as to both
Thou, Adonais; wan they stand and sere
Amid the faint companions of their youth,
With dew all turned to tears; odor, to sighing ruth.

XVII

Thy spirit's sister, the lorn nightingale,
Mourns not her mate with such melodious pain;
Not so the eagle, who like thee could scale
Heaven, and could nourish in the sun's domain
Her mighty youth with morning, doth complain,
Soaring and screaming round her empty nest,
As Albion wails for thee: the curse of Cain
Light on his head who pierced thy innocent breast,
And scared the angel soul that was its earthly guest!

XVIII

Ah woe is me! Winter is come and gone,
But grief returns with the revolving year;
The airs and streams renew their joyous tone;
The ants, the bees, the swallows, reappear;

JOHN KEATS (1795-1821)

Fresh leaves and flowers deck the dead Season's bier;
The amorous birds now pair in every brake,
And build their mossy homes in field and brere;
And the green lizard and the golden snake,
Like unimprisoned flames, out of their trance awake.

XIX

Through wood and stream and field and hill and Ocean,
A quickening life from the Earth's heart has burst
As it has ever done, with change and motion,
From the great morning of the world when first
God dawned on Chaos; in its stream immersed,
The lamps of Heaven flash with a softer light;
All baser things pant with life's sacred thirst,
Diffuse themselves, and spend in love's delight
The beauty and the joy of their renewèd might.

XX

The leprous corpse, touched by this spirit tender,
Exhales itself in flowers of gentle breath;
Like incarnations of the stars, when splendor
Is changed to fragrance, they illumine death
And mock the merry worm that wakes beneath.
Nought we know dies. Shall that alone which knows
Be as a sword consumed before the sheath
By sightless lightning? the intense atom glows
A moment, then is quenched in a most cold repose.

XXI

Alas! that all we loved of him should be,
But for our grief, as if it had not been,
And grief itself be mortal! Woe is me!
Whence are we, and why are we? of what scene
The actors or spectators? Great and mean
Meet massed in death, who lends what life must borrow.
As long as skies are blue and fields are green,
Evening must usher night, night urge the morrow,
Month follow month with woe, and year wake year to sorrow.

JOHN KEATS (1795-1821)

XXII

He will awake no more, oh, never more!
'Wake thou,' cried Misery, 'childless Mother, rise
Out of thy sleep, and slake, in thy heart's core,
A wound more fierce than his with tears and sighs.'
And all the Dreams that watched Urania's eyes,
And all the Echoes whom their sister's song
Had held in holy silence, cried, 'Arise!'
Swift as a Thought by the snake Memory stung,
From her ambrosial rest the fading Splendor sprung.

XXIII

She rose like an autumnal Night, that springs
Out of the East, and follows wild and drear
The golden Day, which, on eternal wings,
Even as a ghost abandoning a bier,
Had left the Earth a corpse.—sorrow and fear
So struck, so roused, so rapped Urania;
So saddened round her like an atmosphere
Of stormy mist; so swept her on her way
Even to the mournful place where Adonais lay.

XXIV

Out of her secret Paradise she sped,
Through camps and cities rough with stone, and steel,
And human hearts which, to her airy tread
Yielding not, wounded the invisible
Palms of her tender feet where'er they fell;
And barbèd tongues, and thoughts more sharp than they,
Rent the soft Form they never could repel,
Whose sacred blood, like the young tears of May,
Paved with eternal flowers that undeserving way.

XXV

In the death-chamber for a moment Death,
Shamed by the presence of that living Might,
Blushed to annihilation, and the breath
Revisited those lips, and life's pale light

JOHN KEATS (1795-1821)

Flashed through those limbs, so late her dear delight.
'Leave me not wild and drear and comfortless,
As silent lightning leaves the starless night!
Leave me not!' cried Urania; her distress
Roused Death; Death rose and smiled, and met her vain caress.

XXVI

'Stay yet awhile! speak to me once again;
Kiss me, so long but as a kiss may live;
And in my heartless breast and burning brain
That word, that kiss, shall all thoughts else survive,
With food of saddest memory kept alive,
Now thou art dead, as if it were a part
Of thee, my Adonais!   I would give
All that I am to be as thou now art!
But I am chained to Time, and cannot thence depart!

XXVII

'O gentle child, beautiful as thou wert,
Why didst thou leave the trodden paths of men
Too soon, and with weak hands though mighty heart
Dare the unpastured dragon in his den?
Defenceless as thou wert, oh, where was then
Wisdom the mirrored shield, or scorn the spear?
Or hadst thou waited the full cycle, when
Thy spirit should have filled its crescent sphere,
The monsters of life's waste had fled from thee like deer.

XXVIII

'The herded wolves, bold only to pursue;
The obscene ravens, clamorous o'er the dead;
The vultures, to the conqueror's banner true,
Who feed where Desolation first has fed,
And whose wings rain contagion;—how they fled,
When, like Apollo, from his golden bow
The Pythian of the age one arrow sped
And smiled!—The spoilers tempt no second blow,
They fawn on the proud feet that spurn them lying low.

[239]

JOHN KEATS (1795–1821)

XXIX

'The sun comes forth, and many reptiles spawn;
He sets, and each ephemeral insect then
Is gathered into death without a dawn,
And the immortal stars awake again;
So is it in the world of living men:
A godlike mind soars forth, in its delight
Making earth bare and veiling heaven, and when
It sinks, the swarms that dimmed or shared its light
Leave to its kindred lamps the spirit's awful night.'

XXX

Thus ceased she; and the mountain shepherds came,
Their garlands sere, their magic mantles rent;
The Pilgrim of Eternity, whose fame
Over his living head like Heaven is bent,
An early but enduring monument,
Came, veiling all the lightnings of his song
In sorrow; from her wilds Ierne sent
The sweetest lyrist of her saddest wrong,
And love taught grief to fall like music from his tongue.

XXXI

'Midst others of less note, came one frail Form,
A phantom among men; companionless
As the last cloud of an expiring storm
Whose thunder is its knell; he, as I guess,
Had gazed on Nature's naked loveliness,
Actæon-like, and now he fled astray
With feeble steps o'er the world's wilderness,
And his own thoughts, along that rugged way,
Pursued, like raging hounds, their father and their prey.

XXXII

A pard-like Spirit beautiful and swift—
A love in desolation masked;—a Power
Girt round with weakness;—it can scarce uplift
The weight of the superincumbent hour;

JOHN KEATS (1795–1821)

It is a dying lamp, a falling shower,
A breaking billow;—even whilst we speak
Is it not broken? On the withering flower
The killing sun smiles brightly; on a cheek
The life can burn in blood, even while the heart may break.

XXXIII

His head was bound with pansies over-blown,
And faded violets, white, and pied, and blue;
And a light spear topped with a cypress cone,
Round whose rude shaft dark ivy-tresses grew
Yet dripping with the forest's noonday dew,
Vibrated, as the ever-beating heart
Shook the weak hand that grasped it; of that crew
He came the last, neglected and apart;
A herd-abandoned deer struck by the hunter's dart.

XXXIV

All stood aloof, and at his partial moan
Smiled through their tears; well knew that gentle band
Who in another's fate now wept his own,
As in the accents of an unknown land
He sung new sorrow; sad Urania scanned
The Stranger's mien, and murmured: 'Who art thou?'
He answered not, but with a sudden hand
Made bare his branded and ensanguined brow,
Which was like Cain's or Christ's—oh! that it should be so!

XXXV

What softer voice is hushed over the dead?
Athwart what brow is that dark mantle thrown?
What form leans sadly o'er the white death-bed,
In mockery of monumental stone,
The heavy heart heaving without a moan?
If it be He, who, gentlest of the wise,
Taught, soothed, loved, honored the departed one,
Let me not vex with inharmonious sighs
The silence of that heart's accepted sacrifice.

JOHN KEATS (1795-1821)

XXXVI

Our Adonais has drunk poison—oh,
What deaf and viperous murderer could crown
Life's early cup with such a draught of woe?
The nameless worm would now itself disown;
It felt, yet could escape the magic tone
Whose prelude held all envy, hate, and wrong,
But what was howling in one breast alone,
Silent with expectation of the song,
Whose master's hand is cold, whose silver lyre unstrung.

XXXVII

Live thou, whose infamy is not thy fame!
Live! fear no heavier chastisement from me,
Thou noteless blot on a remembered name!
But be thyself, and know thyself to be!
And ever at thy season be thou free
To spill the venom when thy fangs o'er flow;
Remorse and Self-contempt shall cling to thee;
Hot Shame shall burn upon thy secret brow,
And like a beaten hound tremble thou shalt—as now.

XXXVIII

Nor let us weep that our delight is fled
Far from these carrion kites that scream below;
He wakes or sleeps with the enduring dead;
Thou canst not soar where he is sitting now.
Dust to the dust! but the pure spirit shall flow
Back to the burning fountain whence it came,
A portion of the Eternal, which must glow
Through time and change, unquenchably the same,
Whilst thy cold embers choke the sordid hearth of shame.

XXXIX

Peace, peace! he is not dead, he doth not sleep—
He hath awakened from the dream of life—
'T is we, who, lost in stormy visions, keep
With phantoms an unprofitable strife,

JOHN KEATS (1795-1821)

And in mad trance strike with our spirit's knife
Invulnerable nothings. *We* decay
Like corpses in a charnel; fear and grief
Convulse us and consume us day by day,
And cold hopes swarm like worms within our living clay.

XL

He has outsoared the shadow of our night;
Envy and calumny and hate and pain,
And that unrest which men miscall delight,
Can touch him not and torture not again;
From the contagion of the world's slow stain
He is secure, and now can never mourn
A heart grown cold, a head grown gray in vain;
Nor, when the spirit's self has ceased to burn,
With sparkless ashes load an unlamented urn.

XLI

He lives, he wakes—'t is Death is dead, not he;
Mourn not for Adonais.—Thou young Dawn,
Turn all thy dew to splendor, for from thee
The spirit thou lamentest is not gone;
Ye caverns and ye forests, cease to moan!
Cease, ye faint flowers and fountains, and thou Air,
Which like a mourning veil thy scarf hadst thrown
O'er the abandoned Earth, now leave it bare
Even to the joyous stars which smile on its despair!

XLII

He is made one with Nature: there is heard
His voice in all her music, from the moan
Of thunder to the song of night's sweet bird;
He is a presence to be felt and known
In darkness and in light, from herb and stone,
Spreading itself where'er that Power may move
Which has withdrawn his being to its own;
Which wields the world with never-wearied love,
Sustains it from beneath, and kindles it above.

JOHN KEATS (1795-1821)

XLIII

He is a portion of the loveliness
Which once he made more lovely; he doth bear
His part, while the one Spirit's plastic stress
Sweeps through the dull dense world, compelling there
All new successions to the forms they wear,
Torturing the unwilling dross that checks its flight
To its own likeness, as each mass may bear,
And bursting in its beauty and its might
From trees and beasts and men into the Heaven's light.

XLIV

The splendors of the firmament of time
May be eclipsed, but are extinguished not;
Like stars to their appointed height they climb,
And death is a low mist which cannot blot
The brightness it may veil. When lofty thought
Lifts a young heart above its mortal lair,
And love and life contend in it for what
Shall be its earthly doom, the dead live there
And move like winds of light on dark and stormy air.

XLV

The inheritors of unfulfilled renown
Rose from their thrones, built beyond mortal thought,
Far in the Unapparent. Chatterton
Rose pale,—his solemn agony had not
Yet faded from him; Sidney, as he fought
And as he fell and as he lived and loved
Sublimely mild, a Spirit without spot,
Arose; and Lucan, by his death approved;
Oblivion as they rose shrank like a thing reproved.

XLVI

And many more, whose names on Earth are dark
But whose transmitted effluence cannot die
So long as fire outlives the parent spark,
Rose, robed in dazzling immortality.

[244]

JOHN KEATS (1795–1821)

    'Thou art become as one of us,' they cry;
    'It was for thee yon kingless sphere has long
    Swung blind in unascended majesty,
    Silent alone amid an Heaven of song.
  Assume thy wingèd throne, thou Vesper of our throng!'

XLVII

  Who mourns for Adonais? Oh, come forth,
  Fond wretch! and know thyself and him aright.
  Clasp with thy panting soul the pendulous Earth;
  As from a centre, dart thy spirit's light
  Beyond all worlds, until its spacious might
  Satiate the void circumference; then shrink
  Even to a point within our day and night;
  And keep thy heart light lest it make thee sink
When hope has kindled hope, and lured thee to the brink.

XLVIII

  Or go to Rome, which is the sepulchre,
  Oh, not of him, but of our joy; 't is nought
  That ages, empires, and religions, there
  Lie buried in the ravage they have wrought;
  For such as he can lend,—they borrow not
  Glory from those who made the world their prey;
  And he is gathered to the kings of thought
  Who waged contention with their time's decay,
And of the past are all that cannot pass away.

XLIX

  Go thou to Rome,—at once the Paradise,
  The grave, the city, and the wilderness;
  And where its wrecks like shattered mountains rise,
  And flowering weeds and fragrant copses dress
  The bones of Desolation's nakedness,
  Pass, till the Spirit of the spot shall lead
  Thy footsteps to a slope of green access,
  Where, like an infant's smile, over the dead
A light of laughing flowers along the grass is spread;

JOHN KEATS (1795-1821)

L

And gray walls moulder round, on which dull Time
Feeds, like slow fire upon a hoary brand;
And one keen pyramid with wedge sublime,
Pavilioning the dust of him who planned
This refuge for his memory, doth stand
Like flame transformed to marble; and beneath,
A field is spread, on which a newer band
Have pitched in Heaven's smile their camp of death,
Welcoming him we lose with scarce extinguished breath.

LI

Here pause: these graves are all too young as yet
To have outgrown the sorrow which consigned
Its charge to each; and if the seal is set,
Here, on one fountain of a mourning mind,
Break it not thou! too surely shalt thou find
Thine own well full, if thou returnest home,
Of tears and gall. From the world's bitter wind
Seek shelter in the shadow of the tomb.
What Adonais is, why fear we to become?

LII

The One remains, the many change and pass;
Heaven's light forever shines, Earth's shadows fly;
Life, like a dome of many-colored glass,
Stains the white radiance of Eternity,
Until Death tramples it to fragments.—Die,
If thou wouldst be with that which thou dost seek!
Follow where all is fled!—Rome's azure sky,
Flowers, ruins, statues, music, words, are weak
The glory they transfuse with fitting truth to speak.

LIII

Why linger, why turn back, why shrink, my Heart?
Thy hopes are gone before; from all things here
They have departed; thou shouldst now depart!
A light is passed from the revolving year,

JOHN KEATS (1795-1821)

> And man, and woman; and what still is dear
> Attracts to crush, repels to make thee wither.
> The soft sky smiles,—the low wind whispers near;
> 'T is Adonais calls! oh, hasten thither,
> No more let Life divide what Death can join together.

LIV

> That Light whose smile kindles the Universe,
> That Beauty in which all things work and move,
> That Benediction which the eclipsing Curse
> Of birth can quench not, that sustaining Love
> Which through the web of being blindly wove
> By man and beast and earth and air and sea,
> Burns bright or dim, as each are mirrors of
> The fire for which all thirst, now beams on me,
> Consuming the last clouds of cold mortality.

LV

> The breath whose might I have invoked in song
> Descends on me; my spirit's bark is driven
> Far from the shore, far from the trembling throng
> Whose sails were never to the tempest given;
> The massy earth and spherèd skies are riven!
> I am borne darkly, fearfully, afar;
> Whilst, burning through the inmost veil of Heaven,
> The soul of Adonais, like a star,
> Beacons from the abode where the Eternal are.

PERCY BYSSHE SHELLEY
(1792–1822)

Popularity

> Stand still, true poet that you are!
>   I know you; let me try and draw you.
> Some night you'll fail us: when afar
>   You rise, remember one man saw you,
> Knew you, and named a star!

JOHN KEATS (1795-1821)

My star, God's glow-worm! Why extend
   That loving hand of his which leads you,
Yet locks you safe from end to end
   Of this dark world, unless he needs you,
Just saves your light to spend?

His clenched hand shall unclose at last,
   I know, and let out all the beauty:
My poet holds the future fast,
   Accepts the coming ages' duty,
Their present for this past.

That day, the earth's feast-master's brow
   Shall clear, to God the challice raising;
"Others give best at first, but thou
   Forever set'st our table praising,
Keep'st the good wine till now!"

Meantime, I'll draw you as you stand,
   With few or none to watch and wonder:
I'll say—a fisher, on the sand
   By Tyre the old, with ocean-plunder,
A netful, brought to land.

Who has not heard how Tyrian shells
   Enclosed the blue, that dye of dyes
Whereof one drop worked miracles,
   And colored like Astarte's eyes
Raw silk the merchant sells?

And each bystander of them all
   Could criticise, and quote tradition
How depths of blue sublimed some pall
   —To get which, pricked a king's ambition;
Worth sceptre, crown and ball.

Yet there's the dye, in that rough mesh,
   The sea has only just o'er-whispered!
Live whelks, each lip's beard dripping fresh,
   As if they still the water's lisp heard
Through foam the rock-weeds thresh.

JOHN KEATS (1795-1821)

    Enough to furnish Solomon
       Such hangings for his cedar-house,
    That, when gold-robed he took the throne
       In that abyss of blue, the Spouse
    Might swear his presence shone

    Most like the centre-spike of gold
       Which burns deep in the bluebell's womb
    What time, with ardors manifold,
       The bee goes singing to her groom,
    Drunken and overbold.

    Mere conches! not fit for warp or woof!
       Till cunning come to pound and squeeze
    And clarify,—refine to proof
       The liquor filtered by degrees,
    While the world stands aloof.

    And there's the extract, flasked and fine,
       And priced and salable at last!
    And Hobbs, Nobbs, Stokes and Nokes combine
       To paint the future from the past,
    Put blue into their line.

    Hobbs hints blue,—straight he turtle eats:
       Nobbs prints blue,—claret crowns his cup:
    Nokes outdares Stokes in azure feats,—
       Both gorge. Who fished the murex up?
    What porridge had John Keats?

                             Robert Browning
                                 (1812-1889)

After a Lecture on Keats

"Purpureos spargam flores"

    The wreath that star-crowned Shelley gave
    Is lying on thy Roman grave,
    Yet on its turf young April sets
    Her store of slender violets;
    Though all the gods their garlands shower,
    I too may bring one purple flower.

JOHN KEATS (1795–1821)

—Alas! what blossom shall I bring,
That opens in my Northern spring?
The garden beds have all run wild,
So trim when I was yet a child;
Flat plantains and unseemly stalks
Have crept across the gravel walks;
The vines are dead, long, long ago,
The almond buds no longer blow.
No more upon its mound I see
The azure, plume-bound fleur-de-lis;
Where once the tulips used to show,
In straggling tufts the pansies grow;
The grass has quenched my white-rayed gem,
The flowering "Star of Bethlehem,"
Though its long blade of glossy green
And pallid stripe may still be seen.
Nature, who treads her nobles down,
And gives their birthright to the clown,
Has sown her base-born weedy things
Above the garden's queens and kings.
—Yet one sweet flower of ancient race
Springs in the old familiar place.
When snows were melting down the vale,
And Earth unlaced her icy mail,
And March his stormy trumpet blew,
And tender green came peeping through,
I loved the earliest one to seek
That broke the soil with emerald beak,
And watch the trembling bells so blue
Spread on the column as it grew.
Meek child of earth! thou wilt not shame
The sweet, dead poet's holy name;
The God of music gave thee birth,
Called from the crimson-spotted earth,
Where, sobbing his young life away,
His own fair Hyacinthus lay.
—The hyacinth my garden gave
Shall lie upon that Roman grave!

Oliver Wendell Holmes
(1809–1894)

JOHN KEATS (1795-1821)

John Keats

The weltering London ways where children weep
   And girls whom none call maidens laugh,—strange road
   Miring his outward steps, who inly trode
The bright Castalian brink and Latmos' steep:—
Even such his life's cross-paths; till deathly deep
   He toiled through sands and Lethe; and long pain,
   Weary with labor spurned and love found vain,
In dead Rome's sheltering shadow wrapped his sleep.
O pang-dowered Poet, whose reverberant lips
And heart-strung lyre awoke the Moon's eclipse,—
   Thou whom the daisies glory in growing o'er,—
Their fragrance clings around thy name, not writ
But rumor'd in water, while the fame of it
   Along Time's flood goes echoing evermore.
DANTE GABRIEL ROSSETTI
(1828-1882)

To John Keats

Great master! Boyish, sympathetic man!
   Whose orbed and ripened genius lightly hung
   From life's slim, twisted tendril and there swung
In crimson-sphered completeness; guardian
Of crystal portals through whose openings fan
   The spiced winds which blew when earth was young,
   Scattering wreaths of stars, as Jove once flung
A golden shower from heights cerulean.
   Crumbled before thy majesty we bow.
   Forget thy empurpled state, thy panoply
Of greatness, and be merciful and near;
   A youth who trudged the highroad we tread now
   Singing the miles behind him; so may we
Faint throbbings of thy music overhear.
AMY LOWELL
(1874-1925)

JOHN KEATS (1795–1821)

On Reading Keats in War Time

As one long lost in no-man's-land of war
Dreams of a cup of pure forgetful wine,
Dark waters deeper than the ancient Rhine
Where Saturnalian maidens swam before
The age of knowledge, and all your golden lore
Held in the splendor of a castle's shine
At sunset on a crag of somber pine—
But wakes to death and thirst and cannon's roar;
So I have come upon your book and drunk
Even to the dregs of melancholy bliss
Your poetry, Keats, and smoothing down your page,
Thought how a soldier leaner than a monk
Still loves, though time without the lover's kiss
Pours out its viscous hemlock on our age.

                          KARL JAY SHAPIRO
                                (1913–   )

JAMES HOGG (1770–1835)

Extempore Effusion upon the Death of James Hogg

When first, descending from the moorlands,
I saw the Stream of Yarrow glide
Along a bare and open valley,
The Ettrick Shepherd was my guide.

When last along its banks I wandered
Through groves that had begun to shed
Their golden leaves upon the pathways,
My steps the Border-minstrel led.

The mighty Minstrel breathes no longer,
'Mid mouldering ruins low he lies;
And death upon the braes of Yarrow,
Has closed the Shepherd-poet's eyes:

JAMES HOGG (1770–1835)

Nor has the rolling year twice measured,
From sign to sign, its stedfast course,
Since every mortal power of Coleridge
Was frozen at its marvellous source;

The rapt One, of the godlike forehead,
The heaven-eyed creature sleeps in earth:
And Lamb, the frolic and the gentle,
Has vanished from his lonely hearth.

Like clouds that rake the mountain-summits,
Or waves that own no curbing hand,
How fast has brother followed brother
From sunshine to the sunless land!

Yet I, whose lids from infant slumber
Were earlier raised, remain to hear
A timid voice, that asks in whispers,
"Who next will drop and disappear?"

Our haughty life is crowned with darkness,
Like London with its own black wreath,
On which with thee, O Crabbe! forthlooking,
I gazed from Hampstead's breezy heath.

As if but yesterday departed,
Thou too art gone before; but why,
O'er ripe fruit, seasonably gathered,
Should frail survivors heave a sigh?

Mourn rather for that holy Spirit,
Sweet as the spring, as ocean deep;
For Her who, ere her summer faded,
Has sunk into a breathless sleep.

No more of old romantic sorrows,
For slaughtered Youth or love-lorn Maid!
With sharper grief is Yarrow smitten,
And Ettrick mourns with her their Poet dead.

WILLIAM WORDSWORTH
(1770–1850)

VII

GIACOMO LEOPARDI (1798–1837)

To Giacomo Leopardi

Cold was thy thought, O stricken son
Of Italy, cold as the moon
That naked, barren, frozen, on
This fertile earth, the boon
Of silver light
Sheds by night,—
Touching the million shaken leaves
That crown our woods; while every fold
Of buttressed Alp soft charm receives,
Till near things look like lands far sought.
Yes, thy thought ached, it was so cold;
And winsome movement, and choice sound,
In harmonies divinely wrought,
Could they be born of that profound
Despair which they so clearly taught?
Nay, suffering, like a nightmare still,
Turned all thy youth's warm radiance chill,
—As yon dead moon turns the sun's beams
Aside in cold yet lucid streams,
Whose loveliness from farther came
Than that dead planet's cratered side;
A globe of glory all one flame
Is in their brightness still implied.
So in the beauty of thine odes
Man's glowing eager spirit shines,
While yet its strange deflection loads
With added charm their play, refines
Their luminous force, till they,
Fair as moonlight,
Infuse the night

GIACOMO LEOPARDI (1798-1837)

>Of our roused sorrow, sadness, and
>Remembered pain, where they expand
>Brilliance, both solemn and serene,
>Grand as the presence of Night's queen.
>
>> T. S. MOORE
>> (1870-   )

HEINRICH HEINE (1797-1856)

Heine's Grave

"*Henri Heine*"—'tis here!
The black tombstone, the name
Carved there—no more! and the smooth,
Swarded alleys, the lines
Touch'd with yellow by hot
Summer, but under them still,
In September's bright afternoon,
Shadow, and verdure, and cool.
Trim Montmartre! the faint
Murmur of Paris outside;
Crisp everlasting-flowers,
Yellow and black, on the graves.

Half blind, palsied, in pain,
Hither to come, from the streets'
Uproar, surely not loath
Wast thou, Heine!—to lie
Quiet, to ask for closed
Shutters, and darken'd room,
And cool drinks, and an eased
Posture, and opium, no more;
Hither to come, and to sleep
Under the wings of Renown.

Ah! not little, when pain
Is most quelling, and man
Easily quell'd, and the fine
Temper of genius so soon
Thrills at each smart, is the praise

HEINRICH HEINE (1797–1856)

Not to have yielded to pain!
No small boast, for a weak
Son of mankind, to the earth
Pinn'd by the thunder, to rear
His bolt-scathed front to the stars;
And, undaunted, retort
'Gainst thick-crashing, insane,
Tyrannous tempests of bale,
Arrowy lightnings of soul.

Hark! through the alley resounds
Mocking laughter! A film
Creeps o'er the sunshine; a breeze
Ruffles the warm afternoon,
Saddens my soul with its chill.
Gibing of spirits in scorn
Shakes every leaf of the grove,
Mars the benignant repose
Of this amiable home of the dead.

Bitter spirits, ye claim
Heine?—Alas, he is yours!
Only a moment I long'd
Here in the quiet to snatch
From such mates the outworn
Poet, and steep him in calm.
Only a moment! I knew
Whose he was who is here
Buried—I knew he was yours!
Ah, I knew that I saw
Here no sepulchre built
In the laurell'd rock, o'er the blue
Naples bay, for a sweet
Tender Virgil! no tomb
On Ravenna sands, in the shade
Of Ravenna pines, for a high
Austere Dante! no grave
By the Avon side, in the bright
Stratford meadows, for thee,
Shakespeare! loveliest of souls,
Peerless in radiance, in joy!

HEINRICH HEINE (1797–1856)

What, then, so harsh and malign,
Heine! distils from thy life?
Poisons the peace of thy grave?

I chide with thee not, that thy sharp
Upbraidings often assail'd
England, my country—for we,
Heavy and sad, for her sons,
Long since, deep in our hearts,
Echo the blame of her foes.
We, too, sigh that she flags;
We, too, say that she now—
Scarce comprehending the voice
Of her greatest, golden-mouth'd sons
Of a former age any more—
Stupidly travels her round
Of mechanic business, and lets
Slow die out of her life
Glory, and genius, and joy.

So thou arraign'st her, her foe;
So we arraign her, her sons.
Yes, we arraign her! but she,
The weary Titan, with deaf
Ears, and labour-dimm'd eyes,
Regarding neither to right
Nor left, goes passively by,
Staggering on to her goal;
Bearing on shoulders immense,
Atlanteän, the load,
Wellnigh not to be borne,
Of the too vast orb of her fate.

But was it thou—I think
Surely it was!—that bard
Unnamed, who, Goethe said,
Had every other gift, but wanted love;
Love, without which the tongue
Even of angels sounds amiss?

HEINRICH HEINE (1797–1856)

Charm is the glory which makes
Song of the poet divine,
Love is the fountain of charm.
How without charm wilt thou draw,
Poet! the world to thy way?
Not by the lightnings of wit—
Not by the thunder of scorn!
These to the world, too, are given;
Wit it possesses, and scorn—
Charm is the poet's alone.
*Hollow and dull are the great,
And artists envious, and the mob profane.*
We know all this, we know!
Can'st thou from heaven, O child
Of light! but this to declare?
Alas, to help us forget
Such barren knowledge awhile,
God gave the poet his song!

Therefore a secret unrest
Tortured thee, brilliant and bold!
Therefore triumph itself
Tasted amiss to thy soul.
Therefore, with blood of thy foes,
Trickled in silence thine own.
Therefore the victor's heart
Broke on the field of his fame.

Ah! as of old, from the pomp
Of Italian Milan, the fair
Flower of marble of white
Southern palaces—steps
Border'd by statues, and walks
Terraced, and orange-bowers
Heavy with fragrance—the blond
German Kaiser full oft
Long'd himself back to the fields,
Rivers, and high-roof'd towns
Of his native Germany; so,
So, how often! from hot

HEINRICH HEINE (1797-1856)

    Paris drawing-rooms, and lamps
Blazing, and brilliant crowds,
Starr'd and jewell'd, of men
Famous, of women the queens
Of dazzling converse—from fumes
Of praise, hot, heady fumes, to the poor brain
That mount, that madden—how oft
Heine's spirit outworn
Long'd itself out of the din,
Back to the tranquil, the cool
Far German home of his youth!

    See! in the May-afternoon,
O'er the fresh, short turf of the Hartz,
A youth, with the foot of youth,
Heine! thou climbest again!
Up, through the tall dark firs
Warming their heads in the sun,
Chequering the grass with their shade—
Up, by the stream, with its huge
Moss-hung boulders, and thin
Musical water half-hid—
Up, o'er the rock-strewn slope,
With the sinking sun, and the air
Chill, and the shadows now
Long on the grey hill-side—
To the stone-roof'd hut at the top!

    Or, yet later, in watch
On the roof of the Brocken-tower
Thou standest, gazing!—to see
The broad red sun, over field,
Forest, and city, and spire,
And mist-track'd stream of the wide
Wide German land, going down
In a bank of vapours—again
Standest, at nightfall, alone!

    Or, next morning, with limbs
Rested by slumber, and heart

HEINRICH HEINE (1797–1856)

Freshen'd and light with the May,
O'er the gracious spurs coming down
Of the Lower Hartz, among oaks
And beechen coverts, and copse
Of hazels green in whose depth
Ilse, the fairy transform'd,
In a thousand water-breaks light
Pours her petulant youth—
Climbing the rock which juts
O'er the valley—the dizzily perch'd
Rock—to its iron cross
Once more thou cling'st; to the Cross
Clingest! with smiles, with a sigh!

Goethe, too, had been there.
In the long-past winter he came
To the frozen Hartz, with his soul
Passionate, eager—his youth
All in ferment!—but he
Destined to work and to live
Left it, and thou, alas!
Only to laugh and to die.

But something prompts me: Not thus
Take leave of Heine! not thus
Speak the last word at his grave!
Not in pity, and not
With half censure—with awe
Hail, as it passes from earth
Scattering lightnings, that soul!

The Spirit of the world,
Beholding the absurdity of men—
Their vaunts, their feats—let a sardonic smile,
For one short moment, wander o'er his lips.
That smile was Heine!—for its earthly hour
The strange guest sparkled; now 'tis pass'd away.

That was Heine! and we,
Myriads who live, who have lived,
What are we all, but a mood,

HEINRICH HEINE (1797-1856)

A single mood, of the life
Of the Spirit in whom we exist,
Who alone is all things in one?

Spirit, who fillest us all!
Spirit, who utterest in each
New-coming son of mankind
Such of thy thoughts as thou wilt!
O thou, one of whose moods,
Bitter and strange, was the life
Of Heine—his strange, alas,
His bitter life!—may a life
Other and milder be mine!
May'st thou a mood more serene,
Happier, have utter'd in mine!
May'st thou the rapture of peace
Deep have embreathed at its core;
Made it a ray of thy thought,
Made it a beat of thy joy!

MATTHEW ARNOLD
(1822-1888)

THOMAS HOOD (1799-1845)

To the Memory of Hood

Another star 'neath Time's horizon dropped,
   To gleam o'er unknown lands and seas;
Another heart that beat for freedom stopped,—
   What mournful words are these!

O Love Divine, that claspest our tired earth,
   And lullest it upon thy heart,
Thou knowest how much a gentle soul is worth
   To teach men what thou art!

His was a spirit that to all thy poor
   Was kind as slumber after pain:
Why ope so soon thy heaven-deep Quiet's door
   And call him home again?

THOMAS HOOD (1799-1845)

Freedom needs all her poets: it is they
  Who give her aspirations wings,
And to the wiser law of music sway
  Her wild imaginings.

Yet thou hast called him, nor art thou unkind,
  O Love Divine, for 't is thy will
That gracious natures leave their love behind
  To work for Mercy still.

Let laurelled marbles weigh on other tombs,
  Let anthems peal for other dead,
Rustling the bannered depth of minster-glooms
  With their exulting spread.

His epitaph shall mock the short-lived stone,
  No lichen shall its lines efface,
He needs these few and simple lines alone
  To mark his resting-place:—

"Here lies a Poet. Stranger, if to thee
  His claim to memory be obscure,
If thou wouldst learn how truly great was he,
  Go, ask it of the poor."

JAMES RUSSELL LOWELL
(1819-1891)

Thomas Hood

The man who cloaked his bitterness within
This winding-sheet of puns and pleasantries,
God never gave to look with common eyes
Upon a world of anguish and of sin:
His brother was the branded man of Lynn;
And there are woven with his jollities
The nameless and eternal tragedies
That render hope and hopelessness akin.
We laugh, and crown him; but anon we feel
A still chord sorrow-swept,—a weird unrest;
And thin dim shadows home to midnight steal,
As if the very ghost of mirth were dead—

THOMAS HOOD (1799–1845)

> As if the joys of time to dreams had fled,
> Or sailed away with Ines to the West.
> EDWIN ARLINGTON ROBINSON
(1869–1935)

[MISCELLANY]

from "A Vision of Poets"

....................these were poets true,
Who died for Beauty as martyrs do
For Truth—the ends being scarcely two.

Here Homer, with a broad suspense
Of thunderous brows, and lips intense
Of garrulous god-innocence.

There Shakespeare, on whose forehead climb
The crowns o' the world: O eyes sublime
With tears and laughters for all time!

Here Æschylus, the women swooned
To see so awful, when he frowned
As the gods did: he standeth crowned.

Euripides, with close and mild
Scholastic lips, that could be wild
And laugh or sob out like a child

Even in the classes. Sophocles,
With that king's-look which down the trees
Followed the dark effigies

Of the lost Theban. Hesiod old,
Who, somewhat blind and deaf and cold,
Cared most for gods and bulls. And bold

Electric Pindar, quick as fear,
With race-dust on his cheeks, and clear
Slant startled eyes that seem to hear

The chariot rounding the last goal,
To hurtle past it in his soul.
And Sappho, with that gloriole

["A VISION OF POETS"]

Of ebon hair on calmèd brows—
O poet-woman! none foregoes
The leap, attaining the repose.

Theocritus, with glittering locks
Dropped sideway, as betwixt the rocks
He watched the visionary flocks.

And Aristophanes, who took
The world with mirth, and laughter-struck
The hollow caves of Thought and woke

The infinite echoes hid in each.
And Virgil: shade of Mantuan beech
Did help the shade of bay to reach

And knit around his forehead high:
For his gods wore less majesty
Than his brown bees hummed deathlessly.

Lucretius, nobler than his mood,
Who dropped his plummet down the broad
Deep universe and said 'No God—'

Finding no bottom: he denied
Divinely the divine, and died
Chief poet on the Tiber-side

By grace of God: his face is stern
As one compelled, in spite of scorn,
To teach a truth he would not learn.

And Ossian, dimly seen or guessed;
Once counted greater than the rest,
When mountain-winds blew out his vest.

And Spenser drooped his dreaming head
(With languid sleep-smile you had said
From his own verse ungenderèd)

["A VISION OF POETS"]

On Ariosto's, till they ran
Their curls in one: the Italian
Shot nimbler heat of bolder man

From his fine lids. And Dante stern
And sweet, whose spirit was an urn
For wine and milk poured out in turn.

Hard-souled Alfieri; and fancy-willed
Boiardo, who with laughter filled
The pauses of the jostled shield.

And Berni, with a hand stretched out
To sleek that storm. And, not without
The wreath he died in and the doubt

He died by, Tasso, bard and lover,
Whose visions were too thin to cover
The face of a false woman over.

And soft Racine; and grave Corneille,
The orator of rhymes, whose wail
Scarce shook his purple. And Petrarch pale,

From whose brain-lighted heart were thrown
A thousand thoughts beneath the sun,
Each lucid with the name of One.

And Camoens, with that look he had,
Compelling India's Genius sad
From the wave through the Lusiad,—

The murmurs of the storm-cape ocean
Indrawn in vibrative emotion
Along the verse. And, while devotion

In his wild eyes fantastic shone
Under the tonsure blown upon
By airs celestial, Calderon.

["A VISION OF POETS"]

And bold De Vega, who breathed quick
Verse after verse, till death's old trick
Put pause to life and rhetoric.

And Goethe, with that reaching eye
His soul reached out from, far and high,
And fell from inner entity.

And Schiller, with heroic front
Worthy of Plutarch's kiss upon 't,
Too large for wreath of modern wont.

And Chaucer, with his infantine
Familiar clasp of things divine;
That mark upon his lip is wine.

Here, Milton's eyes strike piercing-dim:
The shapes of suns and stars did swim
Like clouds from them, and granted him

God for sole vision. Cowley, there,
Whose active fancy debonair
Drew straws like amber—foul to fair.

Drayton and Browne, with smiles they drew
From outward nature, still kept new
From their own inward nature true.

And Marlowe, Webster, Fletcher, Ben,
Whose fire-hearts sowed our furrows when
The world was worthy of such men.

And Burns, with pungent passionings
Set in his eyes: deep lyric springs
Are of the fire-mount's issuings.

And Shelley, in his white ideal,
All statue-blind. And Keats the real
Adonis with the hymeneal

["A VISION OF POETS"]

>Fresh vernal buds half sunk between
>His youthful curls, kissed straight and sheen
>In his Rome-grave, by Venus queen.
>
>And poor, proud Byron, sad as grave
>And salt as life; forlornly brave,
>And quivering with the dart he drave.
>
>And visionary Coleridge, who
>Did sweep his thoughts as angels do
>Their wings with cadence up the Blue.
>
>These poets faced (and many more)
>The lighted altar looming o'er
>The clouds of incense dim and hoar:
>
>And all their faces, in the lull
>Of natural things, looked wonderful
>With life and death and deathless rule.
>
>>ELIZABETH BARRETT BROWNING
>>(1806–1861)

1843

ELIZABETH BARRETT BROWNING (1806–1861)

[Her "Last Poem"—]

>Her "Last Poems"—
>Poets ended
>Silver perished with her tongue,
>Not on record bubbled other
>Flute, or Woman so divine;
>Not unto its summer morning
>Robin uttered half the tune—
>Gushed too free for the adoring,
>From the Anglo-Florentine.
>Late the praise—
>'Tis dull conferring
>On a Head too high a crown,
>Diadem or Ducal showing,

ELIZABETH BARRETT BROWNING (1806–1861)

  Be its grave sufficient sign.
  Yet if we, no Poet's kinsman
  Suffocate with easy woe,
  What and if oneself a Bridegroom
  Put her down, in Italy?
EMILY DICKINSON
(1830–1886)

E. B. B.

The white-rose garland at her feet,
 The crown of laurel at her head,
Her noble life on earth complete,
 Lay her in the last low bed
For the slumber calm and deep:
"He giveth His beloved sleep."

Soldiers find their fittest grave
 In the field whereon they died;
So her spirit pure and brave
 Leaves the clay it glorified
To the land for which she fought
With such grand impassioned thought.

Keats and Shelley sleep at Rome,
 She in well-loved Tuscan earth;
Finding all their death's long home
 Far from their old home of birth.
Italy, you hold in trust
Very sacred English dust.

Therefore this one prayer I breathe,—
 That you yet may worthy prove
Of the heirlooms they bequeath
 Who have loved you with such love:
Fairest land while land of slaves
Yields their free souls no fit graves.
JAMES THOMSON
(1834–1882)

[MISCELLANY]

from "A Fable for Critics"

"There comes Emerson first, whose rich words, every one,
Are like gold nails in temples to hang trophies on,
Whose prose is grand verse, while his verse, the Lord knows,
Is some of it pr— No, 'tis not even prose;
I'm speaking of meters; some poems have welled
From those rare depths of soul that have ne'er been excelled;
They're not epics, but that doesn't matter a pin,
In creating, the only hard thing's to begin;
A grass-blade's no easier to make than an oak;
If you've once found the way, you've achieved the grand stroke;
In the worst of his poems are mines of rich matter,
But thrown in a heap with a crash and a clatter;
Now it is not one thing nor another alone
Makes a poem, but rather the general tone,
The something pervading, uniting the whole,
The before unconceived, unconceivable soul,
So that just in removing this trifle or that, you
Take away, as it were, a chief limb of the statue;
Roots, wood, bark, and leaves singly perfect may be,
But, clapt hodge-podge together, they don't make a tree.

"But, to come back to Emerson (whom, by the way,
I believe we left waiting),—his is, we may say,
A Greek head on right Yankee shoulders, whose range
Has Olympus for one pole, for t'other the Exchange;
He seems, to my thinking (although I'm afraid
The comparison must, long ere this, have been made),
A Plotinus-Montaigne, where the Egyptian's gold mist
And the Gascon's shrewd with check-by-jowl coexist;
All admire, and yet scarcely six converts he's got
To I don't (nor they either) exactly know what;
For though he builds glorious temples, 'tis odd
He leaves never a doorway to get in a god.
'Tis refreshing to old-fashioned people like me
To meet such a primitive Pagan as he,
In whose mind all creation is duly respected
As parts of himself—just a little projected;

["A FABLE FOR CRITICS"]

And who's willing to worship the stars and the sun,
A convert to—nothing but Emerson.
So perfect a balance there is in his head,
That he talks of things sometimes as if they were dead;
Life, nature, love, God, and affairs of that sort,
He looks at as merely ideas; in short,
As if they were fossils stuck round in a cabinet,
Of such vast extent that our earth's a mere dab in it;
Composed just as he is inclined to conjecture her,
Namely, one part pure earth, ninety-nine parts pure lecturer;
You are filled with delight at his clear demonstration,
Each figure, word, gesture, just fits the occasion,
With the quiet precision of science he'll sort 'em,
But you can't help suspecting the whole a *post mortem*.

* * * * *

"There is Bryant, as quiet, as cool, and as dignified,
As a smooth, silent iceberg, that never is ignified,
Save when by reflection 'tis kindled o' nights
With a semblance of flame by the chill Northern Lights.
He may rank (Griswold says so) first bard of your nation
(There's no doubt that he stands in supreme ice-olation),
Your topmost Parnassus he may set his heel on,—
But no warm applauses come, peal following peal on,
He's too smooth and too polished to hang any zeal on:
Unqualified merits, I'll grant, if you choose, he has 'em,
But he lacks the one merit of kindling enthusiasm;
If he stir you at all, it is just, on my soul,
Like being stirred up with the very North Pole.

"He is very nice reading in summer, but *inter
Nos*, we don't want *extra* freezing in winter;
Take him up in the depth of July, my advice is,
When you feel an Egyptian devotion to ices.
But, deduct all you can, there's enough that's right good in him,
He has a true soul for field, river, and wood in him;
And his heart, in the midst of brick walls, or where'er it is,
Glows, softens, and thrills with the tenderest charities—
To you mortals that delve in this trade-ridden planet?
No, to old Berkshire's hills, with their limestone and granite.

["A FABLE FOR CRITICS"]

If you're one who *in loco* (add *foco* here) *desipis*,
You will get of his outermost heart (as I guess) a piece;
But you'd get deeper down if you came as a precipice,
And would break the last seal of its inwardest fountain,
If you only could palm yourself off for a mountain.
Mr. Quivis, or somebody quite as discerning,
Some scholar who's hourly expecting his learning,
Calls B. the American Wordsworth; but Wordsworth
May be rated at more than your whole tuneful herd's worth.
No, don't be absurd, he's an excellent Bryant;
But, my friends, you'll endanger the life of your client,
By attempting to stretch him up into a giant:
If you choose to compare him, I think there are two persons fit for a parallel—Thompson and Cowper;
I don't mean exactly,—there's something of each,
There's T.'s love of nature, C.'s penchant to preach;
Just mix up their minds so that C.'s spice of craziness
Shall balance and neutralize T.'s turn for laziness,
And it gives you a brain cool, quite frictionless, quiet
Whose internal police nips the buds of all riot,—
A brain like a permanent strait jacket put on
The heart that strives vainly to burst off a button,—
A brain which, without being slow or mechanic,
Does more than a larger less drilled, more volcanic;
He's a Cowper condensed, with no craziness bitten,
And the advantage that Wordsworth before him had written.

"But, my dear little bardlings, don't prick up your ears
Nor suppose I would rank you and Bryant as peers;
If I call him an iceberg, I don't mean to say
There is nothing in that which is grand in its way;
He is almost the one of your poets that knows
How much grace, strength, and dignity lie in Repose;
If he sometimes fall short, he is too wise to mar
His thought's modest fullness by going too far;
'Twould be well if your authors should all make a trial
Of what virtue there is in severe self-denial,
And measure their writings by Hesiod's staff,
Which teaches that all has less value than half.

["A FABLE FOR CRITICS"]

"There is Whittier, whose swelling and vehement heart
Strains the strait-breasted drab of the Quaker apart,
And reveals the live Man, still supreme and erect,
Underneath the bemummying wrappers of sect;
There was ne'er a man born who had more of the swing
Of the true lyric bard and all that kind of thing;
And his failures arise (though he seem not to know it)
From the very same cause that has made him a poet,—
A fervor of mind which knows no separation
'Twixt simple excitement and pure inspiration,
As my Pythoness erst sometimes erred from not knowing
If 'twere I or mere wind through her tripod was blowing;
Let his mind once get head in its favorite direction
And the torrent of verse bursts the dams of reflection,
While, borne with the rush of the meter along,
The poet may chance to go right or go wrong,
Content with the whirl and delirium of song;
Then his grammar's not always correct, nor his rhymes
And he's prone to repeat his own lyrics sometimes,
Not his best, though, for those are struck off at white heats
When the heart in his breast like a triphammer beats,
And can ne'er be repeated again any more
Than they could have been carefully plotted before:
Like old what's-his-name there at the battle of Hastings
(Who, however, gave more than mere rhythmical bastings),
Our Quaker leads off metaphorical fights
For reform and whatever they call human rights,
Both singing and striking in front of the war,
And hitting his foes with the mallet of Thor;
Anne haec, one exclaims, on beholding his knocks,
Vestis filii tui, O leather-clad Fox?
Can that be thy son, in the battle's mid din,
Preaching brotherly love and then driving it in
To the brain of the tough old Goliath of sin,
With the smoothest of pebbles from Castaly's spring
Impressed on his hard moral sense with a sling?

"All honor and praise to the right-hearted bard
Who was true to The Voice when such service was hard,

["A FABLE FOR CRITICS"]

Who himself was so free he dared sing for the slave
When to look but a protest in silence was brave;
All honor and praise to the women and men
Who spoke out for the dumb and the downtrodden then!
It needs not to name them, already for each
I see History preparing the statue and niche;
They were harsh, but shall *you* be so shocked at hard words
Who have beaten your pruning hooks up into swords,
Whose rewards and hurrahs men are surer to gain
By the reaping of men and of women than grain?
Why should *you* stand aghast at their fierce wordy war, if
You scalp one another for Bank or for Tariff?
Your calling them cutthroats and knaves all day long
Doesn't prove that the use of hard language is wrong;
While the World's heart beats quicker to think of such men
As signed Tyranny's doom with a bloody steel pen,
While on Fourth of Julys beardless orators fright one
With hints at Harmodius and Aristogeiton,
You need not look shy at your sisters and brothers
Who stab with sharp words for the freedom of others;—
No, a wreath, twine a wreath for the loyal and true
Who, for sake of the many, dared stand with the few,
Not of blood-spattered laurel for enemies braved,
But of broad, peaceful oak leaves for citizens saved!

* * * * *

"There comes Poe, with his raven, like Barnaby Rudge,
Three-fifths of him genius and two-fifths sheer fudge,
Who talks like a book of iambs and pentameters,
In a way to make people of common sense damn meters,
Who has written some things quite the best of their kind,
But the heart somehow seems all squeezed out by the mind,
Who—But hey-day! What's this? Messieurs Mathews and Poe,
You mustn't fling mud balls at Longfellow so,
Does it make a man worse that his character's such
As to make his friends love him (as you think) too much?
Why, there is not a bard at this moment alive
More willing than he that his fellows should thrive;
While you are abusing him thus, even now
He would help either one of you out of a slough;

["A FABLE FOR CRITICS"]

You may say that he's smooth and all that till you're hoarse,
But remember that elegance also is force;
After polishing granite as much as you will,
The heart keeps its tough old persistency still;
Deduct all you can, *that* still keeps you at bay;
Why, he'll live till men weary of Collins and Gray.
I'm not overfond of Greek meters in English,
To me rhyme's a gain, so it be not too jinglish,
And your modern hexameter verses are no more
Like Greek ones than sleek Mr. Pope is like Homer;
As the roar of the sea to the coo of a pigeon is,
So, compared to your moderns, sounds old Melesigenes;
I may be too partial, the reason, perhaps, o't is
That I've heard the old blind man recite his own rhapsodies,
And my ear with that music impregnate may be,
Like the poor exiled shell with the soul of the sea,
Or as one can't bear Strauss when his nature is cloven
To its deeps within deeps by the stroke of Beethoven;
But, set that aside, and 'tis truth that I speak,
Had Theocritus written in English, not Greek,
I believe that his exquisite sense would scarce change a line
In that rare, tender, virginlike pastoral *Evangeline.*
That's not ancient nor modern, its place is apart
Where time has no sway, in the realm of pure Art,
'Tis a shrine of retreat from Earth's hubbub and strife
As quiet and chaste as the author's own life.

JAMES RUSSELL LOWELL
(1819–1891)

EDGAR ALLAN POE (1809–1849)

Poe's Cottage at Fordham

Here lived the soul enchanted
  By melody of song;
Here dwelt the spirit haunted
  By a demoniac throng;
Here sang the lips elated;
Here grief and death were sated;
Here loved and here unmated
  Was he, so frail, so strong.

EDGAR ALLAN POE (1809-1849)

    Here wintry winds and cheerless
        The dying firelight blew,
    While he whose song was peerless
        Dreamed the drear midnight through,
    And from dull embers chilling
    Crept shadows darkly filling
    The silent place, and thrilling
        His fancy as they grew.

    Here, with brow bared to heaven,
        In starry night he stood,
    With the lost star of seven
        Feeling sad brotherhood.
    Here in the sobbing showers
    Of dark autumnal hours
    He heard suspected powers
        Shriek through the stormy wood.

    From visions of Apollo
        And of Astarte's bliss,
    He gazed into the hollow
        And hopeless vale of Dis;
    And though earth were surrounded
    By heaven, it still was mounded
    With graves. His soul had sounded
        The dolorous abyss.

    Proud, mad, but not defiant,
        He touched at heaven and hell.
    Fate found a rare soul pliant
        And rung her changes well.
    Alternately his lyre,
    Stranded with strings of fire,
    Led earth's most happy choir,
        Or flashed with Israfel.

    No singer of old story
        Luting accustomed lays,
    No harper for new glory,
        No mendicant for praise,

EDGAR ALLAN POE (1809-1849)

>   He struck high chords and splendid,
>   Wherein were fiercely blended
>   Tones that unfinished ended
>   With his unfinished days.
>
>   Here through this lowly portal,
>   Made sacred by his name,
>   Unheralded immortal
>   The mortal went and came.
>   And fate that then denied him,
>   And envy that decried him,
>   And malice that belied him,
>   Have cenotaphed his fame.
>
>   JOHN HENRY BONER
>   (1845-1903)

Israfel

Picture the grave in his diabolical dream
Where death would come with clues and scenery,
The bulbous forehead and the crooked mouth
Leaking a poison, the translucent hands.

Perhaps like Juliet he could come alive
To hate Longfellow and to outrage life,
But dare not from his wretched rusty stone,
Landmark for girls developing in slums.

Here he is local color, another crank;
Pawnshops and whores and sour little bars
Accept him. Neither alarming nor prophetic,
He pleases like a wop or a jack-o-lantern.

Others up town forgive his nasty eyes
Because he was sick and had a mind to err;
But he was never dirty like Hawthorne,
But boyish with his spooks and funerals

And clammy virgins. What else were his codes
But diagrams of hideouts of the mind
Plugged up with corpses and expensive junk,
Prosopopoeia to keep himself at bay?

EDGAR ALLAN POE (1809-1849)

    Think of him as a cicerone with data
    False as a waxworks and that understood
    Ask pitifully for pain. Or think that now
    Four cities claim him as France recommended.
                                KARL JAY SHAPIRO
                                        (1913-   )

HENRY WADSWORTH LONGFELLOW (1807-1882)

To H. W. L.

On His Birthday, 27th February, 1867.

I need not praise the sweetness of his song,
    Where limpid verse to limpid verse succeeds
Smooth as our Charles, when, fearing lest he wrong
The new moon's mirrored skiff, he slides along,
    Full without noise, and whispers in his reeds.

With loving breath of all the winds his name
    Is blown about the world, but to his friends
A sweeter secret hides behind his fame,
And Love steals shyly through the loud acclaim
    To murmur a *God bless you!* and there ends.

As I muse backward up the checkered years
    Wherein so much was given, so much was lost,
Blessings in both kinds, such as cheapen tears,—
But hush! this is not for profaner ears;
    Let them drink molten pearls nor dream the cost.

Some suck up poison from a sorrow's core,
    As naught but nightshade grew upon earth's ground;
Love turned all his to heart's-ease, and the more
Fate tried his bastions, she but forced a door
    Leading to sweeter manhood and more sound.

Even as a wind-waved fountain's swaying shade
    Seems of mixed race, a gray wraith shot with sun,
So through his trial faith translucent rayed
Till darkness, half disnatured so, betrayed
    A heart of sunshine that would fain o'errun.

HENRY WADSWORTH LONGFELLOW (1807-1882)

Surely if skill in song the shears may stay
   And of its purpose cheat the charmed abyss,
If our poor life be lengthened by a lay,
He shall not go, although his presence may,
   And the next age in praise shall double this.

Long days be his, and each as lusty-sweet
   As gracious natures find his song to be;
May Age steal on with softly-cadenced feet
Falling in music, as for him were meet
   Whose choicest verse is harsher-toned than he!

                        JAMES RUSSELL LOWELL
                               (1819-1891)

[MISCELLANY]

The Crystal

At midnight, death's and truth's unlocking time,
When far within the spirit's hearing rolls
The great soft rumble of the course of things—
A bulk of silence in a mask of sound,—
When darkness clears our vision that by day
Is sun-blind, and the soul's a ravening owl
For truth and flitteth here and there about
Low-lying woody tracts of time and oft
Is minded for to sit upon a bough,
Dry-dead and sharp, of some long-stricken tree
And muse in that gaunt place,—'twas then my heart,
Deep in the meditative dark, cried out:

"Ye companies of governor-spirits grave,
Bards, and old bringers-down of flaming news
From steep-wall'd heavens, holy malcontents,
Sweet seers, and stellar visionaries, all
That brood about the skies of poesy,
Full bright ye shine, insuperable stars;
Yet, if a man look hard upon you, none
With total lustre blazeth, no, not one
But hath some heinous freckle of the flesh

["THE CRYSTAL"]

Upon his shining cheek, not one but winks
His ray, opaqued with intermittent mist
Of defect; yea, you masters all must ask
Some sweet forgiveness, which we leap to give,
We lovers of you, heavenly-glad to meet
Your largesse so with love, and interplight
Your geniuses with our mortalities.

Thus unto thee, O sweetest Shakspere sole,
A hundred hurts a day I do forgive
('Tis little, but, enchantment! 'tis for thee):
Small curious quibble; Juliet's prurient pun
In the poor, pale face of Romeo's fancied death;
Cold rant of Richard; Henry's fustian roar
Which frights away that sleep he invocates;
Wronged Valentine's unnatural haste to yield;
Too-silly shifts of maids that mask as men
In faint disguises that could ne'er disguise—
Viola, Julia, Portia, Rosalind;
Fatigues most drear, and needless overtax
Of speech obscure that had as lief be plain;
Last I forgive (with more delight, because
'Tis more to do) the labored-lewd discourse
That e'en thy young invention's youngest heir
Besmirched the world with.

      Father Homer, thee,
Thee also I forgive thy sandy wastes
Of prose and catalogue, thy drear harangues
That tease the patience of the centuries,
Thy sleazy scrap of story,—but a rogue's
Rape of a light-o'-love,—too soiled a patch
To broider with the gods.

      Thee, Socrates,
Thou dear and very strong one, I forgive
Thy year-worn cloak, thine iron stringencies
That were but dandy upside-down, thy words
Of truth that, mildlier spoke, had mainlier wrought.

["THE CRYSTAL"]

So, Buddha, beautiful! I pardon thee
That all the All thou hadst for needy man
Was Nothing, and thy Best of being was
But not to be.

          Worn Dante, I forgive
The implacable hates that in thy horrid hells
Or burn or freeze thy fellows, never loosed
By death, nor time, nor love.

                     And I forgive
Thee, Milton, those thy comic-dreadful wars
Where, armed with gross and inconclusive steel,
Immortals smite immortals mortalwise
And fill all heaven with folly.

                 Also thee,
Brave Æschylus, thee I forgive, for that
Thine eye, by bare bright justice basilisked,
Turned not, nor ever learned to look where Love
Stands shining.

          So, unto thee, Lucretius mine
(For oh, what heart hath loved thee like to this
That's now complaining?), freely I forgive
Thy logic poor, thine error rich, thine earth
Whose graves eat souls and all.

                 Yea, all you hearts
Of beauty, and sweet righteous lovers large:
Aurelius fine, oft superfine; mild Saint
A Kempis, overmild; Epictetus,
Whiles low in thought, still with old slavery tinct;
Rapt Behmen, rapt too far; high Swedenborg,
O'ertoppling; Langley, that with but a touch
Of art hadst sung Piers Plowman to the top
Of English songs, whereof 'tis dearest, now,
And most adorable; Cædmon, in the morn
A-calling angels with the cow-herd's call
That late brought up the cattle; Emerson,

["THE CRYSTAL"]

> Most wise, that yet, in finding Wisdom, lost
> Thy Self, sometimes; tense Keats, with angels' nerves
> Where men's were better; Tennyson, largest voice
> Since Milton, yet some register of wit
> Wanting;—all, all, I pardon, ere 'tis asked,
> Your more or less, your little mole that marks
> You brother and your kinship seals to man.
>
> But Thee, but Thee, O sovereign Seer of time,
> But Thee, O poets' Poet, Wisdom's Tongue,
> But Thee, O man's best Man, O love's best Love,
> O perfect life in perfect labor writ,
> O all men's Comrade, Servant, King, or Priest,—
> What *if* or *yet*, what mole, what flaw, what lapse,
> What least defect or shadow of defect,
> What rumor, tattled by an enemy,
> Of inference loose, what lack of grace
> Even in torture's grasp, or sleep's, or death's,—
> Oh, what amiss may I forgive in Thee,
> Jesus, good Paragon, thou Crystal Christ?"

Baltimore, 1880

SIDNEY LANIER
(1842–1881)

ALFRED, LORD TENNYSON (1809–1892)

Wapentake

To Alfred Tennyson

> Poet! I come to touch thy lance with mine;
>   Not as a knight, who on the listed field
>   Of tourney touched his adversary's shield
>   In token of defiance, but in sign
> Of homage to the mastery, which is thine,
>   In English song; nor will I keep concealed,
>   And voiceless as a rivulet frost-congealed,
>   My admiration for thy verse divine.
> Not of the howling dervishes of song,
>   Who craze the brain with their delirious dance,
>   Art thou, O sweet historian of the heart!

ALFRED, LORD TENNYSON (1809–1892)

> Therefore to thee the laurel-leaves belong,
> To thee our love and our allegiance,
> For thy allegiance to the poet's art.
> HENRY WADSWORTH LONGFELLOW
(1807–1882)

Alfred Tennyson

Tears, idle tears! Ah, who shall bid us weep,
Now that thy lyre, O prophet, is unstrung?
What voice shall rouse the dull world from its sleep
And lead its requiem as when Grief was young,
And thou in thy rapt youth, Time's bards among,
Captured our ears, and we looked up and heard
Spring's sweetest music, on thy mourning tongue
And knew thee for Pain's paradisal bird.
We are alone without thee in our tears,
Alone in our mute chauntings. Vows are vain
To tell thee how we loved thee in those years
Nor dream to look upon thy like again.
We know not how to weep without thy aid,
Since all that tears would tell thyself hast said.
WILFRID SCAWEN BLUNT
(1840–1922)

ROBERT BROWNING (1812–1889)

To Robert Browning

There is delight in singing, tho' none hear
Beside the singer; and there is delight
In praising, tho' the praiser sit alone
And see the prais'd far off him, far above.
Shakespeare is not our poet, but the world's,
Therefore on him no speech! and brief for thee,
Browning! Since Chaucer was alive and hale,
No man hath walked along our roads with step
So active, so inquiring eye, or tongue
So varied in discourse. But warmer climes
Give brighter plumage, strong wing: the breeze

[282]

ROBERT BROWNING (1812–1889)

> Of Alpine heights thou playest with, borne on
> Beyond Sorrento and Amalfi, where
> The Siren waits thee, singing song for song.
> WALTER SAVAGE LANDOR
(1775–1864)

From "Sonnets from the Portuguese"

IV

Thou hast thy calling to some palace-floor,
Most gracious singer of high poems! where
The dancers will break footing, from the care
Of watching up thy pregnant lips for more.
And dost thou lift this house's latch too poor
For hand of thine? and canst thou think and bear
To let thy music drop here unaware
In folds of golden fulness at my door?
Look up and see the casement broken in,
The bats and owlets builders in the roof!
My cricket chirps against thy mandolin.
Hush, call no echo up in further proof
Of desolation! there's a voice within
That weeps . . . as thou must sing . . . alone, aloof.

XVII

My poet, thou canst touch on all the notes
God set between his After and Before,
And strike up and strike off the general roar
Of the rushing worlds a melody that floats
In a serene air purely. Antidotes
Of medicated music, answering for
Mankind's forlornest uses, thou canst pour
From thence into their ears. God's will devotes
Thine to such ends, and mine to wait on thine.
How, Dearest, wilt thou have me for most use?
A hope, to sing by gladly? or a fine
Sad memory, with thy songs to interfuse?
A shade, in which to sing—of palm or pine?
A grave, on which to rest from singing? Choose.
ELIZABETH BARRETT BROWNING
(1806–1861)

EDWARD FITZGERALD (1809–1883)

To E. Fitzgerald

Old Fitz, who from your suburb grange,
  Where once I tarried for a while,
Glance at the wheeling orb of change,
  And greet it with a kindly smile;
Whom yet I see as there you sit
  Beneath your sheltering garden-tree,
And watch your doves about you flit,
  And plant on shoulder, hand, and knee,
Or on your head their rosy feet,
  As if they knew your diet spares
Whatever moved in that full sheet
  Let down to Peter at his prayers;
Who live on milk and meal and grass;
  And once for ten long weeks I tried
Your table of Pythagoras,
  And seem'd at first 'a thing enskied,'
As Shakespeare has it, airy-light
  To float above the ways of men,
Then fell from that half-spiritual height
  Chill'd, till I tasted flesh again
One night when earth was winter-black,
  And all the heavens flash'd in frost;
And on me, half-asleep, came back
  That wholesome heat the blood had lost,
And set me climbing icy capes
  And glaciers, over which there roll'd
To meet me long-arm'd vines with grapes
  Of Eshcol hugeness; for the cold
Without, and warmth within me, wrought
  To mould the dream; but none can say
That Lenten fare makes Lenten thought,
  Who reads your golden Eastern lay,
Than which I know no version done
  In English more divinely well;
A planet equal to the sun
  Which cast it, that large infidel
Your Omar; and your Omar drew

EDWARD FITZGERALD (1809-1883)

  Full-handed plaudits from our best
 In modern letters, and from two,
  Old friends outvaluing all the rest,
 Two voices heard on earth no more;
  But we old friends are still alive,
 And I am nearing seventy-four,
  While you have touch'd at seventy-five,
 And so I send a birthday line
  Of greeting; and my son, who dipt
 In some forgotten book of mine
  With sallow scraps of manuscript,
 And dating many a year ago,
  Has hit on this, which you will take,
 My Fitz, and welcome, as I know,
  Less for its own than for the sake
 Of one recalling gracious times,
  When, in our younger London days,
 You found some merit in my rhymes,
  And I more pleasure in your praise.

1883
       ALFRED, LORD TENNYSON
         (1809-1892)

EDWARD LEAR (1812-1888)

Edward Lear

Left his friend to breakfast alone on the white
Italian shore, his Terrible Demon arose
Over his shoulder; he wept to himself in the night,
A dirty landscape-painter who hated his nose.

The legions of cruel inquisitive They
Were so many and big like dogs; he was upset
By Germans and boats; affection was miles away:
But guided by tears he successfully reached his Regret.

How prodigious the welcome was. Flowers took his hat
And bore him off to introduce him to the tongs;
The demon's false nose made the table laugh; a cat

EDWARD LEAR (1812–1888)

Soon had him waltzing madly, let him squeeze her hand;
Words pushed him to the piano to sing comic songs;
And children swarmed to him like settlers. He became a land.
W. H. AUDEN
(1907–   )

VICTOR HUGO (1802–1885)

To Victor Hugo

Victor in Drama, Victor in Romance,
Cloud-weaver of phantasmal hopes and fears,
French of the French, and Lord of human tears;
Child-lover; Bard whose fame-lit laurels glance
Darkening the wreaths of all that would advance,
Beyond our strait, their claim to be thy peers;
Weird Titan by thy winter weight of years
As yet unbroken, stormy voice of France!
Who dost not love our England—so they say;
I know not—England, France, all man to be
Will make one people ere man's race be run:
And I, desiring that diviner day,
Yield thee full thanks for thy full courtesy
To younger England in the boy my son.
ALFRED, LORD TENNYSON
(1809–1892)

To Victor Hugo

In the fair days when God
  By man as godlike trod,
And each alike was Greek, alike was free,
  God's lightning spared, they said,
  Alone the happier head
Whose laurels screened it; fruitless grace for thee,
  To whom the high gods gave of right
Their thunders and their laurels and their light.

  Sunbeams and bays before
  Our master's servants wore,
For these Apollo left in all men's lands;

VICTOR HUGO (1802–1885)

    But far from these ere now
    And watched with jealous brow
Lay the blind lightnings shut between God's hands,
    And only loosed on slaves and kings
The terror of the tempest of their wings.

    Born in those younger years
    That shone with storms of spears
And shook in the wind blown from a dead world's pyre,
    When by her back-blown hair
    Napoleon caught the fair
And fierce Republic with her feet of fire,
    And stayed with iron words and hands
Her flight, and freedom in a thousand lands:

    Thou sawest the tides of things
    Close over heads of kings,
And thine hand felt the thunder, and to thee
    Laurels and lightnings were
    As sunbeams and soft air
Mixed each in other, or as mist with sea
    Mixed, or as memory with desire,
Or the lute's pulses with the louder lyre.

    For thee man's spirit stood
    Disrobed of flesh and blood,
And bare the heart of the most secret hours;
    And to thine hand more tame
    Than birds in winter came
High hopes and unknown flying forms of powers,
    And from thy table fed, and sang
Till with the tune men's ears took fire and rang.

    Even all men's eyes and ears
    With fiery sound and tears
Waxed hot, and cheeks caught flame and eyelid light,
    At those high songs of thine
    That stung the sense like wine,
Or fell more soft than dew or snow by night,
    Or wailed as in some flooded cave
Sobs the strong broken spirit of a wave.

VICTOR HUGO (1802–1885)

But we, our master, we
  Whose hearts, uplift to thee,
Ache with the pulse of thy remembered song,
  We ask not nor await
  From the clenched hands of fate,
As thou, remission of the world's old wrong;
  Respite we ask not, nor release;
Freedom a man may have, he shall not peace.

  Though thy most fiery hope
  Storm heaven, to set wide ope
The all-sought-for gate whence God or Chance debars
  All feet of men, all eyes—
  The old night resumes her skies,
Her hollow hiding-place of clouds and stars,
  Where nought save these is sure in sight;
And, paven with death, our days are roofed with night.

  One thing we can; to be
  Awhile, as men may, free;
But not by hope or pleasure the most stern
  Goddess, most awful-eyed,
  Sits, but on either side
Sit sorrow and the wrath of hearts that burn,
  Sad faith that cannot hope or fear,
And memory grey with many a flowerless year.

  Not that in stranger's wise
  I lift not loving eyes
To the fair foster-mother France, that gave
  Beyond the pale fleet foam
  Help to my sires and home,
Whose great sweet breast could shelter those and save
  Whom from her nursing breasts and hands
Their land cast forth of old on gentler lands.

  Not without thoughts that ache
  For theirs and for thy sake,
I, born of exiles, hail thy banished head;

VICTOR HUGO (1802–1885)

    I whose young song took flight
    Toward the great heat and light
On me a child from thy far splendour shed,
    From thine high place of soul and song,
Which, fallen on eyes yet feeble, made them strong.

    Ah, not with lessening love
    For memories born hereof,
I look to that sweet mother-land, and see
    The old fields and fair full streams,
    And skies, but fled like dreams
The feet of freedom and the thought of thee;
    And all between the skies and graves
The mirth of mockers and the shame of slaves.

    She, killed with noisome air,
    Even she! and still so fair,
Who said "Let there be freedom," and there was
    Freedom; and as a lance
    The fiery eyes of France
Touched the world's sleep and as a sleep made pass
    Forth of men's heavier ears and eyes
Smitten with fire and thunder from new skies.

    Are they men's friends indeed
    Who watch them weep and bleed?
Because thou hast loved us, shall the gods love thee?
    Thou, first of men and friend,
    Seest thou, even thou, the end?
Thou knowest what hath been, knowest thou what shall be?
    Evils may pass and hopes endure;
But fate is dim, and all the gods obscure.

    O nursed in airs apart,
    O poet highest of heart,
Hast thou seen time, who hast seen so many things?
    Are not the years more wise,
    More sad than keenest eyes,
The years with soundless feet and sounding wings?
    Passing we hear them not, but past
The clamour of them thrills us, and their blast.

VICTOR HUGO (1802–1885)

  Thou art chief of us, and lord;
   Thy song is as a sword
Keen-edged and scented in the blade from flowers;
  Thou art lord and king; but we
   Lift younger eyes, and see
Less of high hope, less light on wandering hours;
  Hours that have borne men down so long,
Seen the right fail, and watched uplift the wrong.

  But thine imperial soul,
   As years and ruins roll
To the same end, and all things and all dreams
   With the same wreck and roar
   Drift on the dim same shore,
Still in the bitter foam and brackish streams
  Tracks the fresh water-spring to be
And sudden sweeter fountains in the sea.

  As once the high God bound
   With many a rivet round
Man's saviour, and with iron nailed him through,
   At the wild end of things,
   Where even his own bird's wings
Flagged, whence the sea shone like a drop of dew,
   From Caucasus beheld below
Past fathoms of unfathomable snow;

  So the strong God, the chance
   Central of circumstance,
Still shows him exile who will not be slave;
   All thy great fame and thee
   Girt by the dim strait sea
With multitudinous walls of wandering wave;
  Shows us our greatest from his throne
Fate-stricken, and rejected of his own.

  Yea, he is strong, thou say'st,
   A mystery many-faced,
The wild beasts know him and the wild birds flee;
   The blind night sees him, death
   Shrinks beaten at his breath,
And his right hand is heavy on the sea:

VICTOR HUGO (1802–1885)

We know he hath made us, and is king;
We know not if he care for anything.

    Thus much, no more, we know;
    He bade what is be so,
Bade light be and bade night be, one by one;
    Bade hope and fear, bade ill
    And good redeem and kill,
Till all men be aweary of the sun
    And his world burn in its own flame
And bear no witness longer of his name.

    Yet though all this be thus,
    Be those men praised of us
Who have loved and wrought and sorrowed and not sinned
    For fame or fear or gold,
    Nor waxed for winter cold,
Nor changed for changes of the worldly wind;
    Praised above men of men be these,
Till this one world and work we know shall cease.

    Yea, one thing more than this,
    We know that one thing is,
The splendour of a spirit without blame,
    That not the labouring years
    Blind-born, nor any fears,
Nor men nor any gods can tire or tame;
    But purer power with fiery breath
Fills, and exalts above the gulfs of death.

    Praised above men be thou,
    Whose laurel-laden brow,
Made for the morning, droops not in the night;
    Praised and beloved, that none
    Of all thy great things done
Flies higher than thy most equal spirit's flight;
    Praised, that nor doubt nor hope could bend
Earth's loftiest head, found upright to the end.

                  ALGERNON CHARLES SWINBURNE
                          (1837–1909)

CHARLES BAUDELAIRE (1821–1867)

Ave atque Vale
(In Memory of Charles Baudelaire)

Shall I strew on thee rose or rue or laurel,
    Brother, on this that was the veil of thee?
    Or quiet sea-flower moulded by the sea,
Or simplest growth of meadow-sweet or sorrel,
    Such as the summer-sleepy Dryads weave,
    Waked up by snow-soft sudden rains at eve?
Or wilt thou rather, as on earth before,
    Half-faded fiery blossoms, pale with heat
    And full of bitter summer, but more sweet
To thee than gleanings of a northern shore
    Trod by no tropic feet?

For always thee the fervid languid glories
    Allured of heavier suns in mightier skies;
    Thine ears knew all the wandering watery sighs
Where the sea sobs round Lesbian promontories,
    The barren kiss of piteous wave to wave
    That knows not where is that Leucadian grave
Which hides too deep the supreme head of song.
    Ah, salt and sterile as her kisses were,
    The wild sea winds her and the green gulfs bear
Hither and thither, and vex and work her wrong,
    Blind gods that cannot spare.

Thou sawest, in thine old singing season, brother,
    Secrets and sorrows unbeheld of us:
    Fierce loves, and lovely leaf-buds poisonous,
Bare to thy subtler eye, but for none other
    Blowing by night in some unbreathed-in clime,
    The hidden harvest of luxurious time,
Sin without shape, and pleasure without speech;
    And where strange dreams in a tumultuous sleep
    Make the shut eyes of stricken spirits weep;
And with each face thou sawest the shadow on each,
    Seeing as men sow men reap.

CHARLES BAUDELAIRE (1821-1867)

O sleepless heart and sombre soul unsleeping,
   That were athirst for sleep and no more life
   And no more love, for peace and no more strife!
Now the dim gods of death have in their keeping
   Spirit and body and all the springs of song,
   It is well now where love can do no wrong,
Where stingless pleasure has no foam or fang
   Behind the unopening closure of her lips?
   Is it not well where soul from body slips
And flesh from bone divides without a pang
   As dew from flower-bell drips?

It is enough; the end and the beginning
   Are one thing to thee, who art past the end.
   O hand unclasp'd of unbeholden friend,
For thee no fruits to pluck, no palms for winning,
   No triumph and no labour and no lust,
   Only dead yew-leaves and a little dust.
O quiet eyes wherein the light saith naught,
   Whereto the day is dumb, nor any night
   With obscure finger silences your sight,
Nor in your speech the sudden soul speaks thought,
   Sleep, and have sleep for light.

Now all strange hours and all strange loves are over,
   Dreams and desires and sombre songs and sweet,
   Hast thou found place at the great knees and feet
Of some pale Titan-woman like a lover,
   Such as thy vision here solicited,
   Under the shadow of her fair vast head,
The deep division of prodigious breasts,
   The solemn slope of mighty limbs asleep,
   The weight of awful tresses that still keep
The savour and shade of old-world pine-forests
   Where the wet hill-winds weep?

Hast thou found any likeness for thy vision?
   O gardener of strange flowers, what bud, what bloom,
   Hast thou found sown, what gather'd in the gloom?

CHARLES BAUDELAIRE (1821-1867)

What of despair, of rapture, of derision,
    What of life is there, what of ill or good?
    Are the fruits gray like dust or bright like blood?
Does the dim ground grow any seed of ours,
    The faint fields quicken any terrene root,
    In low lands where the sun and moon are mute
And all the stars keep silence? Are there flowers
    At all, or any fruit?

Alas, but though my flying song flies after,
    O sweet strange elder singer, thy more fleet
    Singing, and footprints of thy fleeter feet,
Some dim derision of mysterious laughter
    From the blind tongueless warders of the dead,
    Some gainless glimpse of Proserpine's veil'd head,
Some little sound of unregarded tears
    Wept by effaced unprofitable eyes,
    And from pale mouths some cadence of dead sighs—
These only, these the heakening spirit hears,
    Sees only such things rise.

Thou are too far for wings of words to follow,
    Far too far off for thought or any prayer.
    What ails us with thee, who art wind and air?
What ails us gazing where all seen is hollow?
    Yet with some fancy, yet with some desire,
    Dreams pursue death as winds a flying fire,
Our dreams pursue our dead and do not find.
    Still, and more swift than they, the thin flame flies,
    The low light fails us in elusive skies,
Still the foil'd earnest ear is deaf, and blind
    Are still the eluded eyes.

Not thee, O never thee, in all time's changes,
    Not thee, but this the sound of thy sad soul,
    The shadow of thy swift spirit, this shut scroll
I lay my hand on, and not death estranges
    My spirit from communion of thy song—
    These memories and these melodies that throng

CHARLES BAUDELAIRE (1821–1867)

Veil'd porches of a Muse funereal—
   These I salute, these touch, these clasp and fold
   As though a hand were in my hand to hold,
Or through mine ears a mourning musical
   Of many mourners roll'd.

I among these, I also, in such station
   As when the pyre was charr'd, and piled the sods,
   And offering to the dead made, and their gods,
The old mourners had, standing to make libation,
   I stand, and to the Gods and to the dead
   Do reverence without prayer or praise, and shed
Offering to these unknown, the gods of gloom,
   And what of honey and spice my seed-lands bear,
   And what I may of fruits in this chill'd air,
And lay, Orestes-like, across the tomb
   A curl of sever'd hair.

But by no hand nor any treason stricken,
   Not like the low-lying head of Him, the King,
   The flame that made of Troy a ruinous thing,
Thou liest and on this dust no tears could quicken.
   There fall no tears like theirs that all men hear
   Fall tear by sweet imperishable tear
Down the opening leaves of holy poet's pages.
   Thee not Orestes, not Electra mourns;
   But bending us-ward with memorial urns
The most high Muses that fulfil all ages
   Weep, and our God's heart yearns.

For, sparing of his sacred strength, not often
   Among us darkling here the lord of light
   Makes manifest his music and his might
In hearts that open and in lips that soften
   With the soft flame and heat of songs that shine.
   Thy lips indeed he touch'd with bitter wine,
And nourish'd them indeed with bitter bread;
   Yet surely from his hand thy soul's food came,
   The fire that scarr'd thy spirit at his flame

CHARLES BAUDELAIRE (1821–1867)

Was lighted, and thine hungering heart he fed
Who feeds our hearts with fame.

Therefore he too now at thy soul's sunsetting,
   God of all suns and songs, he too bends down
   To mix his laurel with thy cypress crown,
And save thy dust from blame and from forgetting.
   Therefore he too, seeing all thou wert and art,
   Compassionate, with sad and sacred heart,
Mourns thee of many his children the last dead,
   And hallows with strange tears and alien sighs
   Thine unmelodious mouth and sunless eyes,
And over thine irrevocable head
   Sheds light from the under skies.

And one weeps with him in the ways Lethean,
   And stains with tears her changing bosom chill;
   That obscure Venus of the hollow hill,
That thing transform'd which was the Cytherean,
   With lips that lost their Grecian laugh divine
   Long since, and face no more call'd Erycine—
A ghost, a bitter and luxurious god.
   Thee also with fair flesh and singing spell
   Did she, a sad and second prey, compel
Into the footless places once more trod,
   And shadows hot from hell.

And now no sacred staff shall break in blossom,
   No choral salutation lure to light
   A spirit sick with perfume and sweet night
And love's tired eyes and hands and barren bosom.
   There is no help for these things; none to mend,
   And none to mar; not all our songs, O friend,
Will make death clear or make life durable.
   Howbeit with rose and ivy and wild vine
   And with wild notes about this dust of thine
At least I fill the place where white dreams dwell
   And wreathe an unseen shrine.

CHARLES BAUDELAIRE (1821-1867)

>Sleep; and if life was bitter to thee, pardon,
> If sweet, give thanks; thou hast no more to live;
> And to give thanks is good, and to forgive.
>Out of the mystic and the mournful garden
> Where all day through thine hands in barren braid
> Wove the sick flowers of secrecy and shade,
>Green buds of sorrow and sin, and remnants gray,
> Sweet-smelling, pale with poison, sanguine-hearted,
> Passions that sprang from sleep and thoughts that started,
>Shall death not bring us all as thee one day
> Among the days departed?
>
>For thee, O now a silent soul, my brother,
> Take at my hands this garland, and farewell.
> Thin is the leaf, and chill the wintry smell,
>And chill the solemn earth, a fatal mother,
> With sadder than the Niobean womb,
> And in the hollow of her breasts a tomb.
>Content thee, howsoe'er, whose days are done;
> There lies not any troublous thing before,
> Nor sight nor sound to war against thee more,
>For whom all winds are quiet as the sun,
> All waters as the shore.
>   ALGERNON CHARLES SWINBURNE
>   (1837-1909)

Baudelaire

>Baudelaire, I wish that I could learn from you
>   how, on the words, to make a chisel pounce,
>and smash a hammer till the shape came through
>   like some Greek runner struggling out of bronze.
>I wish, like you, that I could make my line
>   cool as a statue, yet subtly warm
>with something even you could not divine
>   until it flashed, and took your heart by storm.
>Smooth and deliberate with the classic curve,
>   resolving the mute obstinacy of metal,

CHARLES BAUDELAIRE (1821-1867)

> your enigmatic materpieces swerve
> out of the climate of sound, and, swaying a little,
> compose themselves with the conclusive air
> of dominated marble, Baudelaire.
> HUMBERT WOLFE
(1885–   )

WALT WHITMAN (1819-1892)

Ode To Walt Whitman
(May 31, 1819–March 26, 1892)

I

Now comes Fourth Month and the early buds on the trees.
By the roads of Long Island, the forsythia has flowered,
In the North, the cold will be breaking; even in Maine
The cold will be breaking soon; the young, bull-voiced freshets
Roar from green mountains, gorging the chilly brooks
With the brown, trout-feeding waters, the unlocked springs;
Now Mississippi stretches with the Spring rains. . . .

It is forty years and more,
The time of the ripeness and withering of a man,
Since you lay in the house in Camden and heard, at last,
The great, slow footstep, splashing the Third Month snow
In the little, commonplace street
—Town snow, already trampled and growing old,
Soot-flecked and dingy, patterned with passing feet,
The bullet-pocks of rain, the strong urine of horses,
The slashing, bright steel runners of small boys' sleds
Hitching on behind the fast cutters.
They dragged their sleds to the tops of the hills and yelled
The Indian yell of all boyhood, for pure joy
Of the cold and the last gold light and the swift rush down
Belly-flopping into darkness, into bedtime.
You saw them come home, late, hungry and burning-cheeked,
The boys and girls, the strong children,
Dusty with snow, their mittens wet with the silver drops of thawed
  snow.

WALT WHITMAN (1819–1892)

All winter long, you had heard their sharp footsteps passing,
The skating crunch of their runners,
An old man, tied to a house, after many years,
An old man with his rivery, clean white hair,
His bright eyes, his majestic poverty,
His fresh pink skin like the first strawberry-bloom,
His innocent, large, easy old man's clothes
—Brown splotches on the hands of clean old men
At County Farms or sitting on warm park-benches
Like patient flies, talking of their good sons,
"Yes, my son's good to me"—
An old man, poor, without sons, waiting achingly
For spring to warm his lameness,
For spring to flourish,
And yet, when the eyes glowed, neither old nor tied.

All winter long there had been footsteps passing,
Steps of postmen and neighbors, quick steps of friends,
All winter long you had waited that great, snow-treading step,
The enemy, the vast comrade,
The step behind, in the wards, when the low lamp flickered
And the sick boy gasped for breath,
"*Lean on me! Lean upon my shoulder! By God, you shall not die!*"
The step ahead, on the long, wave-thundering beaches of Paumanok,
Invisible, printless, weighty,
The shape half-seen through the wet, sweet sea-fog of youth,
Night's angel and the dark Sea's
The grand, remorseless treader,
Magnificent Death.

"Let me taste all, my flesh and my fat are sweet,
My body hardy as lilac, the strong flower.
I have tasted the calamus; I can taste the nightbane."

Always the water about you since you were born,
The endless lapping of water, the strong motion,
The gulls by the ferries knew you, and the wild sea-birds,
The sandpiper, printing the beach with delicate prints.

WALT WHITMAN (1819-1892)

At last, old, wheeled to the wharf, you still watched the water,
The tanned boys, flat-bodied, diving, the passage of ships,
The proud port, distant, the people, the work of harbors. . . .

"I have picked out a bit of hill with a southern exposure.
I like to be near the trees.   I like to be near
The water-sound of the trees."

Now, all was the same in the cluttered, three-windowed room,
Low-ceiled, getting the sun like a schooner's cabin,
The crowding photos hiding the ugly wall-paper.
The floor-litter, the strong chair, timbered like a ship,
The hairy black-and-silver of the old wolfskin;
In the back-yard, neither lilac nor pear yet bloomed
But the branch of the lilac swelling with first sap;
And there, in the house, the figures, the nurse, the woman,
The passing doctor, the friends, the little clan,
The disciple with the notebook who's always there.

All these and the pain and the water-bed to ease you
And you said it rustled of oceans and were glad
And the pain shut and relaxed and shut once more.

"Old body, counsellor, why do you thus torment me?
Have we not been friends from our youth?"

But now it came,
Slow, perceived by no others,
The splashing step through the grey, soft, Saturday rain,
Inexorable footstep of the huge friend.
"Are you there at last, fine enemy?
Ah, haste, friend, hasten, come closer!
Breathe upon me with your grave, your releasing lips!
I have heard and spoken; watched the bodies of boys
Flash in the copper sun and dive to green waters,
Seen the fine ships and the strong matrons and the tall axemen,
The young girls, free, athletic; the drunkard, retching
In his poor dream; the thief taken by officers;
The President, calm, grave, advising the nation;

WALT WHITMAN (1819–1892)

The infant, with milk-wet lips in his bee-like slumber.
They are mine; all, all are mine; must I leave them, truly?
I have cherished them in my veins like milk and fruit.
I have warmed them at my bare breast like the eggs of pigeons.
The great plains of the buffalo are mine, the towns, the hills, the ship-bearing waters.
These States are my wandering sons.
I had them in my youth; I cannot desert them.
The green leaf of America is printed on my heart forever."

Now it entered the house, it marched upon the stair.
By the bedside the faces dimmed, the huge shoulder blotting them,
—It is so they die on the plains, the great, old buffalo,
The herd-leaders, the beasts with the kingly eyes,
Innocent, curly-browed,
They sink to the earth like mountains, hairy and silent,
And their tongues are cut by the hunter.
                              Oh, singing tongue!
Great tongue of bronze and salt and the free grasses,
Tongue of America, speaking for the first time,
Must the hunter have you at last?

Now, face to face, you saw him
And lifted the right arm once, as a pilot lifts it,
Signalling with the bell,
In the passage at night, on the river known yet unknown,
—Perhaps to touch his shoulder, perhaps in pain—
Then the rain fell on the roof and the twilight darkened
And they said that in death you looked like a marvelous old, wise child.

2

It is Fourth Month now and spring in another century,
Let us go to the hillside and ask; he will like to hear us;
"Is it good, the sleep?"
                    "It is good, the sleep and the waking.
I have picked out a bit of hill where the south sun warms me.
I like to be near the trees."

WALT WHITMAN (1819–1892)

Nay, let him ask, rather.
"Is it well with you, comrades?
The cities great, portentous, humming with action?
The bridges mightily spanning wide-breasted rivers?
The great plains growing the wheat, the old lilac hardy, well-budded?
Is it well with these States?"

"The cities are great, portentous, a world-marvel,
The bridges arched like the necks of beautiful horses.
We have made the dry land bloom and the dead land blossom."

"Is it well with these States?"

"The old wound of your war is healed and we are one nation.
We have linked the whole land with the steel and the hard highways.
We have fought new wars and won them. In the French field
There are bones of Texarkana and Little Falls,
Aliens, our own; in the low-lying Belgian ground;
In the cold sea of the English; in dark-faced islands.
Men speak of them well or ill; they themselves are silent."

"Is it well with these States?"

"We have made many, fine new toys.
We—
There is a rust on the land.
A rust and a creeping blight and a scaled evil,
For six years eating, yet deeper than those six years,
Men labor to master it but it is not mastered.
There is the soft, grey, foul tent of the hatching worm
Shrouding the elm, the chestnut, the Southern cypress.
There is shadow in the bright sun, there is shadow upon the streets.
They burn the grain in the furnace while men go hungry.
They pile the cloth of the looms while men go ragged.
We walk naked in our plenty."

"My tan-faced children?"

WALT WHITMAN (1819–1892)

"These are your tan-faced children.
These skilled men, idle, with the holes in their shoes.
These drifters from State to State, these wolvish, bewildered boys
Who ride the blinds and the box-cars from jail to jail,
Burnt in their youth like cinders of hot smokestacks,
Learning the thief's crouch and the cadger's whine,
Dishonored, abandoned, disinherited.
These, dying in the bright sunlight they cannot eat,
Or the strong men, sitting at home, their hands clasping nothing,
Looking at their lost hands.
These are your tan-faced children, the parched young,
The old man rooting in waste-heaps, the family rotting
In the flat, before eviction,
With the toys of plenty about them,
The shiny toys making ice and music and light,
But no price for the shiny toys and the last can empty.
The sleepers in blind corners of the night.
The women with dry breasts and phantom eyes.
The walkers upon nothing, the four million.
These are your tan-faced children."

"But the land?"

"Over the great plains of the buffalo-land,
The dust-storm blows, the choking, sifting, small dust.
The skin of that land is ploughed by the dry, fierce wind
And blown away, like a torrent;
It drifts foot-high above the young sprouts of grain
And the water fouls, the horses stumble and sicken,
The wash-board cattle stagger and die of drought.
We tore the buffalo's pasture with the steel blade.
We made the waste land blossom and it has blossomed.
That was our fate; now that land takes its own revenge,
And the giant dust-flower blooms above five States."

"But the gains of the years, who got them?"

"Many, great gains.
Many, yet few; they robbed us in the broad daylight,
Saying, 'Give us this and that; we are kings and titans;

WALT WHITMAN (1819-1892)

We know the ropes; we are solid; we are hard-headed;
We will build you cities and railroads.'—as if *they* built them!
They, the preying men, the men whose hearts were like engines,
Gouging the hills for gold, laying waste the timber,
The men like band-saws, moving over the land.
And, after them, the others,
Soft-bodied, lacking even the pirate's candor,
Men of paper, robbing by paper, with paper faces,
Rustling like frightened paper when the storm broke.
The men with the jaws of moth and aphis and beetle,
Boring the dusty, secret hole in the corn,
Fixed, sucking the land, with neither wish nor pride
But the wish to suck and continue.
They have been sprayed, a little.
But they say they will have the land back again, these men."

"There were many such in my time.
I have seen the rich arrogant and the poor oppressed.
I have seen democracy, also. I have seen
The good man slain, the knave and the fool in power,
The democratic vista botched by the people,
Yet not despaired, loving the giant land,
Though I prophesied to these States."

"Now they say we must have one tyranny or another
And a dark bell rings in our hearts."

"Was the blood spilt for nothing, then?"

3

Under dry winter
Arbutus grows.
It is careless of man.
It is careless of man.

Man can tear it,
Crush it, destroy it;
Uproot the trailers,
The thumb-shaped leafings.

WALT WHITMAN (1819–1892)

A man in grey clothes
May come there also,
Lie all day there
In weak spring sunlight.

White, firm-muscled,
The flesh of his body;
Wind, sun, earth
In him, possessing him.

In his heart
A flock of birds crying.
In his belly
The new grass growing.

In his skull
Sunlight and silence,
Like a vast room
Full of sunlight and silence.

In the lines of his palms
The roads of America,
In the knots of his hands
The anger of America.

In the sweat of his flesh
The sorrows of America,
In the seed of his loins
The glory of America.

The sap of the birch-tree
Is in his pelt,
The maple, the red-bud
Are his nails and parings.

He grows through the earth and is part of it like the roots of new
  grass.

Little arbutus
Delicate, tinted,
Tiny, tender,
Fragile, immortal.

WALT WHITMAN (1819-1892)

If you can grow,
A man can grow
Not like others
But like a man.

Man is a bull
But he has not slain you
And this man lies
Like a lover beside you.

Beside the arbutus,
The green-leaved Spring,
He lies like a lover
By his young bride,
In the white hour,
The white, first waking.

4

They say, they say, they say and let them say.
Call you a revolutionist—you were one—
A nationalist—you were one—a man of peace,
A man describing battles, an old fraud,
A Charlus, an adept self-advertiser,
A "good, grey poet"—oh, God save us all!
God save us from the memoirs and the memories!
And yet, they count. They have to. If they didn't
There'd be no Ph.Ds. And each disciple
Jealously guards his own particular store
Of acorns fallen from the oak's abundance
And spits and scratches at the other gatherers.
"I was there when he died!"
                        "He was not there when he died!"
"It was me he trusted, me! X got on his nerves!
He couldn't stand X in the room!"
                          "Y's well-intentioned
But a notorious liar—and, as for Z . . ."

So all disciples, always and forever.
—And the dire court at Longwood, those last years,
The skull of Sterne, grinning at the anatomists,
Poe's hospital-bed, the madness of the Dean,

WALT WHITMAN (1819-1892)

The bright, coughing blood Keats wrote in to the girl,
The terrible corpse of France, shrunk, naked and solitary—
Oh, yes, you were spared some things.
Though why did Mrs. Davis sue the estate
And what did you mean when you said—
                              And who cares?
You're still the giant lode we quarry
For gold, fools' gold and all the earthy metals,
The matchless mine.
Still the trail-breaker, still the rolling river.

You and your land, your turbulent, seeking land
Where anything can grow.

And they have wasted the pasture and the fresh valley,
Stunk the river, shot the ten thousand sky-darkening pigeons
To build sham castles for imitation Medici
And the rugged sons of the rugged sons of death.
The slum, the sharecropper's cabin, the senseless tower,
The factory town with the dirty stoops of twilight,
The yelling cheapness, the bitter want among plenty,
But never Monticello, never again.
And there are many years in the dust of America
And they are not ended yet.

Far north, far north are the sources of the great river,
The headwaters, the cold lakes,
By the little sweet-tasting brooks of the blond country,
The country of snow and wheat,
Or west among the black mountains, the glacial springs.
Far north and west they lie and few come to them, few taste them,
But, day and night, they flow south,
By the French grave and the Indian, steadily flowing,
By the forgotten camps of the broken heart,
By the countries of black earth, fertile, and yellow earth and red earth,
A growing, a swelling torrent:
Rivers meet it, and tiny rivulets,
Meet it, stain it,
Great rivers, rivers of pride, come bowing their watery heads
Like muddy gift-bearers, bringing their secret burdens,

WALT WHITMAN (1819–1892)

Rivers from the high horse-plains and the deep, green Eastern pastures
Sink into it and are lost and rejoice and shout with it, shout within it,
They and their secret gifts,
A fleck of gold from Montana, a sliver of steel from Pittsburgh,
A wheat-grain from Minnesota, an apple-blossom from Tennessee,
Roiled, mixed with the mud and earth of the changing bottoms
In the vast, rending floods,
But rolling, rolling from Arkansas, Kansas, Iowa,
Rolling from Ohio, Wisconsin, Illinois,
Rolling and shouting:
Till, at last, it is Mississippi,
The Father of Waters; the matchless; the great flood
Dyed with the earth of States; with the dust and the sun and the seed of half the States;
The huge heart-vein, pulsing and pulsing; gigantic; ever broader, ever mightier;
It rolls past broken landings and camellia-smelling woods; strange birds fly over it;
It rolls through the tropic magic, the almost-jungle, the warm darkness breeding the warm, enormous stars;
It rolls to the blue Gulf; ocean; and the painted birds fly.
The grey moss mixes with it, the hawk's feather has fallen in it,
The cardinal feather, the feather of the small thrush
Singing spring to New England,
The apple-pip and the pepper-seed and the checkerberry,
And always the water flowing, earthy, majestic,
Fed with snow and heat, dew and moonlight.
Always the wide, sure water,
Over the rotted deer-horn
The gold, Spanish money,
The long-rusted iron of many undertakings,
Over De Soto's bones and Joliet's wonder,
And the long forest-years before them, the brief years after,
The broad flood, the eternal motion, the restless-hearted
Always, forever, Mississippi, the god.

STEPHEN VINCENT BENÉT
(1898–1943)

April, 1935

EMILY DICKINSON (1830–1886)

To Emily Dickinson

You who desired so much—in vain to ask
Yet fed your hunger like an endless task
Dared dignify the labor, bless the quest—
Achieved that stillness ultimately best,
Being, of all, least sought for: Emily, hear!
O sweet dead silencer, most suddenly clear
When singing that Eternity possessed
And plundered momently in every breast;
—Truly no flower yet withers in your hand,
The harvest you described and understand
Needs more than wit to gather, love to bind.
Some reconcilement of remotest mind
Leaves Ormus rubyless, and Ophir chill.
Else tears heap all within one clay-cold hill.

Hart Crane
(1899–1932)

Emily Dickinson

Demonic Yankee who could taste
In daily bread eternity,
Wary of words and the nerve's waste,
True spinster of mortality.
Drunk with the unbrewed midnight air,
Wandering on her garden gravel,
She harrowed her own home to dare
An inner continent for travel.
Narrow in her salt blood she bore
The seven seas and their loud lash,
Gay at her girlhood waist she wore
World wrapped around her like a sash.
With death she put a wool coat on
For warmth, and walked into the sun.

Paul Engle
(1908–   )

PAUL VERLAINE (1844–1896)

Verlaine

Why do you dig like long-clawed scavengers
To touch the covered corpse of him that fled
The uplands for the fens, and rioted
Like a sick satyr with doom's worshippers?
Come! let the grass grow there; and leave his verse
To tell the story of the life he led.
Let the man go: let the dead flesh be dead,
And let the worms be its biographers.
Song sloughs away the sin to find redress
In art's complete remembrance: nothing clings
For long but laurel to the stricken brow
That felt the Muse's finger; nothing less
Than hell's fulfilment of the end of things
Can blot the star that shines on Paris now.

EDWIN ARLINGTON ROBINSON
(1869–1935)

JEAN ARTHUR RIMBAUD (1854–1891)

Rimbaud

The nights, the railway-arches, the bad sky,
His horrible companions did not know it;
But in that child the rhetorician's lie
Burst like a pipe: the cold had made a poet.

Drinks bought him by his weak and lyric friend
His senses systematically deranged,
To all accustomed nonsense put an end;
Till he from lyre and weakness was estranged.

Verse was a special illness of the ear;
Integrity was not enough; that seemed
The hell of childhood: he must try again.

Now, galloping through Africa, he dreamed
Of a new self, the son, the engineer,
His truth acceptable to lying men.

W. H. AUDEN
(1907–   )

JEAN ARTHUR RIMBAUD (1854-1891)
Preludes for Memnon
LVI

Rimbaud and Verlaine, precious pair of poets,
Genius in both (but what is genius?) playing
Chess on a marble table at an inn
With chestnut blossom falling in blond beer
And on their hair and between knight and bishop—
Sunlight squared between them on the chess-board
Cirrus in heaven, and a squeal of music
Blown from the leathern door of Ste. Sulpice—

Discussing, between moves, iamb and spondee
Anacoluthon and the open vowel
God the great peacock with his angel peacocks
And his dependent peacocks the bright stars:
Disputing too of fate as Plato loved it,
Or Sophocles, who hated and admired,
Or Socrates, who loved and was amused:

Verlaine puts down his pawn upon a leaf
And closes his long eyes, which are dishonest,
And says "Rimbaud, there is one thing to do:
We must take rhetoric, and wring its neck! . . .
Rimbaud considers gravely, moves his Queen;
And then removes himself to Timbuctoo.

And Verlaine dead,—with all his jades and mauves;
And Rimbaud dead in Marseilles with a vision,
His leg cut off, as once before his heart;
And all reported by a later lackey,
Whose virtue is his tardiness in time.

Let us describe the evening as it is:—
The stars disposed in heaven as they are:
Verlaine and Shakspeare rotting, where they rot,
Rimbaud remembered, and too soon forgot;

Order in all things, logic in the dark;
Arrangement in the atom and the spark;
Time in the heart and sequence in the brain—

JEAN ARTHUR RIMBAUD (1854-1891)

> Such as destroyed Rimbaud and fooled Verlaine.
> And let us then take godhead by the neck—
> And strangle it, and with it, rhetoric.
>
> CONRAD AIKEN
(1889–   )

OSCAR WILDE (1856-1900)

The Dead Poet

> I dreamed of him last night, I saw his face
> All radiant and unshadowed of distress,
> And as of old, in music measureless,
> I heard his golden voice and marked him trace
> Under the common thing the hidden grace,
> And conjure wonder out of emptiness,
> Till mean things put on beauty like a dress
> And all the world was an enchanted place.
> And then methought outside a fast-locked gate
> I mourned the loss of unrecorded words,
> Forgotten tales and mysteries half said.
> Wonders that might have been articulate,
> And voiceless thoughts like murdered singing birds.
> And so I woke and knew that he was dead.
>
> LORD ALFRED DOUGLAS
(1870–   )

LIONEL JOHNSON (1867-1902)

Lionel Johnson

> There was a murkier tinge in London's air
> As if the honest fog blushed black for shame.
> Fools sang of sin, for other fools' acclaim,
> And Milton's wreath was tossed to Baudelaire.
> The flowers of evil blossomed everywhere,
> But in their midst a radiant lily came
> Candescent, pure, a cup of living flame,
> Bloomed for a day, and left the earth more fair
> And was it Charles, the "fair and fatal King,"
> Who bade thee welcome to the lovely land?

LIONEL JOHNSON (1867–1902)

>Or did Lord David cease to harp and sing
>To take in his thine emulative hand?
>Or did Our Lady's smile shine forth, to bring
>Her lyric Knight within her choir to stand?
>
>>JOYCE KILMER
>>(1886–1918)

[MISCELLANY]

From "Ode for the Diamond Jubilee of Queen Victoria, 1897"

First went the holy poets, two on two,
And music, sown along the hardened ground,
Budded like frequence of glad daisies, where
Those sacred feet did fare;
Arcadian pipe, and psaltery, around,
And stringèd viol, sound
To make for them melodious due.
In the first twain of those great ranks of death
Went One, the impress recent on his hair
Where it was dinted by the Laureate wreath:
Who sang those goddesses with splendours bare
On Ida hill, before the Trojan boy;
And many a lovely lay,
Where Beauty did her beauties unarray
In conscious song. I saw young Love his plumes deploy,
And shake their shivering lustres, till the night
Was sprinkled and bedropt with starry play
Of versicoloured light,
To see that Poet pass who sang him well;
And I could hear his heart
Throb like the after-vibrance of a bell.

A Strength beside this Beauty, Browning went,
With shrewd looks and intent,
And mediating still some gnarlèd theme.

[FROM "ODE FOR THE DIAMOND JUBILEE"]

Then came, somewhat apart,
In a fastidious dream,
Arnold, with a half-discontented calm,
Binding up wounds, but pouring in no balm.
The fervid breathing of Elizabeth
Broke on Christina's gentle-taken breath.
Rossetti, whose heart stirred within his breast
Like lightning in a cloud, a Spirit without rest,
Came on disranked; Song's hand was in his hair,
Lest Art should have withdrawn him from the band,
Save for her strong command;
And in his eyes high Sadness made its lair.
Last came a Shadow tall, with drooping lid,
Which yet not hid
The steel-like flashing of his armèd glance;
Alone he did advance,
And all the throngs gave room
For one that looked with such a captain's mien.
A scornful smile lay keen
On lips that, living, prophesied of doom;
His one hand held a lightning-bolt, the other
A cup of milk and honey blent with fire;
It seemed as in that quire
He had not, nor desired not, any brother.
A space his alien eye surveyed the pride
Of meditated pomp, as one that much
Disdained the sight, methought; then, at a touch,
He turned the heel, and sought with shadowy stride
His station in the dim,
Where the sole-thoughted Dante waited him.

FRANCIS THOMPSON
(1859–1907)

a Shadow tall] Coventry Patmore

VIII

PAUL LAURENCE DUNBAR (1872–1906)

Paul Laurence Dunbar

He came, a youth, singing in the dawn
  Of a new freedom, glowing o'er his lyre,
  Refining, as with great Apollo's fire,
  His people's gift of song. And thereupon,
This Negro singer, come to Helicon
  Constrained the masters, listening to admire,
  And roused a race to wonder and aspire,
  Gazing which way their honest voice was gone,
With ebon face uplit of glory's crest.
  Men marveled at the singer, strong and sweet,
  Who brought the cabin's mirth, the tuneful night,
But faced the morning, beautiful with light,
To die while shadows yet fell toward the west,
  And leave his laurels at his people's feet.

Dunbar, no poet wears your laurels now;
  None rises, singing, from your race like you.
  Dark melodist, immortal, though the dew
  Fell early on the bays upon your brow,
And tinged with pathos every halcyon vow
  And brave endeavor. Silence o'er you threw
  Flowerets of love. Or, if an envious few
  Of your own people brought no garlands, how
Could Malice smite him whom the gods had crowned?
  If, like the meadow-lark, your flight was low
  Your flooded lyrics half the hilltops drowned;
A wide world heard you, and it loved you so
  It stilled its heart to list the strains you sang,
  And o'er your happy songs its plaudits rang.

                    JAMES D. CORROTHERS
                        (1869–1919)

ALGERNON CHARLES SWINBURNE (1837–1909)

A Singer Asleep

In this fair niche above the unslumbering sea,
That sentrys up and down all night, all day,
From cove to promontory, from ness to bay,
The Fates have fitly bidden that he should be
   Pillowed eternally.

It was as though a garland of red roses
Had fallen about the hood of some smug nun
When irresponsibly dropped as from the sun,
In fulth of numbers freaked with musical closes,
   Upon Victoria's formal middle time
   His leaves of rhythm and rhyme.

O that far morning of a summer day
When, down a terraced street whose pavements lay
Glassing the sunshine into my bent eyes,
I walked and read with a quick glad surprise
   New words, in classic guise,—

The passionate pages of his earlier years,
Fraught with hot sighs, sad laughters, kisses, tears;
Fresh-fluted notes, yet from a minstrel who
Blew them not naïvely, but as one who knew
   Full well why thus he blew.

I still can hear the brabble and the roar
At those thy tunes, O still one, now passed through
That fitful fire of tongues then entered new!
Their power is spent like spindrift on this shore;
   Thine swells yet more and more.

His singing-mistress verily was no other
Than she the Lesbian, she the music-mother
Of all the tribe that feel in melodies;
Who leapt, love-anguished, from the Leucadian steep
Into the rambling world-encircled deep
   Which hides her where none sees.

ALGERNON CHARLES SWINBURNE (1837-1909)

    And one can hold in thought that nightly here
    His phantom may draw down to the water's brim,
    And hers come up to meet it, as a dim
    Lone shine upon the heaving hydrosphere,
    And mariners wonder as they traverse near,
      Unknowing of her and him.

    One dreams him sighing to her spectral form:
    'O teacher, where lies hid thy burning line;
    Where are those songs, O poetess divine
    Whose very orts are love incarnadine?'
    And her smile back: 'Disciple true and warm,
      Sufficient now are thine.' . . .

    So here, beneath the waking constellations,
    Where the waves peal their everlasting strains,
    And their dull subterrene reverberations
    Shake him when storms make mountains of their plains—
    Him once their peer in sad improvisations,
    And deft as wind to cleave their frothy manes—
    I leave him, while the daylight gleam declines
      Upon the capes and chines.

                              Thomas Hardy
                              (1840-1928)

RUPERT BROOKE (1887-1915)

Rupert Brooke

I

    Your face was lifted to the golden sky
      Ablaze beyond the black roofs of the square
      As flame on flame leapt, flourishing in air
    Its tumult of red stars exultantly
    To the cold constellations dim and high:
      And as we neared the roaring ruddy flare
      Kindled to gold your throat and brow and hair
    Until you burned, a flame of ecstasy.

RUPERT BROOKE (1887-1915)

The golden head goes down into the night
   Quenched in cold gloom—and yet again you stand
Beside me now with lifted face alight,
   As, flame to flame, and fire to fire you burn ...
Then, recollecting, laughingly you turn,
And look into my eyes and take my hand.

II

Once in my garret—you being far away
   Tramping the hills and breathing upland air,
   Or so I fancied—brooding in my chair,
I watched the London sunshine feeble and grey
Dapple my desk, too tired to labour more,
   When, looking up, I saw you standing there
   Although I'd caught no footstep on the stair,
Like sudden April at my open door.

Though now beyond earth's farthest hills you fare,
   Song-crowned, immortal, sometimes it seems to me
That, if I listen very quietly,
   Perhaps I'll hear a light foot on the stair
   And see you, standing with your angel air,
Fresh from the uplands of eternity.

III

Your eyes rejoiced in colour's ecstasy,
   Fulfilling even their uttermost desire,
   When, over a great sunlit field afire
With windy poppies streaming like a sea
Of scarlet flame that flaunted riotously
   Among green orchards of that western shire,
   You gazed as though your heart could never tire
Of life's red flood in summer revelry.

And as I watched you, little thought had I
   How soon beneath the dim low-drifting sky
Your soul should wander down the darkling way,
   With eyes that peer a little wistfully,
   Half-glad, half-sad, remembering, as they see
Lethean poppies, shrivelling ashen grey.

RUPERT BROOKE (1887–1915)

IV

October chestnuts showered their perishing gold
   Over us as beside the stream we lay
   In the Old Vicarage garden that blue day,
Talking of verse and all the manifold
Delights a little net of words may hold,
   While in the sunlight water-voles at play
   Dived under a trailing crimson bramble-spray,
And walnuts thudded ripe on soft black mould.

Your soul goes down unto a darker stream
   Alone, O friend, yet even in death's deep night
Your eyes may grow accustomed to the dark
   And Styx for you may have the ripple and gleam
   Of your familiar river, and Charon's bark
Tarry by that old garden of your delight.
WILFRID WILSON GIBSON
(1878–   )

FRANCIS LEDWIDGE (1891–1917)

For Francis Ledwidge

(Killed in action July 31, 1917)

You fell; and on a distant field, shell-shatter'd,
Soaked with blood; while, in your dying, Erin
Knew naught of you, nor folded you for rest.
You will not sleep beneath a mound where kings
Were coffn'd long ago in carven stone
And dream in peace amid an emerald land
Of many memories and swift-wing'd song.
And yet I think that you are not forgotten;
For even in the Irish air there will be
Somewhat of you; in the wide beam of sunlight
Streaming athwart the mountain to the fields
Furrowed and brown, where languid rooks, and gulls
With their sharp crying, circle, or sit and sun
Themselves. The song of birds shall speak of you:
The blackbird chirping cheerily of spring,

FRANCIS LEDWIDGE (1891–1917)

>When hawthorn blows and gorse runs through the hedge;
>The lark lost in the morning; and the stream
>Sparkling, or dark with pools, where salmon leap.
>You will not be forgotten; for your songs
>Have brought the beauty of the Irish land
>To many dimming eyes and homesick hearts.
>Poet and Soldier, could your land forget?
>For you each morning shall her fields be wet.
>
>>NORREYS JEPHSON O'CONOR
>>(1885–   )

GERARD MANLEY HOPKINS (1844–1889)

Father Gerard Hopkins, S.J.

>Why didst thou carve thy speech laboriously,
>>And match and blend thy words with curious art?
>>For Song, one saith, is but a human heart
>Speaking aloud, undisciplined and free.
>Nay, God be praised, Who fixed thy task for thee!
>>Austere, ecstatic craftsman, set apart
>>From all who traffic in Apollo's mart,
>On thy phrased paten shall the Splendour be!
>Now, carelessly we throw a rhyme to God,
>>Singing His praise when other songs are done.
>But thou, who knewest paths Teresa trod,
>>Losing thyself, what is it thou hast won?
>O bleeding feet, with peace and glory shod!
>O happy moth, that flew into the Sun!
>
>>JOYCE KILMER
>>(1886–1918)

AUSTIN DOBSON (1840–1921)

Austin Dobson

Austin Dobson, a writer of light verse.—Newspaper obituary.

>>Ah! would that poets could write
>>>In ink as clear as Dobson's was:
>>Master of airy fancy, light
>>>As morning cobwebs on the grass.

AUSTIN DOBSON (1840–1921)

> Tenderest trifler! how he caught
> (So charmingly, so many times)
> The swift, reluctant birds of thought
> In the bright cages of his rhymes.
>
> And Time, that jingles in his purse
> Mixed coinages, both new and old,
> Makes change with bronze or silver verse
> But spends not his, a coin of gold!
>
> CHRISTOPHER MORLEY
(1890–   )

ALICE MEYNELL (1847–1922)

On Looking at a Copy of Alice Meynell's Poems Given Me Years Ago by a Friend

Upon this greying page you wrote
A whispered greeting, long ago.
Faint pencil-marks run to and fro
Scoring the lines I loved to quote.

A sea-shore of white shoaling sand,
Blue creeks zigzagging through marsh-grasses,
Sandpipers, and a wind which passes
Cloudily silent up the land.

Upon the high edge of the sea
A great four-master sleeps; three hours
Her bowsprit has not cleared those flowers.
I read and look alternately.

It all comes back again, but dim
As pictures on a winking wall,
Hidden save when the dark clouds fall
Or crack to show the moon's bright rim.

I well remember what I was,
And what I wanted. You, unwise
With sore unwisdom, had no eyes
For what was patently the cause.

ALICE MEYNELL (1847-1922)

So are we sport of others' blindness,
We who could see right well alone.
What were you made of—wood or stone?
Yet I remember you with kindness.

You gave this book to me to ease
The smart in me you could not heal.
Your gift a mirror—woe or weal.
We sat beneath the apple-trees.

And I remember how they rang,
These words, like bronze cathedral bells
Down ancient lawns, or citadels
Thundering with gongs where choirs sang.

Silent the sea, the earth, the sky,
And in my heart a silent weeping.
Who has not sown can know no reaping!
Bitter conclusion and no lie.

O heart that sorrows, heart that bleeds,
Heart that was never mine, your words
Were like the pecking autumn birds
Stealing away my garnered seeds.

No future where there is no past!
O cherishing grief which laid me bare,
I wrapped you like a wintry air
About me.   Poor enthusiast!

How strange that tumult, looking back.
The ink is pale, the letters fade.
The verses seem to be well made,
But I have lived the almanac.

And you are dead these drifted years,
How many I forget.   And she
Who wrote the book, her tragedy
Long since dried up its scalding tears.

ALICE MEYNELL (1847–1922)

    I read of her death yesterday,
    Frail lady whom I never knew
    And knew so well. Would I could strew
    Her grave with pansies, blue and grey.

    Would I could stand a little space
    Under a blowing brightening sky,
    And watch the sad leaves fall and lie
    Gently upon that lonely place.

    So cried her heart, a feverish thing.
    But clay is still, and clay is cold,
    And I was young, and I am old,
    And in December what birds sing!

    Go, wistful book, go back again
    Upon your shelf and gather dust.
    I've seen the glitter through the rust
    Of old long years; I've known the pain.

    I've recollected both of you,
    But I shall recollect no more.
    Between us I must shut the door.
    The living have so much to do.

                                   AMY LOWELL
                                    (1874–1925)

T. S. ELIOT (1888–   )
EZRA POUND (1885–   )

                From "A Critical Fable"

    ...."The expatriates
Come next," I began, "but the man who expatiates
Upon them must go all yclad in cold steel
Since these young men are both of them most *difficile*,
And each is possessed of a gift for satire.
Their forked barbs would pierce any usual attire.
In order of merit, if not of publicity,
I will take Eliot first, though it smacks of duplicity

T. S. ELIOT (1888–   )
EZRA POUND (1885–   )

To award Ezra Pound the inferior place
As he simply won't run if not first in a race.
Years ago, 'twould have been the other way round,
With Eliot a rather bad second to Pound.
But Pound has been woefully free with the mustard
And so occupied has quite ruined his custard.
No poems from his pen, just spleen on the loose,
And a man who goes on in that way cooks his goose.
T. S. Eliot's a very unlike proposition,
He has simply won through by process of attrition.
Where Pound played the fool, Eliot acted the wiseacre;
Eliot works in his garden, Pound stultifies his acre.
Eliot's always engaged digging fruit out of dust;
Pound was born in an orchard, but his trees have the rust.
Eliot's mind is perpetually fixed and alert;
Pound goes off anywhere, anyhow, like a squirt.
Pound believes he's a thinker, but he's far too romantic;
Eliot's sure he's a poet when he's only pedantic.
But Eliot has raised pedantry to a pitch,
While Pound has upset romance into a ditch.
Eliot fears to abandon an old masquerade;
Pound's one perfect happiness is to parade.
Eliot's learning was won at a very great price;
What Pound calls his learning he got in a trice.
Eliot knows what he knows, though he cannot digest it;
Pound knows nothing at all, but has frequently guessed it.
Eliot builds up his essays by a process of massing;
Pound's are mostly hot air, what the vulgar call 'gassing.'
Eliot lives like a snail in his shell, pen protruding;
Pound struts like a cock, self-adored, self-deluding.
Pound's darling desire is his ego's projection;
Eliot tortures his soul with a dream of perfection.
Pound's an ardent believer in the value of noise;
Eliot strains every nerve to attain a just poise.
Each despises his fellows, for varying reasons;
Each one is a traitor, but with different treasons.
Each has left his own country, but Pound is quite sick of it,
While for Eliot's sojourn, he is just in the nick of it.

T. S. ELIOT (1888–   )
EZRA POUND (1885–   )

Pound went gunning for trouble, and got it, for cause;
Eliot, far more astute, has deserved his applause.
Each has more brain than heart, but while one man's a critic
The other is more than two-thirds tympanitic.
Both of them are book-men, but where Eliot has found
A horizon in letters, Pound has only found Pound.
Each man feels himself so little complete
That he dreads the least commerce with the man in the street;
Each imagines the world to be leagued in a dim pact
To destroy his immaculate taste by its impact.
To conceive such a notion, one might point out slyly,
Would scarcely occur to an author more highly
Original; such men seldom bother their wits
With outsiders at all, whether fits or misfits.
Where they are, whom they see, is a matter of sheer
Indifference to a poet with his own atmosphere
To exist in, and such have no need to be preachy
Anent commonplaces since they can't write a *cliché-*
In toto, at least, and its *toto* that grounds
All meticulous poets like the Eliots and Pounds.
Taking up Eliot's poetry, it's a blend of intensive
And elegant satire with a would-be offensive
Kind of virulent diatribe, and neither sort's lacking
In the high type of polish we demand of shoe-blacking.
Watteau if you like, arm in arm with Laforgue,
And both of these worthies laid out in a morgue.
The poems are expert even up to a vice,
But they're chilly and dead like corpses on ice.
Now a man who's reluctant to heat his work through,
I submit, is afraid of what that work will do
On its own, with its muscles and sinews unfrozen.
Something, I must think, which he would not have chosen.
Is there barely a clue here that the action of heat
Might reveal him akin to the man in the street?
For his brain—there's no doubt that is up on a steeple,
For his heart might betray him as one of the people.
A fearful dilemma! We can hardly abuse him
For hiding the damaging fact and excuse him

T. S. ELIOT (1888–   )
EZRA POUND (1885–   )

If it really be so, and we've more than a hint of it,
Although I, for one, like him better by dint of it.
Since the poet's not the half of him, we must include
The critical anchorite of his *Sacred Wood*.
'This slim duodecimo you must have your eye on
If you'd be up to date,' say his friends. He's a sly one
To have chosen this format—the book's heavy as iron.
I'm acutely aware that its grave erudition
Is quite in the line of a certain tradition,
That one which is commonly known as tuition.
To read it is much like a lengthy sojourning
In at least two or three institutions of learning.
But, being no schoolboy, I find I'm not burning
For this sort of instruction, and vote for adjourning.
What the fellow's contrived to stuff into his skull
May be certainly classed as a pure miracle,
But the way he imparts it is terribly dull.
This may not be fair, for I've only begun it,
And one should not pronounce on a book till one's done it,
But I've started so often, in so many places,
I think, had there been any livelier spaces
I must have encountered at least one of those
Before falling, I say it with shame, in a doze.
We must take Ezra Pound from a different angle:
He's a belfry of excellent chimes run to jangle
By being too often and hurriedly tugged at,
And even, when more noise was wanted, just slugged at
And hammered with anything there was lying round.
Such delicate bells could not stand so much Pound.
Few men have to their credit more excellent verses
Than he used to write, and even his worse is
Much better than most people's good. He'd a flair
For just the one word indispensably there,
But which few could have hit on. Another distinction
Was the way he preserved fledgeling poets from extinction.
Had he never consented to write when the urge
To produce was not on him, he'd have been on the verge

T. S. ELIOT (1888-   )
EZRA POUND (1885-   )

Of a great reputation by now, but his shoulder
Had always its chip, and Ezra's a scolder.
Off he flew, giving nerves and brain up to the business
In a crowing excitement not unmixed with dizziness,
Whenever he could get any sort of newspaper
To lend him a column and just let him vapor.
But while he was worrying his gift of invention
For adequate means to ensure the prevention
Of anyone's getting what he had not got,
His uncherished talent succumbed to dry rot.
When, after the battle, he would have employed her,
He learnt, to his cost, that he had destroyed her.
Now he does with her ghost, and the ghosts of the hosts
Of troubadours, minstrels, and kings, for he boasts
An acquaintance with persons of whose very names
I am totally ignorant, likewise their fames.
The foremost, of course, is Bertrand de Born,
He's a sort of pervasively huge leprechaun
Popping out from Pound's lines where you never expect him.
He is our poet's chief lar, so we must not neglect him.
There is Pierre de Maensac, and Pierre won the singing—
Where or how I can't guess, but Pound sets his fame ringing
Because he was *dreitz hom* (whatever that is)
And had De Tierci's wife; what happened to his
We don't know, in fact we know nothing quite clearly,
For Pound always treats his ghosts cavalierly.
There is John Borgia's bath, and be sure that he needed it;
Aurunculeia's shoe, but no one much heeded it.
There's a chap named Navighero and another Barabello,
Who prods a Pope's elephant; and one Mozarello;
Savairic Mauleon—Good Lord, what a dance
Of impossible names! First I think we're in France,
Then he slides in Odysseus, and Eros, and Atthis—
But I'm not to be fooled in my Greek, that's what that is.
Yet, look, there's Italian sticking out in italics
And French in plain type, the foreign vocalics
Do give one the feeling of infinite background,
When it's all just a trick of that consummate quack, Pound,

T. S. ELIOT (1888–   )
EZRA POUND (1885–   )

To cheat us to thinking there's something behind it.
But, when nothing's to find, it's a hard job to find it.
The tragedy lies in the fact that the man
Had a potentiality such as few can
Look back to or forward to; had he but kept it,
There's no bar in all poetry but he might have leapt it.
Even now, I believe, if he'd let himself grow,
He might start again . . ." "We will have no 'although'
In your gamut of poets. Your man is a victim
Of expatriation, and, as usual, it's licked him.
It has happened more times than I care to reflect,
And the general toll is two countries' neglect."
1922

AMY LOWELL
(1874–1925)

PADRAIC O'CONAIRE (1881–1928)

Padraic O'Conaire—Gaelic Storyteller

(Died in the Fall of 1928)

They've paid the last respects in sad tobacco
And silent is this wake-house in its haze;
They've paid the last respects; and now their whisky
Flings laughing words on mouths of prayer and praise;
And so young couples huddle by the gables,
O let them grope home through the hedgy night—
Alone I'll mourn my old friend, while the cold dawn
Thins out the holy candlelight.

Respects are paid to one loved by the people;
Ah, was he not—among our mighty poor—
The sudden wealth cast on those pools of darkness,
Those bearing, just, a star's faint signature;
And so he was to me, close friend, near brother,
Dear Padraic of the wide and sea-cold eyes—
So lovable, so courteous and noble,
The very West was in his soft replies.

PADRAIC O'CONAIRE (1881-1928)

They'll miss his heavy stick and stride in Wicklow—
His story-talking down Winetavern Street,
Where old men sitting in the wizen daylight
Have kept an edge upon his gentle wit;
While women on the grassy streets of Galway,
Who hearken for his passing—but in vain,
Shall hardly tell his step as shadows vanish
Through archways of forgotten Spain.

Ah, they'll say: Padraic's gone again exploring;
But now down glens of brightness, O he'll find
An ale-house overflowing with wise Gaelic
That's braced in vigour by the bardic mind,
And there his thoughts shall find their own forefathers—
In minds to whom our heights of race belong,
In crafty men, who ribbed a ship or turned
The secret joinery of song.

Alas, death mars the parchment of his forehead;
And yet for him, I know, the earth is mild—
The windy fidgets of September grasses
Can never tease a mind that loved the wild;

So drink his peace—this grey juice of the barley
Runs with a light that ever pleased his eye—
While old flames nod and gossip on the hearthstone
And only the young winds cry.

FREDERICK ROBERT HIGGINS
(1896-1941)

ROBERT BRIDGES (1844-1930)

Robert Bridges

And you, Robert Bridges, you made your last will
    and testament of beauty in the winter of your thought,
but there was no snow of the mind falling upon Boar's Hill,
    nor upon the further fields that your vision sought.
You could have lingered a year with a daffodil,
    pondering on the dust that could be so brightly fraught

ROBERT BRIDGES (1844-1930)

   with unaccountable design, and yet could find the thrill
     of all matter for ever prevailing upon nought.
Long were your years, but their orbit was inwards
     to the quiet at the heart of the cyclone where leaves
   and the butterflies hang as still as in amber,
or as dew on the crocus before it draws sunwards.
   You are flown, you are melted but, when no wind grieves,
     in the calm of the evening we shall remember.
                                    HUMBERT WOLFE
                                            (1885–1940)

D. H. LAWRENCE (1885-1930)

An Elegy for D. H. Lawrence

   Green points on the shrub
   and poor Lawrence dead.
   The night damp and misty
   and Lawrence no more in the world
   to answer April's promise
   with a fury of labor
   against waste, waste and life's
   coldness.

   Once he received a letter—
   he never answered it—
   praising him: so English
   he had thereby raised himself
   to an unenglish greatness.
   Dead now and it grows clearer
   what bitterness drove him.

   This is the time.
   The serpent in the grotto
   water dripping from the stone
   into a pool.
   Mediterranean evenings. Ashes
   of Cretan fires. And to the north
   forsythia hung with
   yellow bells in the cold.

D. H. LAWRENCE (1885–1930)

Poor Lawrence
worn with a fury of sad labor
to create summer from
spring's decay. English
women. Men driven not to love
but to the ends of the earth.
The serpent turning his
stone-like head,
the fixed agate eyes turn also.

And unopened jonquils
hang their folded heads. No
summer. But for Lawrence
full praise in this
half cold half-season—
before trees are in leaf and
tufted grass stars
unevenly the bare ground.

Slowly the serpent leans
to drink by the tinkling water
and forked tongue alert.
Then fold after fold,
glassy strength, passing
a given point,
as by desire drawn
forward bodily, he glides
smoothly in.

To stand by the sea or walk
again along a river's bank and talk
with a companion, to halt
watching where the edge of water
meets and lies upon
the unmoving shore—
Flood waters rise, and will rise,
rip the quiet valley
trap the gypsy and the girl.
She clings drowning to
a bush in flower.

D. H. LAWRENCE (1885–1930)

Remember, now, Lawrence dead.
Blue squills in bloom—to
the scorched aridity of
the Mexican plateau. Or baked
public squares on the cities of
Mediterranean islands
where one waits for busses and
boats come slowly along the water
arriving.

But the sweep of spring over
temperate lands, meadows and woods
where the young walk and talk
incompletely,
straining to no summer,
hearing the frogs, speaking of
birds and insects—

Febrile spring moves not to heat
but always more slowly,
burdened by a weight of leaves.
Nothing now
to burst the bounds—
remains confined by them. Heat,
heat! Unknown. Poor Lawrence,
dead and only the drowned
fallen dancing from the deck
of a pleasure boat
unfading desire.

Rabbits, imaginings, the
drama, literature, satire.
The serpent cannot move
his stony eyes, scarcely sees
but touching the air
with his forked tongue surmises
and his body which dipped
into the cold water
is gone.

D. H. LAWRENCE (1885-1930)

Violently the satiric sun
that leads April not to
the panting dance but to stillness
in, into the brain, dips
and is gone also.
And sisters return
through the dusk
to the measured rancor
of their unbending elders.

Greep, greep, greep the cricket
chants where the snake
with agate eyes leaned to the water.
Sorrow to the young
that Lawrence has passed
unwanted from England.
And in the gardens forsythia
and in the woods
now the crinkled spice-bush
in flower.

WILLIAM CARLOS WILLIAMS
(1883–)

ROBERT FROST (1875–)

A Letter to Robert Frost

Our friendship, Robert, firm through twenty years,
Dares not commend these couplets to your ears:
How celebrate a thing so rich and strange—
Two poets whose affection does not change;
Immune to all the perils Nature sends,
World war and revolution and kind friends.
Something there is that doesn't love a wall;
Your apples and my pines knew none at all,
But grow together in that ghostly lot
Where your Vermont meets my Connecticut.
Ours is a startling friendship, because art,
Mother of quarrels who tears friends apart,
Has bound us ever closer, mind and heart.

ROBERT FROST (1875-   )

Before the War, among those days that seem
Bathed in the slanting afterglow of dream,
Were happy autumn hours when you and I
Walked down that street still bright in memory.
I was a boy apprenticed to my rhymes,
Your fame already rose above our times,
Your shadow walking tall, my shorter gait,—
Both taller now, the difference as great.

Of wisdom I learned much, an artist's creed
Of work the flower, and worldly fame the weed;
I have forgotten phrases; it remains
As part of me, it courses in my veins.
From many conversations I remember
One on a windy day in late November.
The sly recluse of Amherst in those times
Moved me, in spite of questionable rhymes.
We talked of women poets, nothing else,
From Sappho to our friend at Sevenels.
"Miss Dickinson is best!" You shook your head.
"Perhaps a genius, but mad," you said.
Alas for Emily, alas for me,
That now I go much further than agree:
Once irresistible, now merely coy,
Her whims, her verbal airs and graces cloy.
Taste changes. Candid Louis Untermeyer
Consigns his past editions to the fire;
His new anthology, refined and thrifty,
Builds up some poets and dismisses fifty.
And every poet spared, as is but human,
Remarks upon his critical acumen.
Ah, could we know what vogue will be tomorrow,
What plumes of Paradise our pens could borrow!

Yet not alone among the modern names
Does Fashion choose; she rummages in Fame's.
One poet to be praised—and sometimes read—
She chooses, and the rest are safely dead.

"Sevenels"] in Brookline, Massachusetts: the home of Amy Lowell.

ROBERT FROST (1875-   )

One must be sacrificed if one is praised,
As Crashaw mounts, Shelley must be abased.
With what astonishment we witnessed Donne,
A poet we have always counted on,
Whisked from his niche among the second shelves
And placed with Chaucer, Shakespeare,—and ourselves!
While Blake departs, abandoned by the vogue,
To Beulah-land, where Reason is the rogue;
And Hopkins, fashion's choice to follow Donne,
Rattling his rusty iambs, climbs the sun.

Blest be thy name, O Vogue, that canst embalm
A minor poet with a potted palm;
Make me immortal in thy exegesis,—
Or failing that, at least a Doctor's thesis.

Yet, Robert, through the charlatans who swarm
Like blowing gnats before the social storm,
The stout immortals stand in this our time,
With manners, morals, metres,—even rhyme.
Not every age can triumph over death
In the bright train of Queen Elizabeth,
And our ingenious and cynic age
Has not quite lost the better heritage.
Take Robert Bridges, laureate forever,
Calm as the sea and flowing as a river,
Who knew his source and end, but also knew
The homely country he meandered through.
Who, when we thought his broadening current spent,
Flung high that sun-capped wave, his testament,
The Testament of Beauty. Of the few
Titles he gave his poems, all are true.
And Robinson, what other age but this
Has bred so classic an antithesis:
Mild in his manner, mocking in his eye,
Bold in appraisal, and in statement shy,
He knew all men,—the Man against the Sky.
And urbane Santayana, who alone
Among philosophers still seeks their Stone;

ROBERT FROST (1875-   )

    Whose irony, in golden prose alloyed
    With doubt, yet yields not to the acid Freud;
    Who after years of rightful fame defrauded,
    Wrote one bad book at last,—and all applauded.

    If gold gets rusty, what shall iron do?
    If poets, prophets, critics are untrue
    Why blame the statesmen, who in turn reflect
    On dusty mirrors the uncircumspect?
    When poets laugh at metres, with applause,
    Why punish citizens who laugh at laws?
    All follies regimented are akin—
    Free verse and Bolshevism and bad gin.
    Surely a subtle spring, in flow or drought,
    Waters one age or burns another out.
    When worlds go mad, all things go mad together,
    Nations, philosophers, the arts, the weather.

    Beholding war, Nature, who brooks no rival
    In blind destruction, threatens Man's survival.
    While underground he plants his dynamite,
    She answers with an earthquake overnight.
    While from ingenious wings his bombs rain down,
    She rips the clouds apart and cities drown.
    Machine guns clatter, but her ticking worm
    Of death bombards his armies with a germ.
    Nor can the propaganda of slow doubt
    That one by one puts all faith's candles out
    Find Nature unprepared; her insect ranks
    For Man's destructive unbelief give thanks.
    The ant, the termite, and their brotherhood
    Wait busily, as all good soviets should,
    To crack his concrete and to gnaw his wood,
    And after war and storm have done their worst,
    To view the last man, as they viewed the first.

    From such dark thoughts only Dark Ages come;
    I see not yet the end of Christendom;—
    And if an end? In cloistered minds like yours
    The classic wisdom of the past endures;

one bad book at last] *The Last Puritan* by Santayana

ROBERT FROST (1875-   )

The ancient learning from the ancient guilt
Survives, and from slim chances worlds are built.
Black-armored barons, after Rome declined,
Warred on each other and on soul and mind;
Yet while they slept, cell after lonely cell,
Nearsighted eyes bent to the pliant quill.
The barons' mail adorns Park Avenue,
Quite spurious;—the words remain as true
As when, frail thread amid a mad sword-dance,
They led men to the sunlit Renaissance.
The things that make outlive the things that mar,
Rome and Byzantium crashed,—but here we are;
And even the dark spectre of dark ages
Calls forth old warriors who shame our sages:
Which would you choose, to put it in a word,—
To die with Arthur? or to live with Ford?

Men are as cells within a mighty brain
Swept with one thought of happiness or pain;
Thus when the Thinker gazed beyond all time
Egypt and China blossomed at their prime,
Both worshipers of beauty and of peace.
That mood resolved. He meditated Greece,
Whose culture, wedded to the arts of war,
Brought beauty forth and slew the thing it bore.

Less fortunate we who brought forth the machine
And dare not slay it, lest the truth be seen
That we, now helplessly identified
With the machine, would perish if it died.
We watch each other, our fates intertwined:
It feeds us canned goods and we feed it mind;
It kills us and then calls us from the grave
With new machines, lest it should lack a slave.
In war, where no one wins but the machine,
I pondered as I brought the wounded in:
Of these three choices—death, deformity,
Or patched for war again, who would not die?
And now the final triumph: the star actor
In "Steel: a Tragedy," makes God a tractor.

ROBERT FROST (1875-)

Yet let us still believe, in thinking deeper,
These are but twitchings of a troubled sleeper
In whom the nightmare rages, and who can
Tomorrow dream the incredible—a Man.

Why, Robert, look! it's after midnight. Always
At this hour I hear stirrings in the hallways.
You would not mind. If I recall aright
You and Miss Lowell would converse all night,
Seldom agreeing, always the best friends,
That poetry can shape to different ends;
Myself, too sleepy then as now, would run
To catch the last car back at half-past one.
Heigh-ho, I've seen worse things than morbid youth
Inscribes in his dark diary. The truth
Remains that my few perfect moments seem
Eternal, and the bad ones but a dream.
Like Johnson's friend, I woo philosophy,
But cheerfulness breaks in spite of me.
So does the spirit sift a life away
Into its best, preparing for the day
When, from its golden nucleus, shall rise
That happy part attuned to happier skies.

But happier skies? That phrase is fustian stuff,—
This green Connecticut is good enough;
My shining acres and the house I built,
All mine, all earned, all mortgaged to the hilt.
If I may make some changes here and there
When halos play on my unhallowed hair,
New England winters well might be curtailed—
In May it snowed, and in July it hailed.
Rosebugs should all be banished, and with those
The people who see rosebugs on the rose.
And yet I shrink from this celestial boom,
Lest, with improvements, also I assume
Responsibility for things in bloom.
I might forget wax flowers of huckleberry,
I might leave out the fragrance of wild cherry;
In short, I am content to leave to God
The natural world. O that our statesmen would!

ROBERT FROST (1875-   )

And so good night with lullaby, my friend,
Republics fall and even letters end,
And Horace at one elbow sings of home
Far more eternal than the hills of Rome;—
Caesar, in fact, must marvel, looking down,
To find an Ethiope in his Gallic crown.
And Gibbon, at my other elbow, gives
Wry testimony of what dies, what lives,—
A secret not to be imparted, but
Known to Vermont and to Connecticut:
New as tomorrow's dawn, old as the Nile,
In Nefertiti's tears and Shakespeare's smile,
And all so simple in an age of guile;
For Horace on his acres has no fears,
His empire grows through twenty hundred years.

Good night, I take unconsiderable time
A-dying, but in rhymeless years a rhyme
Bids one converse beyond the crack of dawn,—
It now has cracked, and dew is on the lawn.
Since I write oftener than you, I vow
Another letter twenty years from now.

ROBERT HILLYER
(1895-   )

STEPHEN VINCENT BENÉT (1898-1943)

S. V. B.

"This I shall write," he said.
They said, "Vain dreaming!"
So he went down to the dead
And more than their seeming
Brought back in a living book
For the sons of men to share
Where immortal banners shook
Over armies in the air.

"This," said Pain, "you will bear."
He said, "Non dolet.
Shall Man's predestined share
The springing soul let,

STEPHEN VINCENT BENÉT (1898-1943)

Let, hinder, or constrain
From the call of the work at hand?
I shall search your world, O Pain;
I shall understand."

So, throughout all the land,
None brought him in vain
(To weigh in a thoughtful hand)
The living grain;
To find the pearl in the dust,
Or of true gold the token,
With generous word and just
Endlessly spoken.

So flowed in tide unbroken
Glamour of story,
Glory of song—but more
Than glamour or glory:
Wisdom and insight that grew,
An inner truth that spoke:
The fleece that was filled with dew;
The god in the oak.

And legend for his own folk,
Of their toil and their mirth;
Tang of the tongue they spoke,
The savour of their earth;
Till, when foul darkness stirred
To blast all singing.
Men heard his quiet word
Steady and ringing.

Speaking to them of their land,
Of a great wind's breath
That blows from strand to strand
Against evil and death,
And now, like the drums' long roll,
Rises and floods and fills
Body and heart and soul
With the strength of our hills.

STEPHEN VINCENT BENÉT (1898–1943)

So he spoke to the end,
As he lived and wrought:
Simply, and as a friend,
From his burning thought.
But I know what shapes of light
Shine in the dome—
What stars are bright tonight
Where he comes home.

WILLIAM ROSE BENÉT
(1886–   )

WILLIAM BUTLER YEATS (1865–1939)

In Memory of W. B. Yeats
(d. Jan. 1939)

I

He disappeared in the dead of winter:
The brooks were frozen, the air-ports almost deserted,
And snow disfigured the public statues;
The mercury sank in the mouth of the dying day.
O all the instruments agree
The day of his death was a dark cold day.

Far from his illness
The wolves ran on through the evergreen forests,
The peasant river was untempted by the fashionable quays;
By mourning tongues
The death of the poet was kept from his poems.

But for him it was his last afternoon as himself,
An afternoon of nurses and rumours;
The provinces of his body revolted,
The squares of his mind were empty,
Silence invaded the suburbs,
The current of his feeling failed: he became his admirers.

Now he is scattered among a hundred cities
And wholly given over to unfamiliar affections;
To find his happiness in another kind of wood

WILLIAM BUTLER YEATS (1865-1939)

And be punished under a foreign code of conscience.
The words of a dead man
Are modified in the guts of the living.

But in the importance and noise of to-morrow
When the brokers are roaring like beasts on the floor of the Bourse,
And the poor have the sufferings to which they are fairly accustomed,
And each in the cell of himself is almost convinced of his freedom;
A few thousand will think of this day
As one thinks of a day when one did something slightly unusual.

O all the instruments agree
The day of his death was a dark cold day.

2

You were silly like us: your gift survived it all;
The parish of rich women, physical decay,
Yourself; mad Ireland hurt you into poetry.
Now Ireland has her madness and her weather still,
For poetry makes nothing happen: it survives
In the valley of its saying where executives
Would never want to tamper; it flows south
From ranches of isolation and the busy griefs,
Raw towns that we believe and die in; it survives,
A way of happening, a mouth.

3

Earth, receive an honoured guest;
William Yeats is laid to rest:
Let the Irish vessel lie
Emptied of its poetry.

Time that is intolerant
Of the brave and innocent,
And indifferent in a week
To a beautiful physique,

Worships language and forgives
Everyone by whom it lives;
Pardons cowardice, conceit,
Lays its honours at their feet.

WILLIAM BUTLER YEATS (1865-1939)

Time that with this strange excuse
Pardoned Kipling and his views,
And will pardon Paul Claudel,
Pardons him for writing well.

In the nightmare of the dark
All the dogs of Europe bark,
And the living nations wait,
Each sequestered in its hate;

Intellectual disgrace
Stares from every human face,
And the seas of pity lie
Locked and frozen in each eye.

Follow, poet, follow right
To the bottom of the night,
With your unconstraining voice
Still persuade us to rejoice;

With the farming of a verse
Make a vineyard of the curse,
Sing of human unsuccess
In a rapture of distress;

In the deserts of the heart
Let the healing fountain start,
In the prison of his days
Teach the free man how to praise.

W. H. AUDEN
(1907-   )

INDEX OF SUBJECTS

ADDISON, Joseph (1672–1719), 141, 152, 163
ÆSCHYLUS (525–456 B.C.), 15, 263, 280
ALCÆUS (620–580 B.C.), 13
ANACREON (572?–?488 B.C.), 8, 13
ARNOLD, MATTHEW (1822–1888), 313
ARISTOPHANES (448?–?380 B.C.), 264
ARIOSTO, Ludovico (1474–1533), 62, 265
BAUDELAIRE, Charles (1821–1867), 292, 297
BEAUMONT, Francis (1584–1616), 88, 89
BENÉT, Stephen Vincent (1898–1943), 339
BLAKE, William (1757–1827), 189, 190
BRIDGES, Robert (1844–1930), 329, 335
BROOKE, Rupert (1887–1915), 317
BROWNING, Elizabeth Barrett (1806–1861), 267, 268, 313
BROWNING, Robert (1812–1889), 282, 283
BRYANT, William Cullen (1794–1878), 270
BURNS, Robert (1759–1796), 191, 193, 195, 266
BYRON, George Gordon, Lord (1788–1824), 209, 221, 222, 223, 267
CAMOENS, Luiz Vaz de (1524–1580), 59, 265
CAMPION, Thomas (1567–1620), 82
CAREW, Thomas (1595?–?1645), 109
CATULLUS (84?–54 B.C.), 31
CHAPMAN, George (1559?–1634), 80, 81, 82, 105
CHATTERTON, Thomas (1752–1770), 184, 187

CHAUCER, Geoffrey (1340?–1400), 49, 50, 51, 52, 64, 102, 119, 137, 266
COLERIDGE, Samuel Taylor (1772–1834), 211, 213, 214, 267
COLLINS, William (1721–1759), 169
CONGREVE, William (1670–1729), 134, 140
CORNEILLE, Pierre (1606–1684), 153, 265
COWLEY, Abraham (1618–1667), 119, 137, 148, 266
COWPER, William (1731–1800), 180, 182
CRABBE, George (1754–1832), 188
CRASHAW, Richard (1613?–1649), 113, 115
DANIEL, Samuel (c. 1562–1619), 104
DANTE ALIGHIERI (1265–1321), 40, 41, 44, 62, 265, 280
DAVENANT, Sir William (1606–1668), 109
DAVID (10th century B.C.), 1
DEKKER, Thomas (1572?–1632), 83
DENHAM, Sir John (1615–1669), 139
DICKINSON, Emily (1830–1886), 309, 334
DOBSON, Austin (1840–1921), 320
DONNE, John (1573–1631), 95, 98, 99, 335
DRUMMOND, William (1585–1649), 105
DRYDEN, John (1631–1700), 136, 139, 140, 153
DUNBAR, Paul Laurence (1872–1906), 315
DYER, John (1700?–1758), 167
EMERSON, Ralph Waldo (1803–1882), 269
ELIOT, Thomas Stearns, (1888–   ), 323
EURIPIDES (480–406 B.C.), 17, 263

INDEX OF SUBJECTS

FITZGERALD, Edward (1809–1883), 284
FLETCHER, John (1579–1625), 90, 91, 93, 119, 135
FORD, John (1586?–?1638), 101
FROST, Robert (1875–   ), 333
GAY, John (1685–1732), 145
GOETHE, Johann Wolfgang von (1749–1832), 208, 209, 266
GOWER, John (1325?–1408), 102
GRAY, Thomas (1716–1771), 171
HAFIZ (14th century), 48
HEINE, Heinrich (1797–1856), 255
HERBERT, George (1593–1633), 112
HERRICK, Robert (1591–1674), 107
HESIOD (*fl.* 776 B.C.), 263
HOGG, James (1770–1835), 252
HÖLDERLIN, Friedrich (1770–1843), 199
HOMER (9th century B.C.), 4, 5, 16, 37, 263, 279
HOOD, Thomas (1799–1845), 261, 262
HOPKINS, Gerard Manley (1844–1889), 320, 335
HORACE (65–8 B.C.), 34, 339
HUGO, Victor (1802–1885), 286
JACOPONI DA TODI (1230?–1306), 40
JOHNSON, Lionel (1867–1902), 312
JOHNSON, Samuel (1709–1784), 170
JONES, Sir William (1746–1794), 180
JONSON, Ben (1573?–1637), 71, 83, 86, 87, 88, 104, 108, 119, 135
KEATS, John (1795–1821), 231, 232, 247, 249, 251, 252, 266
KILLIGREW, Anne (1660–1685), 130
LANDOR, Walter Savage (1775–1864), 218
LANGLAND, William (1332?–?1400), 280
LAWRENCE, David Herbert (1888–1930), 330
LEAR, Edward (1812–1888), 285
LEDWIDGE, Francis (1891–1917), 319
LEOPARDI, Giacomo (1798–1837), 254
LONGFELLOW, Henry Wadsworth (1807–1882), 273, 277

LOWELL, Amy (1874–1925), 338
LUCAN (39–65), 38
LUCRETIUS (96?–55 B.C.), 22, 30, 44, 264, 280
MARLOWE, Christopher (1564–1593), 67, 68, 103
MARTIAL (1st century A.D.), 36
MASSINGER, Philip (1583–1640), 100
MEYNELL, Alice (1847–1922), 321
MILTON, John (1608–1674), 64, 115, 117, 118, 136, 138, 149, 266, 280
MOORE, Thomas (1779–1852), 220
NASHE, Thomas (1567–1601), 104
O'CONAIRE, Padraic (1881–1928), 328
OLDHAM, John (1653–1683), 130
OMAR KHAYYÁM (12th century), 39, 284
OVID (43 B.C.–A.D. 17), 38
PARNELL, Thomas (1679–1718), 145
PATMORE, Coventry (1823–1896), 314
PETRARCA, Francesco (1304–1374), 46, 47, 64, 265
PINDAR (*c.* 522?–443 B.C.), 11, 13, 263
POE, Edgar Allan (1809–1849), 273, 274, 276
POPE, Alexander (1688–1744), 157, 160, 163, 164, 166
POUND, Ezra (1885–   ), 323
PULCI, Luigi (1431–1487), 64
RACINE, Jean Baptiste (1639–1699), 153, 265
RALEIGH, Sir Walter (1552–1618), 65
RIMBAUD, Jean Arthur (1854–1891), 310, 311
ROBINSON, Edwin Arlington (1869–1935), 335
RONSARD, Pierre de (1524–1585), 58, 59
ROSSETTI, Christina (1830–1894), 314
ROSSETTI, Dante Gabriel (1828–1882), 314
SAPPHO (7th century B.C.), 6, 13, 263, 316
SCHILLER, Friedrich von (1759–1805), 189, 266

INDEX OF SUBJECTS

SCOTT, Sir Walter (1771-1832), 62
SHADWELL, Thomas (1642?-1692), 124
SHAKESPEARE, William (1564-1616), 44, 64, 68, 70, 71, 72, 73, 74, 75, 76, 77, 78, 79, 119, 136, 140, 148, 263, 279
SHELLEY, Percy Bysshe (1792-1822), 223, 225, 227, 228, 229, 230, 266
SIDNEY, Sir Philip (1554-1586), 65, 67, 103
SKELTON, John (1460?-1529), 55, 147
SMART, Christopher (1722-1771), 172
SOPHOCLES (496?-406 B.C.), 15, 16, 263
SOUTHEY, Robert (1774-1843), 214, 216
SPENSER, Edmund (1552?-1599), 62, 64, 103, 119, 137, 149, 264
SWIFT, Jonathan (1667-1745), 144, 152
SWINBURNE, Algernon Charles (1837-1909), 316
TASSO, Torquato (1544-1595), 60, 265
TENNYSON, Alfred, Lord (1809-1892), 281, 282, 313
TERESA, Saint (1515-1582), 58

THEOCRITUS (3rd century B.C.), 19, 20, 21, 264
THOMSON, James (1700-1748), 168
VAUGHAN, Henry (1622-1695), 121, 122, 123
VEGA, Lope de (1562-1635), 266
VERLAINE, Paul (1844-1896), 310, 311
VILLON, François (1431-1489), 53
VIRGIL (70-19 B.C.), 31, 33, 38, 102, 158, 264
WALLER, Edmund (1606-1687), 139
WARNER, William (c. 1558-1609), 104
WARTON, Joseph (1722-1800), 171
WARTON, Thomas, Jr. (1728-1790), 171
WEBSTER, John (1580?-?1625), 98, 99
WHITMAN, Walt (1819-1892), 298
WHITTIER, John Greenleaf (1807-1892), 272
WILDE, Oscar (1856-1900), 312
WORDSWORTH, William (1770-1850), 201, 204, 205, 206, 208, 209
WYATT, Sir Thomas (1503?-1542), 56, 104
YEATS, William Butler (1865-1939), 341

INDEX OF AUTHORS

	PAGE
ADDISON, JOSEPH (1672-1719)	
From "An Account of the Greatest English Poets"	136
AIKEN, CONRAD (1889-)	
Preludes for Memnon, LVI	311
AKENSIDE, MARK (1721-1770)	
From "On Lyric Poetry"	13
ARNOLD, MATTHEW (1822-1888)	
To a Friend	16
Austerity of Poetry	40
Shakspeare	76
From "Stanzas in Memory of the Author of 'Obermann'"	208
Memorial Verses	209
From "Stanzas from the Grande Chartreuse"	223
Heine's Grave	255
AUDEN, WYSTAN HUGH (1907-)	
From "Letter to Lord Byron"	223
Edward Lear	285
Rimbaud	310
In Memory of W. B. Yeats	341
BASSE, WILLIAM (1583-1653)	
Elegy on Mr William Shakespeare	70
BEAUMONT, FRANCIS, (1584-1616)	
Master Francis Beaumont's Letter to Ben Jonson	83
BELL, GERTRUDE LOWTHIAN (1868-1926)	
To Hafiz of Shiraz	48
BENÉT, STEPHEN VINCENT (1898-1943)	
Ode to Walt Whitman	298
BENÉT, WILLIAM ROSE (1886-)	
S. V. B.	339
BLUNDEN, EDMUND CHARLES (1896-)	
The Age of Herbert & Vaughan	123
The Wartons	171
BLUNT, WILFRID SCAWEN (1840-1922)	
Alfred Tennyson	282
BONER, JOHN HENRY (1845-1903)	
Poe's Cottage at Fordham	274
BRIDGES, ROBERT (1844-1930)	
From "The Testament of Beauty"	44
BROWNING, ELIZABETH BARRETT (1806-1861)	
From "Wine of Cyprus"	17
Cowper's Grave	181
On a Portrait of Wordsworth by B. R. Haydon	206
From "A Vision of Poets"	263
From "Sonnets from the Portuguese"	283

INDEX OF AUTHORS

PAGE

BROWNING, ROBERT (1812–1889)
From "Balaustion's Adventure" 17
The Names 76
From "Parleyings with Certain People of Importance" 172
The Lost Leader 205
From "Pauline" 225
Memorabilia 227
Popularity 247

BRYANT, WILLIAM CULLEN (1794–1878)
Dante 40

BYRON, GEORGE GORDON, LORD (1788–1824)
From "Childe Harold's Pilgrimage" 34, 47, 60
From "English Bards and Scotch Reviewers" 188
From "Don Juan" 214
To Thomas Moore [1816] 220
To Thomas Moore [1817] 221

CAREW, THOMAS (1595?–?1645)
An Elegy upon the Death of Doctor Donne, Dean of Paul's 95

CHAUCER, GEOFFREY (1340?–1400)
From "The Hous of Fame" 37

CLARE, JOHN (1793–1864)
Cowper 180

COLERIDGE, HARTLEY (1796–1849)
To Shakespeare 74

COLERIDGE, SAMUEL TAYLOR (1772–1834)
On Donne's Poetry 98
Monody on the Death of Chatterton 184
To the Author of "The Robbers" 189
To William Wordsworth 201

COLLINS, WILLIAM (1721–1759)
Ode on the Death of Mr. Thomson 168

CONSTABLE, HENRY (1562–1613)
On the Death of Sir Philip Sidney 67

CORROTHERS, JAMES D. (1869–1919)
Paul Laurence Dunbar 315

CORY, WILLIAM JOHNSON (1823–1892)
After Reading "Ajax" 16

COWLEY, ABRAHAM (1618–1667)
Elegie upon Anacreon 8
The Praise of Pindar 11
On the Death of Mr. Crashaw 113

COWPER, WILLIAM (1731–1800)
From "Table Talk" 163
Epitaph on Dr. Johnson 170

CRANE, HART (1899–1932)
To Shakespeare 79
To Emily Dickinson 309

CRASHAW, RICHARD (1613?–1649)
From "Upon the Book and Picture of the Seraphical Saint Teresa"   58
On Mr. G. Herbert's Book, entitled "The Temple of Sacred Poems,
sent to a gentlewoman" 112

INDEX OF AUTHORS

	PAGE
DAVIES, JOHN, OF HEREFORD (1565?–1618)	
To Our English Terence, Mr. Will. Shakespeare	68
DENHAM, SIR JOHN (1615–1669)	
On Mr. Abraham Cowley, His Death and Burial amongst the Ancient Poets	119
DICKINSON, EMILY (1830–1886)	
[Her "Last Poems"—]	267
DOBSON, AUSTIN (1840–1921)	
For a Copy of Theocritus	20
To Q. H. F.	34
For a Copy of Herrick	107
DOUGLAS, LORD ALFRED BRUCE (1870–1945)	
The Dead Poet	312
DRAYTON, MICHAEL (1563–1631)	
To My Worthy Friend Mr. George Chapman, and His Translated Hesiod	80
To My Most Dearly-Loved Friend, Henry Reynolds, Esquire, of Poets and Poesy	101
DRYDEN, JOHN (1631–1700)	
Epigram on Milton	117
Mac Flecknoe	124
To the Memory of Mr. Oldham	130
To the Pious Memory of the accomplisht young lady, Mrs. Anne Killigrew	130
To My Dear Friend, Mr. Congreve, on His Comedy Call'd "The Double-Dealer"	134
ELIOT, THOMAS STEARNS (1888–)	
Whispers of Immortality	99
ENGLE, PAUL (1908–)	
Emily Dickinson	309
FITZ-GEFFREY, CHARLES (1575?–1638)	
From "Drake"	4
GAY, JOHN (1685–1732)	
From "Mr. Pope's Welcome from Greece"	160
GIBSON, WILFRID WILSON (1878?–)	
Rupert Brooke	317
GOLDSMITH, OLIVER (1728–1774)	
Epitaph on Dr. Parnell	145
GOSSE, SIR EDMUND (1849–1928)	
Theocritus	21
Madrigal	82
With a Copy of Herrick	107
GRAY, THOMAS (1716–1771)	
From "The Progress of Poesy"	140
GREGORY, HORACE (1898–)	
Praise to John Skelton	55
GREVILLE, FULKE, LORD BROOKE (1554–1628)	
Epitaph on Sir Philip Sidney	65
HARDY, THOMAS (1840–1928)	
To Shakespeare	78
Shelley's Skylark	228
A Singer Asleep	316

INDEX OF AUTHORS

	PAGE
HARVEY, GABRIEL (1545?–?1630)	
To the Learned Shepheard	62
HERRICK, ROBERT (1591–1674)	
An Ode for Ben Jonson	86
His Prayer to Ben Jonson	86
Upon Ben Jonson	87
Upon M. Ben Jonson, Epigram	87
Upon Master Fletchers Incomparable Playes	90
HIGGINS, FREDERICK ROBERT (1896–1941)	
Padraic O'Conaire—Gaelic Storyteller	328
HILLYER, ROBERT (1895–)	
For Maister Geoffrey Chaucer	52
A Letter to Robert Frost	333
HOCCLEVE, THOMAS, (1370?–?1450)	
Lament for Chaucer	49
HOLMES, OLIVER WENDELL (1809–1894)	
After a Lecture on Keats	249
HOWARD, HENRY, EARL OF SURREY (1517?–1547)	
On the Death of Sir T(homas) W(yatt)	56
HUNT, LEIGH (1784–1859)	
The Poets	64
To John Keats	231
JAPP, ALEXANDER HAY (1837–1905)	
Landor	218
JOHNSON, LIONEL PIGOT (1867–1902)	
Lucretius	30
JOHNSON, SAMUEL (1709–1784)	
From "Prologue Spoken by Mr. Garrick"	72
JONES, THOMAS S., JR. (1882–1932)	
George Herbert	112
Richard Crashaw	115
Henry Vaughan	122
JONSON, BEN (1573?–1637)	
To the Memory of My Beloved the Author, Mr. William Shakespeare: and What He Hath Left Us	68
To My Worthy and Honoured Friend, Mr. George Chapman, On His Translation of Hesiod's Works and Days	81
To Francis Beaumont	88
To John Donne	95
KEATS, JOHN (1795–1821)	
To Homer	4
A Dream, after Reading Dante's Episode of Paolo and Francesca	41
Written on the Blank Space at the End of Chaucer's Tale of "The Floure and the Lefe"	51
On Sitting Down to Read "King Lear" Once Again	7
On First Looking into Chapman's Homer	8
Bards of Passion and of Mirth	8
To Chatterton	187
To Byron	222
KENT, CHARLES (1823–1902)	
Pope at Twickenham	164

INDEX OF AUTHORS

	PAGE
KILMER, ALFRED JOYCE (1886–1918)	
Lionel Johnson	312
Father Gerard Hopkins, S. J.	320
LANDOR, WALTER SAVAGE (1775–1864)	
Æschylos and Sophocles	15
On Catullus	31
Shakespeare and Milton	73
To Southey, 1833	216
To Robert Browning	282
LANG, ANDREW (1844–1912)	
The Odyssey	5
Martial in Town	36
Ronsard	58
LANGHORNE, CHARLES HARTLEY (1818–1845)	
Theocritus	19
LANIER, SIDNEY (1842–1881)	
The Crystal	278
LONGFELLOW, HENRY WADSWORTH (1807–1882)	
Divina Commedia	41
Chaucer	51
Milton	118
Robert Burns	193
Wapentake	281
LOVELACE, RICHARD (1681–1658)	
To Fletcher Reviv'd	91
LOWELL, AMY (1874–1925)	
To John Keats	251
On Looking at a Copy of Alice Meynell's Poems Given Me Years Ago by a Friend	321
From "A Critical Fable"	323
LOWELL, JAMES RUSSELL (1819–1891)	
To the Memory of Hood	261
From "A Fable for Critics"	269
To H. W. L.	277
LYDGATE, JOHN (1370?–?1451)	
From "The Fall of Princes"	50
MACKAIL, JOHN WILLIAM (1859–)	
The Aeneid	33
MARVELL, ANDREW (1621–1678)	
On Mr Milton's "Paradise Lost"	115
MELVILLE, HERMAN (1819–1891)	
Camoens	59
MEREDITH, GEORGE (1828–1909)	
The Spirit of Shakespeare	77
MILTON, JOHN (1608–1674)	
On Shakespeare	71
MOORE, THOMAS STURGE (1870–)	
To Giacomo Leopardi	254
MORLEY, CHRISTOPHER (1890–)	
Austin Dobson	320

INDEX OF AUTHORS

	PAGE
MUIR, EDWIN (1887–)	
Hölderlin's Journey	199
MYERS, ERNEST (1844–1921)	
Achilles	5
O'CONOR, NORREYS JEPHSON (1885–)	
For Francis Ledwidge	319
PALGRAVE, FRANCIS TURNER (1824–1897)	
William Wordsworth	206
PARNELL, THOMAS (1679–1718)	
To Mr. Pope	157
POPE, ALEXANDER (1688–1744)	
From "An Essay on Criticism"	34
On Mr. Gay	145
From "Epistle to Dr. Arbuthnot"	146
The First Epistle of the Second Book of Horace	146
RALEIGH, SIR WALTER (1552?–1618)	
A Vision upon the Conceit of "The Faery Queen"	64
ROBINSON, EDWIN ARLINGTON (1869–1935)	
George Crabbe	188
Thomas Hood	262
Verlaine	310
ROGERS, SAMUEL (1763–1855)	
From "Italy"	46
ROSSETTI, DANTE GABRIEL (1828–1882)	
Thomas Chatterton	187
William Blake	190
Samuel Taylor Coleridge	213
Percy Bysshe Shelley	228
John Keats	251
SASSOON, SIEGFRIED (1886–)	
At the Grave of Henry Vaughan	122
SCOTT, JOHN (1730–1783)	
On the Ingenious Mr. Jones	180
SHAKESPEARE, WILLIAM (1564–1616)	
Sonnet 86	80
SHAPIRO, KARL JAY (1913–)	
On Reading Keats in War Time	252
Israfel	276
SHELLEY, PERCY BYSSHE (1792–1822)	
To Wordsworth	204
To [Byron]	221
Sonnet to Byron	222
Adonais	232
SHIRLEY, JAMES (1596–1666)	
To My Friend, Master John Ford	101
SKELTON, JOHN (1460?–1529)	
From "Garlande of Laurell"	50
SMART, CHRISTOPHER (1722–1771)	
From "A Song to David"	1

INDEX OF AUTHORS

PAGE

SPENSER, EDMUND (1552?–1599)
From "The Faerie Queene" 50
To the Right Noble and Valorous Knight, Sir Walter Raleigh 65

STERLING, JOHN (1806–1844)
Shakespeare 75

SUCKLING, SIR JOHN (1609–1642)
A Session of the Poets 108

SWINBURNE, ALGERNON CHARLES (1837–1909)
Sapphics 6
A Ballad of François Villon 53
Christopher Marlowe 67
Thomas Decker 83
Ben Jonson 88
John Webster 98
Philip Massinger 100
In Memory of Walter Savage Landor 218
To Victor Hugo 286
Ave atque Vale 292

TATE, ALLEN (1899–   )
Mr. Pope 166

TENNYSON, ALFRED, LORD (1809–1892)
Lucretius 22
"Frater Ave atque Vale" 31
To Virgil 31
From "A Dream of Fair Women" 52
Milton 118
To Victor Hugo 286

THOMPSON, FRANCIS (1859–1907)
From "Ode for the Diamond Jubilee of Queen Victoria, 1897" 313

THOMSON, JAMES (1834–1882)
William Blake 190
E. B. B. 268

TICKELL, THOMAS (1686–1740)
To the Earl of Warwick on the Death of Mr. Addison 141

VAUGHAN, HENRY (1622–1695)
Upon Mr. *Fletchers* Playes 93

WALLER, EDMUND (1606–1687)
Upon Mr. John Fletcher's Playes 90

WARTON, THOMAS, JR. (1728–1790)
To Mr. Gray 171

WATSON, SIR WILLIAM (1858–1935)
After Reading "Tamburlaine the Great" 68

WATTS-DUNTON, WALTER THEODORE (1832–1914)
Coleridge 214

WHITTIER, JOHN GREENLEAF (1807–1892)
Burns 195

WILLIAMS, WILLIAM CARLOS (1883–   )
An Elegy for D. H. Lawrence 330

INDEX OF AUTHORS

	PAGE
WOLFE, HUMBERT (1885–1940)	
For Omar	39
Ronsard and Hélène	59
Baudelaire	297
Robert Bridges	329
WORDSWORTH, WILLIAM (1770–1850)	
England, 1802	117
To the Poet, John Dyer	167
Remembrance of Collins	169
From "Resolution and Independence"	187
At the Grave of Burns	191
From "The Prelude"	211
Extempore Effusion upon the Death of James Hogg	252
WYLIE, ELINOR MORTON (1885–1928)	
A Red Carpet for Shelley	229
YEATS, WILLIAM BUTLER (1865–1939)	
Swift's Epitaph	144

INDEX OF TITLES

	PAGE
A Ballad of François Villon	53
From "A Critical Fable"	323
A Dream, after Reading Dante's Episode of Paolo and Francesca	41
From "A Dream of Fair Women"	52
From "A Fable for Critics"	269
A Letter to Robert Frost	333
A Red Carpet for Shelley	229
A Session of the Poets	108
A Singer Asleep	316
From "A Song to David"	1
From "A Vision of Poets"	263
A Vision upon the Conceit of "The Faery Queen"	64
Achilles	5
Adonais	232
Æschylos and Sophocles	15
After a Lecture on Keats	249
After Reading "Ajax"	16
After Reading "Tamburlaine the Great"	68
Alfred Tennyson	282
From "An Account of the Greatest English Poets"	136
An Elegy for D. H. Lawrence	330
An Elegy upon the Death of Doctor Donne, Dean of Paul's	95
From "An Essay on Criticism"	34
An Ode for Ben Jonson	86
At the Grave of Burns	191
At the Grave of Henry Vaughan	122
Austerity of Poetry	40
Austin Dobson	320
Ave atque Vale	292
From "Balaustion's Adventure"	17
Bards of Passion and of Mirth	89
Baudelaire	297
Ben Jonson	88
Burns	195
Camoens	59
Chaucer	51
From "Childe Harold's Pilgrimage"	34, 47, 60
Christopher Marlowe	67
Coleridge	214
Cowper	180
Cowper's Grave	181
Dante	40

357

INDEX OF TITLES

	PAGE
Divina Commedia	41
From "Don Juan"	214
From "Drake"	4
E. B. B.	268
Edward Lear	285
Elegie upon Anacreon	8
Elegy on Mr William Shakespeare	70
Emily Dickinson	309
England, 1802	117
From "English Bards and Scotch Reviewers"	188
Epigram on Milton	117
From "Epistle to Dr. Arbuthnot"	146
Epitaph on Dr. Johnson	170
Epitaph on Dr. Parnell	145
Epitaph on Sir Philip Sidney	65
Extempore Effusion upon the Death of James Hogg	252
Father Gerard Hopkins, S. J.	320
For a Copy of Herrick	107
For a Copy of Theocritus	20
For Francis Ledwidge	319
For Maister Geoffrey Chaucer	52
For Omar	39
"Frater Ave atque Vale"	31
From "Garlande of Laurell"	50
George Crabbe	188
George Herbert	112
Heine's Grave	255
Henry Vaughan	122
[Her "Last Poems"—]	267
His Prayer to Ben Jonson	86
Hölderlin's Journey	199
In Memory of W. B. Yeats	341
In Memory of Walter Savage Landor	218
Israfel	276
From "Italy"	46
John Keats	251
John Webster	98
Lament for Chaucer	49
Landor	218
From "Letter to Lord Byron"	223
Lionel Johnson	312
Lucretius	22
Lucretius	30
Mac Flecknoe	124
Madrigal	82
Martial in Town	36
Master Francis Beaumont's Letter to Ben Jonson	83
Memorabilia	227

INDEX OF TITLES

	PAGE
Memorial Verses	209
Milton	118
Milton	118
Monody on the Death of Chatterton	184
Mr. Pope	166
From "Mr. Pope's Welcome from Greece"	160
From "Ode for the Diamond Jubilee of Queen Victoria, 1897"	313
Ode on the Death of Mr. Thomson	168
Ode to Walt Whitman	298
On a Portrait of Wordsworth by B. R. Haydon	206
On Catullus	31
On Donne's Poetry	98
On First Looking into Chapman's Homer	82
On Looking at a Copy of Alice Meynell's Poems Given Me Years Ago by a Friend	321
From "On Lyric Poetry"	13
On Mr. Abraham Cowley, His Death and Burial amongst the Ancient Poets	119
On Mr. G. Herbert's Book, entitled The Temple of Sacred Poems, sent to a gentlewoman	112
On Mr. Gay	145
On Mr Milton's "Paradise Lost"	115
On Reading Keats in War Time	252
On Shakespeare	71
On Sitting Down to Read "King Lear" Once Again	74
On the Death of Mr. Crashaw	113
On the Death of Sir Philip Sidney	67
On the Death of Sir T(homas) W(yatt)	56
On the Ingenious Mr. Jones	180
Padraic O'Conaire—Gaelic Storyteller	328
Paul Laurence Dunbar	315
From "Parleyings with Certain People of Importance"	172
From "Pauline"	225
Percy Bysshe Shelley	228
Philip Massinger	100
Poe's Cottage of Fordham	274
Pope at Twickenham	164
Popularity	247
Praise to John Skelton	55
Preludes for Memnon, LVI	311
From "Prologue Spoken by Mr. Garrick"	72
Remembrance of Collins	169
From "Resolution and Independence"	187
Richard Crashaw	115
Rimbaud	310
Robert Bridges	329
Robert Burns	193
Ronsard	58

INDEX OF TITLES

	PAGE
Ronsard and Hélène	59
Rupert Brooke	317
S. V. B.	339
Samuel Taylor Coleridge	213
Sapphics	6
Shakespeare	75
Shakespeare and Milton	73
Shakspeare	76
Shelley's Skylark	228
Sonnet 86	80
Sonnet to Byron	222
From "Sonnets from the Portuguese"	283
From "Stanzas from the Grande Chartreuse"	223
From "Stanzas in Memory of the Author of 'Obermann'"	208
Swift's Epitaph	144
From "Table Talk"	163
The Aeneid	33
The Age of Herbert & Vaughan	123
The Crystal	278
The Dead Poet	312
From "The Faerie Queene"	50
From "The Fall of Princes"	50
The First Epistle of the Second Book of Horace	146
From "The Hous of Fame"	37
The Lost Leader	205
The Names	76
The Odyssey	5
The Poets	64
The Praise of Pindar	11
From "The Prelude"	211
From "The Progress of Poesy"	140
The Spirit of Shakespeare	77
From "The Testament of Beauty"	44
The Wartons	171
Theocritus	19
Theocritus	21
Thomas Chatterton	187
Thomas Decker	83
Thomas Hood	262
To a Friend	16
To [Byron]	221
To Byron	222
To Chatterton	187
To E. Fitzgerald	284
To Emily Dickinson	309
To Fletcher Reviv'd	91
To Francis Beaumont	88
To Giacomo Leopardi	254

INDEX OF TITLES

	PAGE
To H. W. L.	277
To Hafiz of Shiraz	48
To Homer	4
To John Donne	95
To John Keats	231
To John Keats	251
To Mr. Gray	171
To Mr. Pope	157
To My Dear Friend Mr. Congreve, on His Comedy Call'd "The Double-Dealer"	134
To My Friend, Master John Ford	101
To My Most Dearly-Loved Friend, Henry Reynolds, Esquire, of Poets and Poesy	101
To My Worthy and Honoured Friend, Mr. George Chapman, On His Translation of Hesiod's Works and Days	81
To My Worthy Friend Mr. George Chapman, and His Translated Hesiod	80
To Our English Terence, Mr. Will. Shakespeare	68
To Q. H. F.	34
To Robert Browning	282
To Shakespeare	74
To Shakespeare	78
To Shakespeare	79
To Southey, 1833	216
To the Author of "The Robbers"	189
To the Earl of Warwick on the Death of Mr. Addison	141
To the Learned Shepheard	62
To the Memory of Hood	261
To the Memory of Mr. Oldham	130
To the Memory of My Beloved the Author, Mr. William Shakespeare: and What He Hath Left Us	68
To the Pious Memory of the accomplisht young lady, Mrs. Anne Killigrew	130
To the Poet, John Dyer	167
To the Right Noble and Valorous Knight, Sir Walter Raleigh	65
To Thomas Moore [1816]	220
To Thomas Moore [1817]	221
To Victor Hugo	286
To Victor Hugo	286
To Virgil	31
To William Wordsworth	201
To Wordsworth	204
Upon Ben Jonson	87
Upon M. Ben Jonson, Epigram	87
Upon Master Fletchers Incomparable Playes	90
Upon Mr. *Fletchers* Playes	93
Upon Mr. John Fletcher's Playes	90
From "Upon the Book and Picture of the Seraphical Saint Teresa"	58

INDEX OF TITLES

	PAGE
Verlaine	310
Wapentake	281
Whispers of Immortality	99
William Blake	189
William Blake	190
William Wordsworth	206
From "Wine of Cyprus"	17
With a Copy of Herrick	107
Written on the Blank Space at the End of Chaucer's Tale of "The Floure and the Lefe"	51

INDEX OF FIRST LINES

	PAGE
A bard there was, and that a worthy wight,	52
A session was held the other day,	108
Above the voiceful windings of a river	122
After the rare arch-poet Jonson died,	87
Allas! my worthy maister honorable,	49
Ah, Ben!	86
Ah, did you once see Shelley plain,	227
Ah! would that poets could write	329
All human things are subject to decay,	124
All the night sleep came not upon my eyelids,	6
An old man in a lodge within a park;	51
And ever must I fan this fire?	59
And you, Robert Bridges, you made your last will	329
Another star 'neath Time's horizon dropped,	261
Apollo sings, his harpe resounds; give roome,	90
As Hermes once took to his feathers light,	41
As one long lost in no-man's-land of war	252
As one that for a weary space has lain	5
At midnight, death's and truth's unlocking time,	278
Athwart the sunrise of our western day	5
Back to the flower-town, side by side,	218
Bard of the Fleece, whose skilful genius made	167
Bards of Passion and of Mirth,	89
Baudelaire, I wish that I could learn from you	297
Beyond a hundred years and more,	164
Bird of the bitter bright grey golden morn	53
Bless'd be the great! for those they take away,	146
Bob Southey! You're a poet—Poet-laureate,	214
Bright baffling Soul, least capturable of themes,	78
Broad-based, broad-fronted, bounteous, multiform,	88
But this is nothing; an eccentric joke,	229
By England's lakes, in grey old age,	208
Byron! how sweetly sad thy melody!	222
Can we not force from widowed poetry,	95
Chapman, we find, by thy past-prized fraught,	80
Clouds here and there arisen an hour past noon	100
Cold was thy thought, O stricken son	254
Collyn, I see, by thy new taken taske,	62
Cowper, the poet of the fields	180
Crowned, girdled, garbed and shod with light and fire,	67
Demonic Yankee who could taste	309
Donne, the delight of Phœbus and each muse,	95

INDEX OF FIRST LINES

	PAGE
Far from the sun and summer-gale,	140
Farewell, too little, and too lately known,	130
Ferrara! in thy wide and grass-grown streets,	60
First went the holy poets, two on two,	313
Fletcher, to thee, wee doe not only owe	90
Fresh with all airs of woodland brooks	107
Friend of the wise! and Teacher of the Good!	201
From pastoral meads, from tasks of field and fold,	33
Gentle and grave, in simple dress,	206
Give him the darkest inch your shelf allows,	188
Give pardon, blessèd soul, to my bold cries,	67
Glide gently, thus for ever glide,	169
Goethe in Weimar sleeps, and Greece,	209
Great lamps of silver light his last retreat	115
Great master! Boyish, sympathetic man!	251
Green points on the shrub	330
He came, a youth, singing in the dawn	315
He came to the desert of London town	190
He comes again!	82
He disappeared in the dead of winter:	341
Heart-stealing Homer, marrow of the Muses,	4
"*Henri Heine*"——'tis here!	255
Her "Last Poems"—	267
Here Johnson lies, a sage by all allowed,	170
Here lived the soul enchanted	274
Here lyes Jonson with the rest	87
His Soul fared forth (as from the deep home-grove	213
Horace still charms with graceful negligence,	34
"Horatius Flaccus, B.C. 8,"	34
How have I been Religious? what strange Good	91
How I doe love thee, Beaumont, and thy Muse,	88
How little fades from earth when sink to rest	75
How shall I lament thine end,	8
I dreamed of him last night, I saw his face	312
I like your muse because she's gay and witty,	223
I knew thee not, nor durst *attendance* strive	93
I need not praise the sweetness of his song,	277
I ne'er had ventured e'en to hope for this,	225
I pace the sounding sea-beach and behold	118
I read, before my eyelids dropt their shade,	52
I see amid the fields of Ayr	193
I see thee pine like her in golden story	214
I shiver, Spirit fierce and bold,	191
I thought of Chatterton, the marvellous Boy,	187
I, too, have been a wanderer; but, alas!	211
I weep for Adonais—he is dead!	232
If, dumb too long, the drooping Muse hath stay'd,	141
If I esteemed you less, Envy would kill	222

INDEX OF FIRST LINES

	PAGE
In front of these came Addison. In him	163
In higher natures, poetic or mystical,	44
In the fair days when God	286
In this fair niche above the unslumbering sea,	316
In yonder grave a Druid lies	168
Indweller of a peaceful vale,	216
It is a place where poets crowned may feel the heart's decaying;	181
It seems as if . . . or did the actual chance	172
Just for a handful of silver he left us,	205
Know you, fair, on what you look:	112
Last night, within the stifling train,	36
Left his friend to breakfast alone on the white	285
Like crown'd athlete that in a race has run,	218
Long has thou, friend! been absent from thy soil,	160
Lucilia, wedded to Lucretius, found	22
Lucretius! King of men, that are	30
Many days have come and gone,	107
Master, I see thee with the locks of grey,	58
Methought I saw the grave where Laura lay,	64
Mild hearts! and modest as the evening bell	171
Milton! thou shouldst be living at this hour:	117
Much have I travell'd in the realms of gold,	82
My boat is on the shore,	221
My dearly lovéd friend, how oft have we—	101
No more these simple flowers belong	195
Not that her blooms are mark'd with beauty's hue,	171
Now comes Fourth Month and the early buds on the trees.	298
Now prompts the Muse poetic lays,	184
O Chatterton! how very sad thy fate!	187
O Golden-tongued Romance, with serene lute!	74
O mighty mind, in whose deep stream this age	221
O mighty-mouth'd inventor of harmonies,	118
O noble Chaucer whos pullisshyd eloquence	50
O Singer of the field and fold,	20
O thou, that sit'st upon a throne,	1
O thou undaunted daughter of desires!	53
Of manners gentle, of affections mild;	145
Oft have I seen at some cathedral door	41
Old Chaucer, like the morning star,	119
Old Fitz, who from your suburb grange,	284
Once more I join the Thespian choir,	13
Others abide our question. Thou art free.	76
Our Euripides, the Human,	17
Our friendship, Robert, firm through twenty years,	333
Out of the depths of darkling life where sin	83
Picture the grave in his diabolical dream	276
Pindar is imitable by none;	11
Poet and *Saint!* to thee alone are given	113

INDEX OF FIRST LINES

	PAGE
Poet! I come to touch thy lance with mine;	281
Poet of Nature, thou hast wept to know	204
Praise to John Skelton and	55
Renownèd Spenser, lie a thought more nigh	70
Rimbaud and Verlaine, precious pair of poets,	311
Roman Virgil, thou that singest	31
Row us out from Desenzano, to your Sirmione row!	31
Schiller! that hour I would have wish'd to die.	189
Shakespeare!—to such name's sounding, what succeeds	76
Shall I strew on thee rose or rue or laurel,	292
Silence augmenteth grief, writing increaseth rage,	65
Since, dearest Harry, you will needs request	136
Sith of our language he was the lode-star.	50
So were we at destruction's very edge,	17
Some say, good Will, (which I in sport do sing)	68
Something surrounds him when he walks alone	122
Somewhere afield here something lies	228
Sophocles. Thou goest then, and leavest none behind	15
Stand still, true poet that you are!	247
Standing aloof in giant ignorance,	4
Swift has sailed into his rest;	144
Tears, idle tears! Ah, who shall bid us weep,	282
Tell me not what too well I know	31
That son of Italy who tried to blow,	40
The Asian Muse, a stranger fair!	180
. . . . "The expatriates	323
The man who cloaked his bitterness within	262
The nights, the railway-arches, the bad sky,	310
The poplars and the ancient elms	21
The soul of man is larger than the sky,	74
The sun (which doth the greatest comfort bring	83
The tongue of England, that which myriads	73
The weltering London ways where children weep	251
The white-rose garland at her feet,	268
The world may like, for all I care,	16
The wreath that star-crowned Shelley gave	249
Then farewell, Horace; whom I hated so,	34
Then it was faith and fairness,	123
Theocritus! Theocritus! ah, thou hadst pleasant dreams	19
There be who say, in these enlighten'd days,	188
"There comes Emerson first, whose rich words, every one,	269
There is a tomb in Arqua;—rear'd in air,	47
There is delight in singing, tho' none hear	282
There is, within three leagues and less of Padua	46
There saugh I stonden, out of drede,	37
There was a murkier tinge in London's air	312
. . . . these were poets true,	263
They've paid the last respects in sad tobacco	328

INDEX OF FIRST LINES

	PAGE
"This I shall write," he said.	339
This is the place. Even here the dauntless soul,	189
This pleasant tale is like a little copse:	51
This tomb inscribed to gentle PARNELL's name,	145
Thou hast thy calling to some palace-floor,	283
Thou youngest virgin-daughter of the skies,	130
Three poets, in three distant ages born,	117
Through torrid entrances, past icy poles	79
Thunder: the flesh quails, and the soul bows down	98
Thus said the Poet: "When Death comes to you,	48
Thy greatest knew thee, Mother Earth; unsour'd	77
'Tis well you think me truly one of those,	231
To draw no envy (Shakespeare) on thy name,	68
To praise, yet still with due respect to praise,	157
To thee that are the sommers Nightingale,	65
'Twixt those twin worlds,—the world of Sleep, which gave	228
Unto this altar, rich with thine own spice,	101
Upon this greying page you wrote	321
Victor in Drama, Victor in Romance,	286
Was it the proud full sail of his great verse,	80
Webster was much possessed by death	99
Well then, the promis'd hour is come at last;	134
Were I to name, out of the times gone by,	64
What are you doing now,	220
What helps it now, that Byron bore,	223
What needs my Shakespeare for his honoured bones	71
When Alexander Pope strolled in the city	166
When dawn no longer, with the hunters use,	39
When first, descending from the moorlands,	252
When Hölderlin started from Bordeaux	199
When I a verse shall make,	86
When I beheld the poet blind, yet bold,	115
When Learning's triumph o'er her barb'rous foes	72
While you, great Patron of Mankind! sustain	146
Who, mid the grasses of the field,	40
Who prop, thou ask'st, in these bad days, my mind?—	16
Whose work could this be, CHAPMAN, to refine	81
Why didst thou carve thy speech laboriously,	320
Why do you dig like long-clawed scavengers	310
Whylome, as antique stories tellen us,	50
Wide pastures, thatch of turf, and ancient spire	112
With Donne, whose muse on dromedary trots,	98
With Shakespeare's manhood at a boy's wild heart,—	187
Wordsworth upon Helvellyn! Let the cloud	206
W(yatt) resteth here that quick could never rest;	56
Yon page being closed, my Shakespeare's let me ope.	68
You fell; and on a distant field, shell-shatter'd,	319

INDEX OF FIRST LINES

PAGE

You sang, Ronsard, in your imperial lay 59
You who desired so much—in vain to ask 309
Your face was lifted to the golden sky 317